The Author

Professor ERNST U. VON WEIZSÄCKER held the chair of Interdisciplinary Biology at Essen University before he was appointed President of the new University of Kassel in 1975. After completing his five-year term, he served as a Director at the United Nations Center for Science and Technology for Development. In 1984 he became Director of the Institute for European Environmental Policy in Bonn. Since early 1991 he has been President of the Wuppertal Institute for Climate, Energy and Environment.

He is a member of the Club of Rome. In 1989 he was recipient — together with the Norwegian Prime Minister, Mrs Gro Harlem Brundtland — of the Italian De Natura Prize.

He has published numerous articles, essays and books in the field of environmental policy, the theory of open systems, and technology policy. His most recent book, *Ecological Tax Reform: A Policy Proposal for Sustainable Development* (co-authored with Jochen Jesinghaus) was published by Zed Books in 1992.

Earth Politics

Ernst U. von Weizsäcker

Foreword by the President of the Club of Rome

Zed Books Ltd
London and New Jersey

Earth Politics was first published in English by Zed Books Ltd., 7 Cynthia Street, London N1 9JF, UK and 165 First Avenue, Atlantic Highlands, New Jersey 07716, USA, in 1994.

Based on an earlier version of the work published in German under the title *Erdpolitik: Ökologische Realpolitik an der Schwelle zum Jahrhundert der Umwelt* by Wissenschaftliche Buchgesellschaft, Darmstadt, in 1992.

Copyright © Ernst U. von Weizsäcker 1994
Laserset by Idiom, Plymouth
Cover design by Andrew Corbett
Visuals by Hans Kretschmer
Printed by Biddles Ltd, Guildford and King's Lynn.

A catalogue record for this book is available from the British Library

US CIP data is available from the British Library

ISBN 1 85649 173 0 hb
ISBN 1 85649 174 9 pb

Contents

List of Figures

Preface

'Earth politics', as I use the term in this book, means the necessity of global environmental policies and the political processes that will inevitably be associated with them. The state of the earth imperatively demands global thinking and action. But our political arena, even at the United Nations and other international governmental organisations, ultimately knows only nation states as actors, the sovereign nations which made progress at the Earth Summit of Rio de Janeiro so difficult to achieve.

This book, which in its first German edition was published in 1989, but which has been comprehensively revised and updated for this edition, sets out to propose a pragmatic strategy for earth politics. To define the frame of action some history, especially the fairly recent development of economic thinking, is recalled. Pollution control and the more recent emergence of global environmental concerns are also discussed, as important elements of the overall picture. Chapter 3 in this first part of the book is devoted to European thinking which shaped so much of modern history and to European environmental policy which could theoretically serve as a model for earth politics.

Part Two outlines five fields of environmental crisis. Earth politics must address them all. Possible first steps for solutions are indicated. Part Three turns these initial answers into what is hoped to be a coherent strategy of earth politics under the very obvious rubric that 'prices should tell the ecological truth'. The results of the 1992 Earth Summit are assessed to be unsatisfactory according to this criterion.

Part Four calls for vision beyond today's pragmatism. Technologies, the sciences, human labour and indeed our whole culture will be profoundly transformed once we are underway towards the 'century of the environment', as the twenty-first century is consistently called in this book.

No single author could possibly write authoritatively about all the fields that have to be covered when taking this challenge seriously. These fields include climatology and biodiversity and genetic engineering; international law and fiscal policy; transport and agriculture; energy and the global debt crisis; macroeconomics and business administration; history and futurology; and last, but not least, a sense of political realism under very different cultural and economic conditions is required.

It would have been impossible to bring this manuscript into a publishable form without intense help from expert friends and colleagues. Some of the most important feedback came from Anil Agarwal, David Baldock,

xii *Preface*

George Besch, Willy Bierter, Raimund Bleischwitz, Ernst Brugger, Fritjof Capra, Mary Clark, Ernest Cohen, Jos Delbeke, Frans Duinhouwer, Nigel Haigh, Harald Hohmann, Jochen Jesinghaus, Peter Kramer, Dietrich Kupfer, Michael Marien, Lester Milbrath, Konrad von Moltke, Johannes Opschoor, Hermann Priebe, Wolfgang Sachs, Stephan Schmidheiny, Friedrich Schmidt-Bleek, Helmut Schreiber, Eberhard Seifert, Udo Ernst Simonis, Carl Christian von Weizsäcker, Richard A. Westin, John Whitelegg and Nicholas Yost. I wish to thank them all and acknowledge their extremely helpful comments. Clearly all remaining errors and inconsistencies are my exclusive responsibility.

Special thanks go to my wife, Christine, with whom I am privileged to have maintained a dialogue over more than two decades on the topics of Part Four of the book. She has also by generous practical arrangements enabled me finally to write the manuscript in 1989.

The German *Land*, North Rhine-Westphalia, had the vision and commitment in financially difficult times to create the Wuppertal Institute for Climate, Environment and Energy, an institute almost entirely devoted to policy research for sustainable development. I was honoured in being appointed the founding president of this new institute and being encouraged to get *Earth Politics* published in other languages than just German.

Colin Brown and John Clifford took on the formidable task of translating the book (from its second German edition) into English. They were greatly helped by Francesca Loening and received general guidance from Ulrich Loening, Director of the Centre for Human Ecology at the University of Edinburgh. The final English editing of the manuscript which I updated in August 1992 was done by some of the experts noted above and by Robert Molteno and his team at Zed Books. Hans Kretschmer has been extremely helpful in preparing the visuals for the English edition. Bernhard Rothfos generously sponsored the translation into English and the chapter-by-chapter review by Anglo-Saxon specialists in their respective fields.

I am greatly indebted to all who made this publication possible.

Wuppertal, Germany

Ernst Ulrich von Weizsäcker

Foreword

by *Ricardo Diez-Hochleitner*, President of the Club of Rome

More than 20 years ago, the report *The Limits to Growth*, sponsored by The Club of Rome, triggered for the first time a heated (almost scandalous) debate on the 'world problematique', with particular reference to long-term constraints on linear growth practices and the negative consequences of wasteful consumerism for both the biosphere and human development itself. Now sustainable development has become — after the Rio Earth Summit — the new catchword for a hopeful approach towards protecting the environment, although the global problems we confront are continuing to grow and to become more intricate and complex, causing the present feeling of uncertainty around the world. Moreover, at the root of the present challenges, the main issue is one of ethical and moral values — beginning with solidarity — and of learning how to solve global problems jointly.

Workers and business leaders, consumers and engineers, ecological activists and rural populations, besides many more actors, need to be encouraged to work on viable long-term solutions. But how can they become motivated? Or should they be forced to change? Is intervention by the state necessary for the transition to sustainability? Ernst von Weizsäcker in this book takes a courageous approach: prices must tell the ecological truth for prices are a language anyone — even illiterates — understand. Moreover, sustainable development can become a profitable business under a system of ecologically honest prices, as the author explains. *Earth Politics* thus offers a host of specific and novel proposals, all in line with this general philosophy on prices.

The ideas and previous studies of Professor von Weizsäcker, a distinguished member of The Club of Rome, have already had a major impact on German and European environmental policies. His proposals for a slowly progressing ecological tax reform (see Chapter Eleven of this book) have helped to shape the EC Commission proposal for a Council Directive on a combined energy and carbon tax. What is more, his book offers (in Part Four) a far-reaching vision of what he calls 'the coming of the century of the environment'. May this book help to pave the way to the next century!

PART ONE:

SETTING THE FRAMEWORK

Chapter 1

Towards a Century of the Environment

Introduction: Why Earth Politics?

The Earth Summit has been and gone. With more than a hundred heads of state or heads of government present, it was easily the largest diplomatic event of the century. The summit was devoted to the environment and its links to development, or at least that is how the Northern media presented it. From a Southern perspective, the United Nations Conference on Environment and Development (UNCED), held at Rio de Janeiro from 3 to 14 June 1992, was devoted to development, global inequalities and their links with the environment. The connections between the environment and development are so close and intricate that any attempt to disentangle them can only lead to illogical conclusions and counter-productive solutions.

To show this, let us start by looking at the Southern myopia, which is easy for Northern readers (who probably constitute the larger part of this book's readership) to criticize. The South has tended to define the UNCED agenda as a strategy for overcoming poverty and reversing global economic inequalities. Environmental questions would in this interpretation be subordinated to global economic issues. This view almost invariably leads to a repetition of Indira Gandhi's famous statement twenty years ago at the Stockholm UN Conference on the Human Environment, that 'poverty is the biggest pollution'. That may well be the case in areas where poverty drives people to collect and cut firewood in an unsustainable manner, and in a different sense it is also true to say that poverty under present conditions means high birth rates and resulting population pressure which then leads to further environmental degradation.

On the other hand, *overcoming* poverty in the conventional sense tends further to increase the stress on the environment. It means higher per capita consumption of water, energy, biomass, minerals and higher rates of land use, as well as waste, water and air pollution. Reversing global inequalities does not seem remotely possible in the real world without a massive increase in worldwide consumption rates. Hence giving priority to issues of development and world equity means that the environment is doomed to deteriorate at an accelerated pace.

The Northern myopia is no less fallacious. It essentially consists of saying that environmental protection is of the highest priority (together with birth control — in the developing countries, of course!). Environmental protection, on the other hand, is a high-tech, costly activity which even the North can afford only under conditions of affluence. The South is advised to strive for economic growth (through world market integration and activating the private sector) so as to be able to afford costly Northern pollution-control technologies. As a compromise during an interim period, some official development assistance may be made available for this purpose. This is how the North saw the negotiations at Rio de Janeiro for Agenda 21, that vastly comprehensive programme of action on all conceivable areas of environmental protection.

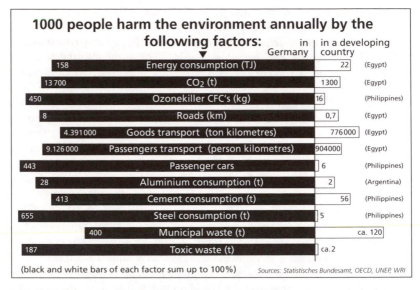

1000 people harm the environment annually by the following factors:

		in Germany	in a developing country	
158	Energy consumption (TJ)		22	(Egypt)
13 700	CO$_2$ (t)		1300	(Egypt)
450	Ozonekiller CFC's (kg)		16	(Philippines)
8	Roads (km)		0,7	(Egypt)
4.391 000	Goods transport (ton kilometres)		776 000	(Egypt)
9.126 000	Passengers transport (person kilometres)		904 000	(Egypt)
443	Passenger cars		6	(Philippines)
28	Aluminium consumption (t)		2	(Argentina)
413	Cement consumption (t)		56	(Philippines)
655	Steel consumption (t)		5	(Philippines)
400	Municipal waste (t)		ca. 120	
187	Toxic waste (t)		ca.2	

(black and white bars of each factor sum up to 100%)   Sources: Statistisches Bundesamt, OECD, UNEP, WRI

Figure 1: One thousand Germans consume roughly ten times more resources than one thousand Argentinians, Egyptians or Filippinos. From a brochure prepared for the Earth Summit by the Wuppertal Institute for Climate, Environment and Energy (Bleischwitz and Schütz, 1992).

But what is meant by affluence? It is essentially the Northern way of life with a healthy diet, high levels of individual mobility, space for living, infrastructure, education and so on. Figure 1 shows that present lifestyles in Germany are associated with consumption rates per capita roughly ten times higher than those in some developing countries. If such German, let alone North American, levels of consumption were extended to some 5.5 billion people, the Earth would in no time be completely exhausted, swamped and overheated, in short destroyed.

Caricaturing the Southern and Northern myopias in this way we have also outlined the dilemma faced by the Earth Summit, and indeed the World Commission on Environment and Development at its establishment in 1984. The World Commission, commonly referred to as the Brundtland Commission after its chairwoman Dr Gro Harlem Brundtland, Prime Minister of Norway, has given prominence to a formula, '*sustainable development*', to overcome both the Southern and the Northern myopias (World Commission 1987). This formula alone, as everybody knows, does not and cannot change the world.

What then can change the world? To escape the dilemma of Northern and Southern myopias and to make sustainable development a *reality*, we need a new set of values, a new culture, a new set of incentives to make those millions of actors both in the North and the South act *differently*. We need to enter and to create a new era of human history. The Earth Summit left us with this challenge. I call it the challenge of Earth Politics.

The Earth Summit has served as a good start for Earth Politics, but more fundamental changes are due. In my view, we shall have to overcome the obsessive way in which we subject everything on Earth to the economy. Economics is the common denominator of the Southern and the Northern myopia. Economics has become the veritable religion of our time.

The Economic Century: An Episode

Each century in modern times has had its own particular character. Our century is the Economic Century. Realists, or those who consider themselves realists, base their actions on economics or use economics as a justification for those actions. The world is divided according to economic criteria. Nowadays it is more important to know whether countries are (economically) 'developed' or 'less developed' than to know about their climate, their government or their religion. The European Union was, of course, founded as an *economic* community. The upheavals in Eastern Europe were, at least in large part, brought about by the hope of economic change. Worldwide, elections are usually decided by economic factors, and most activities of the United Nations agencies and organisations relate to the economic development of the developing countries.

Science and technology, which once belonged intellectually in the realm of the arts, have become crucially important areas of economic activity. Meanwhile, the arts themselves have also become an important sector of the economy. The Beatles were honoured by the Queen for their economic success rather than for what she or the Prime Minister considered to be their artistic merit. Even Christmas is nowadays first and foremost an economic event: it's the day after the last shopping day before Christmas.

In the second half of our century, economics holds us in thrall to such an extent that it never occurs to us that other centuries were shaped by entirely different realities or perceptions of reality. One only has to read the literature and records of past centuries to discover that, contrary to our own economic prejudices and to the Marxist interpretation of history, the economic worldview hardly ever played a *dominant role* in our culture before 1900.

In the seventeenth century — at least in central Europe — *religious wars* determined our culture. To be a realist in the seventeenth century meant to prove oneself worthy of one's denomination. The Counter-Reformation was an ecclesiastical, state and cultural response to the challenge of the Reformation, which itself had shaped the sixteenth century. According to prevailing public perceptions, these religious developments had virtually nothing to do with economics.

The eighteenth century became the *century of the princely courts*. As a realist you kept on good terms with your Prince. Soldiers served the King. Even the Enlightenment, which sowed the seeds for the end to royal absolutism, originated in courtly circles. Voltaire was a favoured guest of Frederick II of Prussia. To be sure, there were already some economists, the physiocrats in France and Adam Smith in Britain. The former, however, were but a passing phase and Adam Smith primarily considered himself a philosopher, although he also represented the advanced British culture of the time which was to discover economics much earlier than other cultures did.

In the nineteenth century the princely courts gave way to *nation states* created by bourgeois revolutions. A realist now defined him- or herself in France as French, in Germany as German, or in Britain as British. Garibaldi and Cavour were the Italian heroes of the time, the men who 'created the Italian nation', as old-fashioned historians would have put it. To be sure the nineteenth century may also be characterised by a phenomenon which is usually seen as an economic phenomenon, namely industrialisation and the emergence of the working class. But workers and industrialists alike found their identity in their nation states. The workers' idea of an international community or solidarity remained a dream.

The European nation states soon discovered how to harness modern industrial and military technology to conquer the world (see Polanyi, 1957, and Chapter 3). An ugly phase followed with imperialism, colonisation, global economic crises, mass unemployment, totalitarianism and last but not least two devastating world wars. The age of the nation state, one should think, had come to a natural end. A new paradigm could move in: economics.

Contrary to our ethical traditions, egotism and the pursuit of short- to medium-term material and financial gain have been accorded a place of honour, through a simplistic interpretation of Adam Smith: the Invisible

Hand of God would ensure that this preoccupation with the pursuit of individual profit would be to the common good. The broad consensus of the system of values to which we adhere in our present century — the century of economics — is based on this anti-ethic (see, e.g. Lux, 1990).

It is easy to understand how the economic paradigm took hold so forcefully after the end of the Second World War. Economic thinking, so gloriously represented by the USA, the liberator of the devastated Old Continent, meant peace, freedom and the prospect of material welfare. International politics was to be redefined in terms of reconstruction and development. The very term 'underdevelopment' in the economic sense was publicly pronounced by President Harry Truman only in 1949 (see *Oxford English Dictionary*, vol. XVIII, p. 960).

World trade, development assistance, infrastructure and technological development: these were just a few of the catchwords of the new economic consensus of the Western world. The United Nations was inaugurated with more or less equal emphasis on security and economic development. At the Bretton Woods Conference in 1944 the new international economic system was defined, including the International Bank for Reconstruction and Development (the World Bank), the International Monetary Fund (IMF) and later the General Agreement of Tariffs and Trade (GATT). The goals of all these new institutions, as of the leading nation of the time, the USA, were peace and prosperity for all. And economics was to be the dominant moving force. Who could deny the spell of such a promise?

From the vantage point offered by so attractive a set of values, it is not difficult to see how the concepts which had shaped the cultures of earlier centuries came to be seen as unenlightened and foolish. But that may not do justice to the people who lived before us. And who knows whether people in future centuries will find our present day economic values and preoccupations even more foolish and unenlightened than the values of religious hypocrisy, princely courts or the nation state?

Indeed, such a judgement of history on our own time is precisely what I fear. Many critics have pointed out that under the veil of seemingly non-political economic values, oppression, conquest and abuse of power continue. However, the real danger, as I see it, is that the supremacy of economics in its present form will cause irreparable damage to the Earth and to the people who live on it and from it, irrespective of the injustice and deprivation which are caused, or at least not prevented, by the dominion of economics.

In the parlance of present-day economics and politics, the realist thinks in the short-term and does for nature, the environment and posterity no more than the legally prescribed minimum. To do more means to commit oneself to expenditure without profit. In many cases it is even regarded as absurd idealism to follow the letter of the law. Indeed, on occasion the authorities in many countries shut their eyes because they are more concerned with short-term prosperity, jobs or tax revenues than with the environment.

The Rape of Nature

It is my thesis that the wonderful days of naive economic consensus are numbered. We are reaching the limits of destructive growth. It is just not possible for the amount of energy, land, water, air and other natural resources consumed by 10 per cent of the world's population — directly or indirectly — to be matched by the remaining 90 per cent without total ecological collapse. And yet this 'standard' is the declared aim or the dream of all development aspirations.

No invisible hand can ward off such an ecological collapse. Merely to sustain the present level of consumption of the top 10 per cent, natural resources are being exploited at a fearful rate. At present approximately 1,000 tons of soil are being washed, blown away or otherwise eroded per second; the Earth is losing some 3,000 square metres of its forests per second, an area almost the size of Britain, each year; each day we wipe out ten, perhaps fifty, species of animal or plant; every second we pump around 1,000 tons of greenhouse gases into the atmosphere (Lester Brown et al. 1988, table 1.1).

Ecological disasters on a local scale make things worse. In Mexico City and Wuhan (China), the air is so badly polluted that hardly a child grows up without suffering from chronic lung disease. The Ivory Coast in West Africa has lost three-quarters of its forests in twenty years. The Wisla River in Poland, once known for the quality of its fish, is now virtually dead and its water is considered unfit even for industrial use. The once forested Riesengebirge between Germany and Bohemia are now largely bare, except where it has not yet been possible to keep up with the felling of the dead or dying trees. The Baltic and the Black Seas are both under severe threat of devastating eutrophication (Alcamo (ed) 1992).

Worst of all, there are the global problems. The ozone layer, which largely screens out cancer-inducing ultraviolet-B-radiation, is being destroyed by man-made chemicals, chiefly chlorofluoro carbons (CFCs). Our global climate has been by and large stable during the present interglacial period, but now there are signs that, by geological standards, the climate is undergoing extraordinarily rapid change as a result of human activity, in a way which could turn whole regions of the earth, including parts of Europe, into steppe or desert and raise the ocean levels to an unpredictable extent (for a balanced reading, see Houghton et al. 1990). Uncounted additional species may become extinct if climatic change progresses at the speed being forecast and leads to an unprecedented shift of biotic zones (Peters and Lovejoy (eds) 1992).

Tragic situations sometimes begin in an invisible way only to become apparent when it is too late to attempt to solve them. William Stigliani (1988) gives the striking example of the build-up of acidity in the Big Moose Lake in New York State. For eighty years increasing quantities of sulphur in the form of sulphurous or sulphuric acids rained down on the region, until finally the buffering capacity of the soil in the catchment area and of the lake itself were exhausted. The last drops of acid rain eventually pushed the lake past the point of no return, since when it has been virtually dead.

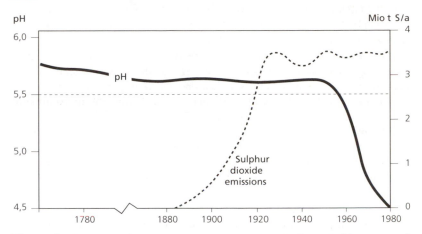

Figure 2: One instance of an ecological time-bomb. It took fifty years of acid rain for the Big Moose Lake to be pushed beyond its limits. Diagram. W. Stigliani (1988).

A similar story can be told of *Waldsterben*, the dieback of forests which became apparent only a decade or two after the process had actually begun. And only now can we see the effect of nitrates which have been seeping into the groundwater for the last ten or twenty years. There are other examples where, over large areas, the considerable ability of the soil to act as buffer has been similarly exhausted: we may already be sitting on hundreds of ecological time bombs threatening the livelihood of our children.

Earth Politics for the Century of the Environment

If the days of the Economic Century are numbered, what of the future? Whether we like it or not, we are now entering a *Century of the Environment*. In this new century, the hallmark of the realist will have to be regard for the environment. Short-term economic goals will naturally remain, but if they are not subordinated to the ecological imperative they will in time lose all credibility.

At first sight, a Century of the Environment seems an optimistic vision, but that is not what I mean to convey by the phrase. What it signifies is the cruel reality of ecological devastation which will confront us in our everyday lives and which will inevitably shape our civilisation if present trends of destruction continue for just another decade or two. And, given the massive momentum behind present trends and the well-known slowness of human beings to change, there is no doubt that this pillage will continue for much more than two decades. This means that, from its very beginning, the twenty-first century will bear the mark of a massively endangered natural environment. This fact will become increasingly dominant in all fields of politics, from foreign affairs and development policy to research, technology and education. In the Century of the Environment it is the ecological imperative which will become the dominant determinant for law and administration, for city planning and agriculture, for the arts and for religion, for technology and indeed for the economy.

The transition from our present Economic Century to the Century of the Environment will not simply follow from somewhat more ambitiously formulated standards for water, air and soil pollutants, nor from symbolically upgrading the post of environment minister in governments throughout the world. Clearly, the transformation has to go much deeper than that. The sooner we make a start, the better our prospects of salvaging for future generations the amenities and the fabulous degree of freedom which, at least in some parts of the world, made the Economic Century so attractive.

The political task associated with this impending transformation is what I call Earth Politics. Earth Politics will have to be very pragmatic. It must take realistic account of the present and its power structure and it must not demand the impossible of either the people or the decision-makers. In order to evaluate the present accurately, Earth Politics must also show an understanding of the past. For this reason, almost every chapter of this book begins with a few words on the historical background. Not least, since its origins lie in the Economic Century, Earth Politics must take into account the contemporary political bias towards economics. It must develop and offer, so far as possible, *economically* viable strategies for the impending transformation.

Earth Politics must be international. We must get out of the habit of thinking in terms of the nation, a concept which had its heyday in the nineteenth century, but at the same time we must respect the human need for a sense of home and place, for linguistic and cultural identity, as well as for community. Simultaneously, much political decision-making should be decentralised: 'Think globally — act locally'.

For all its pragmatism, Earth Politics also needs a *vision*. That vision must be consistent. In particular it will also have to address, and as far as possible resolve, the fundamental contradiction between the level of consumption of today's rich and what is ecologically feasible for five billion, and one day twelve billion people.

The first part of the book seeks to set the ecological and historical framework for Earth Politics. It is worth paying attention to the beginnings of Earth Politics from within traditional environmental politics because it is here — most encouragingly — we discover that it is possible to bring about meaningful change in the economy in a relatively short space of time and without needing a revolution.

The second part then examines five topics or areas of crisis in which classical environmental politics has not been successful; first steps towards solutions in these areas are outlined.

The third section moves on to put these fragmented elements in a coherent context, which is intended to serve as a politically realistic plan of action based on the generally accepted polluter-pays principle of environmental policy. However it is shown that, in spite of assertions to the contrary, classical environmental policy has at best been only half-hearted in translating this principle into reality. This is the basis from which the concept of ecological tax reform is derived and a new direction for foreign policy after the Earth Summit may evolve.

Finally, the fourth section tries to give clearer expression to the vision of Earth Politics, though it can hardly yet lay claim to being regarded as pragmatic or constituting *realpolitik*. A longer-term vision is nevertheless required to impart the sense of direction which is so deplorably lacking in present-day *realpolitik*.

It is to be hoped that this whole construct — the framework, areas of crisis, a plan of action and the vision — will appeal to the consciousness of the reader — the consciousness that 'things can't continue like this', but also that we still have a good chance to set the necessary changes in motion. Such consciousness is crucial for the earth-political change which we now need.

Consciousness — the Starting Point for Change

In the 1960s anyone speaking of the approaching Century of the Environment would have been open to ridicule. The catastrophic figures we now have were not then known, and in some areas things simply were not as bad as they are now.

In the last two decades, however, environmental awareness has been steadily on the increase, though for quite different reasons in different countries. It seems that some time during 1988 a critical threshold was crossed. The media finally discovered the hole in the ozone layer, global warming, the fate of the tropical forests. *Time*, which at the end of the year normally features a Man or (rarely) a Woman of the Year, for the New Year 1989 put the Earth as Planet of the Year on its cover (Figure 5). *Scientific American*, read all over the world with editions in many languages, devoted its entire September 1989 issue to global environmental issues.

Reacting to public pressure, political leaders lifted environmental issues to the top of their agendas. Chancellor Helmut Kohl managed to have the rainforests on the agendas of two subsequent Economic Summits, 1988 and 1989. The political attention to the global ecology culminated at the 1992 Earth Summit of Rio de Janerio, as mentioned at the outset.

The public did not notice at the time that the world economy was tumbling into recession, the deepest since the great Depression. But only a few weeks after the Earth Summit this fact became the dominant public theme in all OECD countries. The environment disappeared from the headlines. Scepticism and short-terminism prevailed. But the state of the environment continues to worsen. Can we afford to ignore this? I believe we cannot.

However, in order for environmental protection to re-gain the hearts and minds of the public, it should be redesigned in a way that helps economic recovery. It is my firm belief that this is possible. In fact, Chapters 11 and 12 of this book outline my proposals for 'economy friendly' environmental policy.

Environmental policies should not be dogmatic. The Earth wants them to be success oriented.

Chapter 2

Classical Environmental Policy: Pollution Control

Silent Spring

Environmental protection has been practised over a longer period than we often appreciate. We have inherited from past millenia such concepts as closed seasons for hunting, fallow years in agriculture and drainage; from past centuries come the ideas of sanitation, safety at work and refuse disposal. The concept of nature conservation goes back to the nineteenth century. Yellowstone Park, the first National Park on Earth, was put under strict protection as early as 1878, but not until this century have we started to think systematically about environmental protection.

Air quality has perhaps the longest history of neglect — after all, friendly winds carried the smoke 'away'. To assist them, smokestacks were built to make for half-way tolerable air in the industrial centres and belching chimneys became proverbial signs of a region's wealth. Only after the London smog in the winter of 1952, which claimed over 4,000 lives, was a measure introduced which reduced air pollution at source rather than distributing it further afield: the burning of cheap, sulphurous coal for cooking and heating was prohibited. People switched to central heating or used gas or electricity, with flame-effect lamps replacing the homely flicker of the open fire. The smog disappeared, and for two decades the British believed they had solved their environmental problems.

In the early 1960s alarm bells started ringing in the United States. For years, a courageous journalist and author, Rachel Carson, had been investigating the creeping chemical contamination of the natural world; she concentrated her researches on the use of agricultural pesticides, and published her findings in a book with the moving and memorable title *Silent Spring* (Carson 1962, see also Hynes, 1989).

The chemical industry's first reaction was to try to limit the book's impact by buying up the entire print-run and swamping the media with meaningless reassurances, but the book still became a bestseller. America was seized by the fear that its national emblem, the bald-headed eagle, would become extinct as a result of the effects of DDT entering the food chain and destroying the bird's egg shells and thereby its progeny. Such fears were in no way lessened by pictures of foam piled high on rivers, of the filth created by Pittsburgh's heavy industry and of the Cuyahooga River which was so polluted that it ignited from time to time.

The public was outraged and many were ready to stage an ecological revolt. Across the length and breadth of the country people began to take the initiative, and American public opinion, forthright and influential as ever, forced the chemical companies into retreat. The use of DDT and some other pesticides was prohibited forthwith, and henceforth detergents had to be biodegradable. Countless legal battles were fought and won by consumers, conservationists and the victims of pollution. Perhaps the most famous battle was the attempt to halt the construction of the Tellico dam because of the threat it posed to the habitat of a small fish, the snail darter. The National Wildlife Federation, the Sierra Club and the National Audubon Society grew to become major national environmental organisations. Other organisations which emerged included Friends of the Earth, headed by the white-haired radical, David Brower, the Conservation Foundation (which was later to merge with WWF USA) and the National Resources Defense Council.

These bodies, along with many others, played a decisive part at both national and local levels in changing the face of American society. (Dunlap and Mertig, 1992). In 1969, the National Environmental Policy Act (NEPA) was adopted, to be followed by the Clean Air Act in 1970 and the Clean Water Act in 1972. Eventually a total of some 13,000 laws, orders and binding court rulings came into being, creating a tight net of environmental law. To help the enforcement of the new laws, a major national environmental authority, the Environmental Protection Agency (EPA) was created, also in 1970. Hundreds of lawyers were employed by the EPA and the Justice Department to bring proceedings against polluters both large and small.

All of this, it is perhaps worth noting, was happening at a time when very little was to be read in the European press about home-grown environmental pollution, and when 'the Americans' were seen in Europe primarily as the belligerent party in Vietnam and, as such, looked on with scorn and contempt.

Stockholm 1972, Japan and Europe

The idea of bringing environmental protection to the United Nations had its roots in North America as well as in Scandinavia. The General Assembly of the UN decided to convene a UN Conference on the Human Environment in the summer of 1972. Sweden, many of whose lakes were threatened by acid rain, invited the family of nations to Stockholm. The Canadian entrepreneur Maurice Strong was appointed Secretary General to the conference and made great efforts to inspire it with the wealth of ideas already at large in North America.

Figure 3: Logo of the United Nations Environment Conference on the Human Environment (UNCHE) in Stockholm, 1972.

Western Europe and Japan, where in the three years preceding the conference environmental thinking had found its way into the political arena, played very active and supportive roles at the Stockholm conference. The developing countries, however, which at that time were full of self-confidence, in contrast to their position in the 1980s, felt that all the talk of environmental protection was a matter for the rich, industrialised North, whilst they in the South had to consider their own economic development as top priority. Brazil, acting as chair for the Group of 77 (the developing countries), branded the West's ecopolitical demands as neo-colonial and wholly unreasonable. The countries of the still homogeneous Eastern bloc declared that environmental problems were caused by capitalism and imperialism and declined to become involved. Despite the many divisions among delegations, some meaningful decisions were reached, including the establishment of the United Nations Environmental Programme (UNEP). As a symbol of good faith to the South, UNEP was located in Nairobi and funded almost exclusively by the Western nations. Maurice Strong became UNEP's Executive Director for the first two years, and was followed by the Egyptian physician, Dr Mostafa Tolba, who has headed UNEP for almost 20 years. Dr Tolba's successor since 1993 is Elizabeth Dowdeswell, from Canada.

Japan's conversion to ecology came five years later than the USA's, but it was none the weaker for that. Mercury and cadmium poisoning on a massive scale had led to hundreds of deaths amongst fisherfolk and workers. Air pollution in the country's major conurbations had become so intolerable that in Tokyo and some other cities policemen had to wear gas masks. There were hundreds of thousands of cases of chronic bronchitis and other respiratory diseases. A number of spectacular court cases followed in which the polluters were required to make public apologies and ordered to pay their victims large amounts in damages. These verdicts, moreover, were not made on the principle of strict causality but on the basis of statistical evidence. This was something of a reversal of the normal application of the burden of proof and set a most important precedent for current discussions about liability in Europe. Japanese industry had to accept the imposition of a hefty sulphur dioxide charge to finance a fund for the health bills of smoke disease patients.

Municipalities in Japan came up with another remarkable idea: operating licenses for polluting industries were made conditional on accepting 'voluntary' but none the less highly restrictive pollution control obligations. In a country where a firm's success relies very much on the stability of its local workforce, the threat of losing a local factory site is a formidable one (see Tsuru and Weidner, 1985).

In Western Europe the origin of environmental thinking was twofold: wildlife conservation and the nightmares of air pollution. Wildlife became a very popular issue in West Germany in the 1960s through the work of Bernhard Grzimek, director of the Frankfurt Zoo, who reached the hearts and minds of many millions with his numerous TV shows and with his film and book *Serengeti Must Not Die*. Jacques Cousteau's diving expeditions and eloquent TV presentations had a similar effect in France when they demonstrated the alarming decline in underwater life which had taken place in the space of a few decades. In Britain and Holland, bird watchers organised to protect migratory birds.

People all over Europe, indeed the world, who were concerned about the fate of the animal kingdom were attracted to the World Wildlife Fund (WWF), now renamed the World Wide Fund for Nature. Greenpeace, the other major international environmental group, started off much later, developing from a small group of Canadian adventurers and idealists. Their spectacular and daring blockades, mostly on the open seas, drew attention to the slaughter of whales and seals, and also to nuclear weapons testing — as well as to Greenpeace itself.

There is no doubt that the WWF, Greenpeace and a number of prominent authors played a decisive role in establishing worldwide recognition of the need for environmental protection and nature conservation on a global scale — and hence for Earth Politics.

By the end of the 1960s the ground was prepared for pollution control in Europe. Air and water pollution and the excessive use of chemicals had become major political issues in nearly all Western European countries. In Germany, Holland and France, a wide range of factors gave birth to environmental politics as we know it today. Foam mountains were seen on the rivers; fish were dying; asthma and bronchitis were rife in the conurbations; urban planning seemed to lead to nothing but ugly concrete uniformity. In addition, the student unrest of 1968 made public demonstrations much easier to organise, so enabling public opinion on environmental issues to express itself.

France was the first European Community (EC) country to create an environment ministry. France also used its presidency of the Community in the second half of 1972 to initiate environmental policy at Community level. At the Versailles Summit in October 1972 (two months after Stockholm) the heads of state and government of the six countries which then were members of the EEC — in the presence of the heads of government of the three countries joining the Community in 1973 — adopted a strong resolution demanding the preparation of an Environmental Action Programme for the Community.

Germany and Holland were strong supporters of this move, partly because their own environmental laws, whether in preparation or already in force, were placing a considerable burden on their industries. German and Dutch industrialists felt it was time for competition within the Community to be placed on an equal footing. European environmentalists therefore found themselves in the same boat as the captains of Dutch and German industry. They had a common interest in the widest possible promotion of high environmental standards throughout the Community. Nothing in this surprising overlap of interests has basically altered to this day. (For a more detailed discussion of EC environmental policy, see Chapter 3.)

Environmental Policy in West Germany

Germany, like other countries, had a history of environmental protection long before the expression was even coined, although earlier practices are hardly models for the present. In 1873, for example, it was maintained that factory workers could safely withstand a concentration of 30,000 milligrams of sulphur dioxide per cubic metre of air, even over long periods. Today, the World Health Organisation recommends average values of up to 0.04–0.06 milligrams per cubic metre.

Modern environmental protection came into being in Northrhine-Westphalia in the 1960s; the first air quality law was adopted in 1963. But six years later, when Willy Brandt, then leader of the opposition at the Federal level, campaigned for 'blue skies over the Ruhr district', he was ridiculed by his pragmatist political adversaries. Following his election in late 1969, he was the first Federal Chancellor to give high priority to environmental protection in a government programme.

In October 1971 a Federal Environment Programme was adopted, which entailed the passing of eighteen major environmental laws over the subsequent five years, including the Waste Disposal Act 1972 (since 1986, the Waste Act); the Federal Emission (Ambient Air Quality) Act of 1974, in conjunction with the 'TA Luft' (Technical Circular on Air); the 1976 amendment to the Water Management Act of 1957 and the Waste Water Charges Act 1976; the Federal Nature Conservation Act 1976. A whole new field of law was thus created over a very short period.

The Federal Environment Programme of 1971 established three principles of environmental policy which remain valid today: the polluter-pays principle, the precautionary principle and the co-operation principle. The co-operation principle means that all relevant bodies, from the federal level to local communities, must co-operate, alongside business and science, in environmental protection. Environmental activists have always been somewhat suspicious of this principle, which they say is responsible for environmental protection in Germany on the margins of economic development.

Despite their many detractors, these laws had considerable effect. Following the adoption of the Detergents Act 1975 and two ensuing regulations, biodegradable detergents allowed the foam to disappear from rivers; the proportion of detergent-based phosphates in urban waste water fell from 50 to 20 per cent within a few years, and has since become still lower.

There was a drastic reduction in the heavy metal content of rivers as industry and local authorities built the prescribed sewage treatment plants, and, of their own volition, sometimes even went further than was demanded by law.

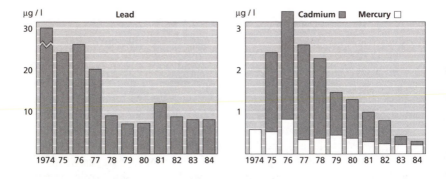

Figure 4: Reducing concentrations of heavy metals in the Rhine. This chart draws on data from the International Commission for Protection of the Rhine, and refers to unfiltered water taken from the Rhine at the Dutch-German border. The reason for the further rise in the values of lead (Pb), cadmium (Cd), and mercury (Hg) in 1976 was the particularly low level of the Rhine.

The air in the agglomerations — not least in the Ruhr — became cleaner, and illicit rubbish tips disappeared one after the other. Today, the biggest headaches for environmental politics are still caused by municipal and hazardous waste, but even these problems should not be insuperable within existing policies. What it all comes down to is that environmental politics has turned into a success story, but one story with a sting in the tail.

By 1975, when the most important laws had been passed or approved by the governing SPD/FDP coalition, a totally new problem was dominating public opinion — the energy crisis and the associated rocketing of fuel prices, which added new burdens to the economy, driving up inflation and leading to a rapid increase in unemployment. Business and union leaders were frequent visitors to ministries and to the Chancellor, warning against burdening industry with any additional costs. Shortly before the summer recess of 1975 Helmut Schmidt summoned the main players in the fields of economics and the environment to Gymnich Castle near Bonn for talks. As a result of the widespread fear of unemployment, no new environmental policy initiatives were undertaken for several years to come (E. Müller, 1986 pp. 51–96). This experience is finding its parallel in the near collapse of German environmental policy during the recession year of 1993 (see Chapter 12). Notwithstanding the governmental stand-still on environmental policy, the later years of Schmidt's chancellorship were by no means insignificant as regards the environmental debate.

Responding to the oil crisis, Germany, like France and other countries, planned an immense build-up of nuclear power so as to become less dependent on foreign energy supplies. But in contrast to France, these plans were hotly debated in Germany, and wherever any electricity generating company or regional government tried to construct a reactor, massive local protest resulted. At Wyhl, Brokdorf, Grohnde, Gorleben and other proposed sites, protesters successfully delayed or even prevented the construction of nuclear installations. Strongly intensified efforts by the contractors to make the reactors safe, perhaps even fool-proof, which added to the costs of nuclear energy, resulted from the protests. Another result was that far fewer reactors were actually built than originally planned, though this turned out to be to Germany's advantage. France, by contrast, had not met significant resistance to its reactor build-up and soon had to cope with costly over-capacity (see also Chapter 5).

These years were also quite significant in classical fields of environmental policy. Two features remain worth mentioning: firstly, the gradual but forceful creation of an environmental administration at Land (or regional) and commune levels, today often envied by foreign visitors, and secondly the gradual switch from ambient quality approaches to emission standards. German activists began to castigate the prevailing 'policy of high smokestacks', just as in the Anglo-Saxon world it became accepted that 'dilution is no solution to pollution'. In water protection, emission standards became official government policy as early as 1975, while in air pollution control it was not until the widespread acknowledgement of the *Waldsterben* or the forest dieback that uniform emission standards became a government doctrine. That was around 1982.

Waldsterben marked the end of the comparatively quiet period of West German environmental policy. All of a sudden, the public was up in arms again. The forests, the home of German myths and fairy tales, were dying. That shock probably went much deeper than the American concern for the bald-headed eagle.

Public debate on the death of forests happened to coincide with the end of the socialist–liberal coalition. The new conservative government composed of the CDU, CSU and FDP faced a broad public demand for decisive action in environmental policies. The Greens made their entry into the Bundestag in 1982. The environment had become even more of a political issue than it had been in the early 1970s, a harbinger for the Century of the Environment.

The Federal Emissions Act and the TA Luft were considerably tightened, and a Large Combustion Plants Regulation was added, involving some twenty billion marks in environmental investments. Germany also fought battles at EC level for the catalytic converter to be made compulsory for motor vehicles. The German public, like that in Scandinavia, Switzerland and Austria, began to believe that the EC was blocking progress on the environment, although this was not exactly a fair assessment (see Chapter 3).

Since May 1987 the Federal environment ministry (which was created only in 1986, in the wake of the Chernobyl disaster) was led by Professor Klaus Töpfer. He quickly developed a good understanding of the functioning of EC environmental policy and soon brought both national and international recognition to this ministry. Helped by the Commission and by France, Denmark and the Netherlands, he pushed the Large Combustion Plants Directive through the EC Council and reached a reasonable compromise on the emissions of small cars (in this instance against resistance from the French side). He also took a leading role internationally on such topics as protection of the North Sea, the rain forests, global warming and the ecological reconstruction of Eastern Europe. At the Earth Summit in Rio de Janeiro he was certainly one of the leading figures representing the North and contributed much to the ultimate success of UNCED.

To sum up, it is no exaggeration to define as 'classical' the course of environmental policy from its beginnings in the late 1960s to date. The dominant topic during this classical period was pollution control.

Why Pollution Control is Just Not Enough

Classical environmental policy remains on the agenda in all major industrialised countries. The US Clean Air Act has been tightened up. The EC's Environmental Impact Assessment Directive is beginning to re-shape planning procedures in all EC countries. Waste reduction has become a popular formula after waste disposal and waste incineration seem to have reached their limits in many countries. Environmental litigation is thriving, and causing serious problems for industry. Green consumer guides are found on bestseller lists. Green investment has become fashionable and is raising the pressure on environmental audits. Product life-cycle analysis is an exciting new topic for environmental analysts and, increasingly, for legislators. It is no longer pollution from the factory alone that is troubling the environmental community but the products themselves which are targeted.

The fall of communism and the opening up of Eastern Europe has given the West the immensely comfortable feeling that market economies have protected the environment much better than state bureaucrats. The ecological tragedies of Eastern Europe also seem to demonstrate that pollution control is truly indispensable and should be continued. Furthermore, the collapse of communism is seen as a most welcome enlargement of the market for pollution-control technologies developed in the West.

Prospering countries and prospering companies seem to be much better than poor ones at controlling pollution and protecting the environment. The moral seems clear: become rich and you will be able to shoulder the cost of protecting the environment.

However, as we pointed out in the first chapter, this formula leaves an unsolved dilemma. Becoming rich in the conventional Western sense means or involves very high levels of consumption. Per capita energy and material consumption of the rich exceed the consumption levels of the poor by a factor of ten or twenty. The environmental destruction outlined in the first chapter of this book can hardly be influenced by making the rich countries yet a little cleaner. When President Bush boasted in Rio de Janeiro of strict pollution control laws in his country, he made hardly any impression on the developing countries. From a global perspective, pollution control laws passed in Europe, North America and Japan are fundamentally inadequate for a number of reasons. They are geographically limited to the rich countries; the poorer nations can easily argue that this sort of protection is beyond their means and in any case belated. They are thematically restricted; the wasteful use of resources, such as energy, minerals, land and water, is effectively not covered (see Part Two of this book). They are mostly limited to specific environmental media (air, water, soil). They involve high administrative costs both for the state and for those regulated; the addressee of the classical environmental legislation is the legal profession rather than the simple, sometimes illiterate, polluter or consumer of natural resources. They tend to frustrate rather than stimulate the productive sectors of the economy.

Pollution control and bureaucratic regulation appear to be incapable of solving the major environmental problems of our time. A fairly fundamental review appears to be necessary for the methods and philosophies of environmental policy. This challenge will be taken up in Part Three of this book.

Chapter 3

Europe

Global Crisis — A European Heritage

In historical terms, European civilisation was a late-comer; China, Egypt, Mesopotamia and India were all civilised areas earlier. When Hannibal marched over the Alps with his column of elephants he came upon tribes to the North who were at a stage in their development comparable to that of the Amazon Indians today.

Although Europe did not 'invent' civilisation, it was none the less responsible for the spreading throughout the world of a particular kind of civilisation. Incredibly different Europeans stand together as the founders or the symbols of that civilisation: Hippocrates and Aristotle, Augustus and Constantine, Charlemagne and William the Conqueror, Cervantes and Shakespeare, Leonardo, Copernicus and Galileo, Columbus and Pizarro, Luther and Erasmus, Machiavelli and Louis XIV, Newton and Kant, Rousseau and Goethe, Robespierre and Napoleon, Rembrandt and Beethoven, Linné and Darwin, Adam Smith and Karl Marx, James Watt and Carnot, Lavoisier and Wöhler, Livingstone and Amundsen, Queen Victoria and Bismarck, Daimler and MacAdam, Henri Dunant and Maria Montessori, Max Planck and Madame Curie, Einstein and Bohr, Pasteur and Pavlov, Hertz and Marconi, Hitler and Stalin, Wernher von Braun and Yuri Gagarin, Heisenberg and Prigogine, Robert Schuman, Dag Hammarskjöld and Mikhail Gorbachev, Picasso and the Beatles, they were or are all Europeans, and their inventions or their influence changed the world.

The development of North and South America, Africa, the Russian/Soviet empire, Australia and Oceania was decisively shaped by European conquerors and European thought. Even Asia, radiating earlier civilisation and inner power, accepted the European contribution of science and technology, military and constitutional structures, economics and a European definition of progress.

If the Century of Religious Wars (as characterised in the first chapter) was a purely European phenomenon, the Century of the Nation State was spread through colonialisation across the whole world; the Economic Century is indisputably a global affair, even if its spiritual fathers, Adam

Smith, David Ricardo, Karl Marx, Vilfredo Pareto, Joseph A. Schumpeter and John Maynard Keynes, were all Europeans.

The great explorers opened the way for the European missionaries and the colonisers and, in their wake, those who plundered the world under the veil of spreading civilisation and a perceived duty to convert the world to Christianity. Armies, colonial companies and European-language administrations secured the conquest.

Even for nature-lovers like Alexander von Humboldt and Charles Darwin, the Earth was first and foremost a treasure trove, a rich seam to be exploited and a subject for study. For their lesser scientific followers, the Earth was there to be exploited in an exciting trophy-hunt in the furtherance of their academic or political careers.

Missionary schools, medicine and colonial farms, mining, railways and cars, guns and bush-knives, alcohol and syphilis, rats, dogs, pigs, goats, chickens and cows, potatoes, wheat and maize, bulldozers and petrol stations, general stores and rough bars, steaks, ketchup and Coca Cola were the fruit of European and, later, American 'civilisation'. 'Out there' and at home, the shirt-sleeved pioneer spirit won great admiration. To have shot an elephant, cut down a rebel, burnt a square mile of jungle or cheated the natives in a trade-deal were all acts of heroism for several generations of Europeans. In Europe we prefer to ignore and repress the terrible side of European expansion and draw attention to the spreading of schools, hospitals and well-functioning administrations. But the quincentenary of Columbus's 'discovery' of America has served as a good opportunity for us in the North to recognise what is dangerously wrong with this view (see Boorstin, 1983; Sale, 1991).

Breath-taking European achievements over four centuries, built on the history of more than two thousand years, have nevertheless loaded a heavy burden of responsibility, indeed of guilt upon us Europeans. It does not need a great stretch of the imagination to see the present environmental crisis as a direct consequence of world-wide European exploitation and colonisation, together with a population explosion which also originated in Europe (see Chapter 8). The environmental crisis is perhaps the most serious historical burden with which Europe is faced.

Post-War Europe

Two world wars, unleashed by Germany, brought a swift end to European domination of the planet. Only in concert with each other was it now possible for Europeans to provide a counterweight to the new Great Powers, and it is now only in concert with the other nations of the world that we Europeans may take responsibility for our planet.

One of the most important contributions Europe can make to a meaningful global environmental policy is for Europeans to admit openly their role during the past five centuries. Moreover, we should be among the first to acknowledge the imperative of *sustainable development* for ourselves.

To what extent have we in Europe taken the road towards environmentally sound development?

The two world wars left a trail of devastation not just in Germany but right across Europe. 1945 was for Germany and her neighbours the time to make a new start. It was also a time for reflection, and one thing was clear to all: inhumanity like that which took place at Auschwitz and Hiroshima must never again be allowed. Depoliticised models of economic reconstruction, agriculture, technology and science were supported wholeheartedly by both the population and the state authorities. The United States was seen by Europeans as the saviour. America sent CARE parcels to Germany rather than demanding war-reparations. The only condition imposed by the victors was that of a democratic constitution, a condition which was gladly fulfilled. For the Americans the concepts of democracy and freedom embrace also that of 'free enterprise' (e.g. Friedman, 1962). This was a new understanding of freedom for most non-Anglo-Saxon Europeans for whom freedom traditionally had much more to do with civil liberties than with business, but it turned out to be very much to the benefit of the West European economies, as soon became apparent in the contrast between East and West. After the Berlin Blockade and the take-over of Czechoslovakia by supporters of Stalin's Soviet Union, the old horrors of National Socialism were soon overshadowed by the fear of Communism.

The Germans and the French, the Italians and the Belgians, the Dutch and the Luxemburgers were of one opinion, that war must become a thing of the past, and they set about building a small European grouping. Concessions were wrung from the Germans and the French: the Germans had for the time being to give up all hope of reunification; the French had to accept limitations to their centuries old concept of national sovereignty and agree to a referendum in the Saar. The Benelux countries and Italy did not have much to lose and so it was possible for an agreement to be reached among the six states on the European Coal and Steel Community, the EEC Treaty and Euratom.

The 1957 EEC Treaty, although politically motivated, was clearly an economic treaty. For Europe it meant the (late) arrival of the Economic Century. Economic expansion was the explicit objective of Article 2 of the Treaty, and since European law was accorded primacy over national law, economic expansion in effect became a quasi-constitutional goal for the member states.

In the early years of the European Economic Community there was virtually no interest in the environmental questions, yet rapid economic development on the American model led to an enormous increase in environmental damage. Energy consumption, traffic, urban sprawl, the use of agrochemicals, air and water pollution and waste all reached hitherto unknown levels, and this at a time which is now recorded in the history books as the happy post-war period of peaceful reconstruction and reconciliation between old enemies.

Above all, there was a spectacular boom in agricultural production. Guaranteed prices set at a high level, together with the exclusion from the EEC of imports which might have competed with the products thus guaranteed, led in time to an ever greater increase in production. The hungry years became a thing of the past. France and Holland pushed agricultural exports within the Community, and what was not consumed went to growing 'mountains' and 'lakes' of food and drink. West Germany and northern Italy meanwhile profited from the enlarged market for their industrial products, and at the same time Belgium and Luxembourg benefited from their position at the centre of the new Europe. Thus each member state had its own reasons for holding back criticism of the development of the market in agricultural products, a development which was, predictably enough, getting out of hand. The crude slogan 'grow or make way' which, through the Mansholt Plan, had become EEC doctrine did not meet too much opposition among farmers; those who had to make way and could not retire early easily found new work in the expanding industrial and service sectors.

The true loser was the environment. Land consolidation, simplified crop rotation, increased application of chemicals, a high level of mechanisation, the division of livestock from plant production and the complete dominance of economics over all other aspects of land management — all these led, it is true, to an unprecedented increase in production, but at the same time they also brought about a disastrous assault on the ecological quality of the land (see further Chapter 7).

In other areas the EEC, by its very existence, contributed to the degradation of the environment. The Treaty concluded by the EEC first in Yaoundé and later in Lomé with the African, Caribbean and Pacific (ACP) developing countries promoted the transport infrastructure and the export of ores and agricultural commodities. Forest clearing, excessive mining and rapidly saturated commodity markets were the inevitable result. This led to falling commodity prices, despite efforts in the Stabex protocols to keep them at reasonably high levels (see further Chapter 8).

The European Community's Regional Policy benefited southern Italy in particular and a few other regions which had been left behind industrially, and had the aim of effecting ever more rapid structural change:

more roads, industrialisation, mechanised agriculture and provision for tourism were the result, all at great cost to the environment.

Energy, one of the most important factors in environmental degradation, was not the subject of Community policy as such. There was, however, always a clear and tacit understanding that the Community should help to make available as much energy as possible at the lowest possible prices. Euratom was a Community for the promotion of nuclear research and energy, while the Coal and Steel Community helped to keep European coal on the market even though it was no longer truly competitive.

Other areas of EEC policy, such as free trade, industrial development and administrative and technical standardisation, which traditionally aimed to promote growth, have either proved directly damaging to the environment, or been at least of no ecological benefit.

Thus the EEC, precisely because it was founded as a community with the express aim of promoting economic expansion and growth, presented from its inception an additional danger to the environment, even though this may not have been apparent to its founding fathers. In the 1960s the EEC enjoyed an almost entirely positive image, and to have drawn up a balance sheet of EEC environmental sins would at that time have appeared to the majority as inappropriate hair-splitting.

EC Environmental Policy — A Model for the World?

The pollution of air, water and soil called, however, for a political answer. By 1972 the time had come for the European Economic Community — or European Community as it later came to be known — to decide on a specific environmental policy. The six heads of government of Belgium, Germany, France, Italy, Luxembourg and the Netherlands met on 19 and 20 October 1972 in Paris and Versailles in the presence of the heads of government of Denmark, Ireland and the United Kingdom. They called on the institutions of the European Community to draw up an environmental action programme by 31 July 1973.

In 1973, by when there were nine member states and ministers with responsibility for the environment, the First Environmental Action Programme was agreed, already establishing the principle that 'the best environmental policy consists in preventing pollution at source.' Technical progress must be so directed 'that its effect on the environment should be taken into account at the lowest possible cost to the community'. It is noteworthy that the Action Programme specifically refers to Article 2 of the EEC Treaty, quoting from it that the Community shall have as its task the promotion of economic expansion, explaining however that this will in future be unthinkable without environmental protection. Only the Maastricht Union Treaty, which entered into force in November 1993, changed Article 2 to specify economic growth as 'sustainable' and 'respecting the environment'.

It was in introducing EC environmental policy that, the directive, a legal instrument which had already been tried and tested in EC law received new prominence. While the directive is not — as is the case with an EC Regulation — directly applicable law, and tends to leave much leeway in terms of implementation, member states are obliged within a given time limit to translate a directive into nationally applicable law, and any individual Community citizen can lodge a complaint with the Commission if she or he considers that a national, regional or local authority has failed to implement a directive. Thereupon, under Article 169 of the EEC Treaty, the European Commission, having established the validity of the complaint, may open proceedings which can lead to a judgment of the European Court of Justice (ECJ) in Luxembourg against the member state in question (Krämer, 1991, also Johnson and Corcelle, 1989). Countries against which judgment has been given in the ECJ have generally taken steps to remedy the omission, although better compliance and perhaps certain sanctions against non-compliers might be thought desirable. The existing procedures are, however, unique in international environmental policy and as such deserve support. The submission to supranational authorities in environmental policy practised in the European Community may well become a legal model for Earth Politics of the future.

The privilege of proposing EU environmental legislation lies with the Commission, and early drafts are routinely discussed with national experts even before these drafts receive the status of a Commission proposal. The European Parliament and the Economic and Social Committee of the EU have to be heard before the appropriate Council of Ministers can finally make its decision (see Haigh, 1989, and see Figure 5).

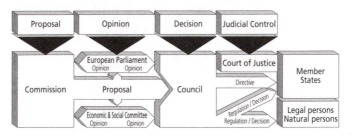

Figure 5: The process and scrutiny of decision-making in the EC. To whom is it directed?

When in 1972 the heads of government, and in 1973 the ministers for the environment, considered an environmental policy for the European Community, they were faced with a problem: the 1957 EEC Treaty made no provision for environmental policy. In order to provide a legal basis for Community environmental legislation, they therefore had to fall back on a flexible interpretation of existing Treaty Articles: the harmonisation of national legislation, as laid down in Article 100 of the EEC Treaty, would also now be applied to provisions covering environmental matters. As we have seen in the preceding chapter, it was primarily Germany and Holland which had an economic interest in such harmonisation.

In cases where no harmonisation pretext could be established, i.e. where the provisions in question did not directly affect the functioning of the common market, there still remained Article 235 of the EEC Treaty which permits member states acting unanimously to take appropriate measures in cases 'where the Treaty has not provided the necessary powers', but only in so far as these measures do not conflict with other treaty articles.

The unanimity required for decision-making in the EEC was not too great a hindrance to progress in 1957 when there were only six closely allied states, but increasingly became a problem after the accession of three new member states in 1973. Denmark on joining had reserved for itself the right of consent by the Market Committee of its national parliament, with the result that most EC legislation could only be adopted after the parliament in Copenhagen had given the green light. Britain, of course, took a notoriously sceptical attitude to many EC developments to such an extent that negotiations were often a long drawn-out affair. EC environment policy therefore got off to a difficult start, and the achievements of such a short period of time are therefore all the more remarkable.

The most important directives of the first four years of EC environmental policy were the Detergents Directive (73/404/EEC); the Surface Water Directive (75/440/EEC), establishing three categories of water quality; the Discharge of Dangerous Substances (in the Aquatic Environment) Directive (76/464/EEC), with its black and grey lists of substances, requiring numerous 'Daughter Directives' (see further pages 31–32); the Bathing Water Directive (76/160/EEC); the Waste Framework Directive (75/442/EEC), requiring waste disposal plans; substantial amendments to the Vehicle Noise Directive (73/350/EEC).

The Second Environmental Action Programme of 1977–81 was a continuation of the first and focused on air quality, control of chemicals, drinking water and nature conservation. Among the resulting directives were the Toxic and Dangerous Waste Directive (78/319/EEC); the Lead in Petrol Directive (78/611/EEC); the first Pesticides Directive (banning DDT, among others; 79/117/EEC); the New Chemicals Directive (79/831 EEC), commonly referred to as the Sixth Amendment (of an earlier Directive, 67/548/EEC) on the classification, packaging and labelling of chemicals; the Sixth Amendment introduced pre-market testing, notification and licensing of new chemicals; the Air Quality Directive (80/779/EEC), fixing air quality standards for SO_2 and suspended particulates; the Directive on a limit value for Lead in the Air (82/884/EEC); the Drinking Water Directive (80/778/EEC) containing highly ambitious standards for pesticide contamination, which eventually led to the ban in several member states of some herbicides of rather subordinate toxicological significance (see also Chapters 7 and 10); the Birds Directive (79/409 EEC, on the conservation of wild birds and their habitats) which is continually violated by virtually all member states (see Chapter 8); various amendments to existing noise directives and regulation 348/81 limiting imports of whale products.

The Third Environmental Action Programme of 1982–86 emphasised for the first time the need truly to implement in practice the directives that had already been adopted. New topics were also addressed, leading to a number of new directives. These include the 'Seveso Directive' (82/501/EEC) covering the prevention of major industrial accidents and emergency response measures; several 'daughter directives' to the Dangerous Substances into Water Directive (e.g. mercury: 82/176/EEC and 84/156/EEC), cadmium 83/513/EEC), lindane/hexachlorocyclohexane 84/491/EEC); the Beverage Containers Directive (85/339 EEC); the Directive on Transfrontier Shipment of Toxic and Dangerous Wastes (84/631); the Sewage Sludge Directive (86/278/EEC); the Nitrogen Dioxide in Air Directive (85/203/EEC); the Environmental Impact Assessment Directive (85/501/EEC); a particularly important directive which had to wait nearly five years for its adoption, owing to the Danish reservations; the new Lead in Petrol Directive (85/210/EEC), requiring lead-free petrol to be offered Community-wide.

When in 1985 the twelve member states were negotiating a fourth Environmental Action Programme, it was already clear that the EEC Treaty would be amended by the Single European Act and that a special environment section would be added to the treaty. The main points of the Fourth Environmental Action Programme were the enforcement of the existing environmental legislation in all countries of the Community. This gave yet more recognition and visibility to a central concern of the Institute for European Environmental Policy, which since 1981 had been studying the implementation of EC environmental legislation at national and local levels. Other major subject areas of the Fourth Action Programme included new initiatives addressing agricultural problems (nitrates, further pesticides and general habitat protection); the deliberate release of genetically modified organisms; environment and employment (a declaration rather than practical policy) and the development of further economic instruments for environmental protection; a cross-media approach to chemicals control; freedom of information and, finally, environmental research.

By the end of 1992 some further important directives have been adopted and decisions taken, among them the decision to set up a European

Environmental Agency (Regulation EEC No. 1210/90); the Large Combustion Plants Directive (88/609/EEC) intended to reduce acid rain by reducing emissions of SO_2 from large combustion plants by 58 per cent between 1980 and 2003; the Directive on the Freedom of Access to Information on the Environment (90/313/EEC), embarrassingly much delayed by Germany, seemingly for fear of floods of public requests that might paralyse the already overloaded administrations; the directive on the deliberate release of genetically engineered organism (90/220/EEC) (see further Chapter 9); the Urban Waste Water Directive (91/271/EEC) which followed the public outcry about the pollution of the Adriatic Sea; the Nitrates from Agriculture Directive (91/676/EEC); the Eco-label Regulation (Reg. EEC No. 880/92); a new Waste Framework Directive (91/165/EEC), with emphasis on waste avoidance and on recycling, plus two Directives on Waste Incineration (89/369/EEC and 89/429/EEC); it has to be said that Denmark and Germany generally feel impeded rather than encouraged by the Community's waste policy, notably by the draft packaging directive proposed in September 1993; the Habitat Directive (flora, fauna, habitats; 92/43/EEC), which sets out to establish a comprehensive nature protection policy for the Community.

A comprehensive treatment of all EC (now EU) directives including their history and their impact on Britain is presented by Nigel Haigh (1989 and 1991).

Uniform Emission Standards Versus Environmental Quality Objectives

Adopting directives was not generally without conflict. On the question of quality objectives versus uniform emission standards, in particular, there has often been a significant disagreement above all between Britain — favouring quality objectives — and Germany — favouring uniform emission standards throughout the Community. The discussion about the Discharge of Dangerous Substances (in the Aquatic Environment) Directive (76/464/EEC) was a case in point. The day before the Directive came before the Council for the first time, on 15 October 1975, a leader appeared in the *Times* under the heading 'The Rhine and the Thames'. It contained sharp attacks on the European Commission for giving precedence to the German principle of emission standards (which, as was well known, had not until then cleaned up the Rhine) over the British principle of quality objectives (with the help of which the Thames had already been made acceptably clean at a relatively reasonable cost).

For the British observer the case was clear: economically inefficient and doctrinaire German environmental policy was to be foisted on the whole EC, to the detriment both of the environment and of the economy.

For German observers, on the other hand, it was incomprehensible that the British were not prepared to accept the evidently logical and practical principle of uniform emission standards.

But reality clearly lies elsewhere. In reality the differing views point first and foremost to a massive conflict of *economic* interests. Equal European water and air quality objectives mean far higher costs for Germany (and Holland) than they do for Britain, where the wind exports the pollution and the short rivers do not accumulate high concentrations of pollutants. For Britain, on the other hand, uniform emission standards are unattractive from a cost-benefit point of view; they either lead to exorbitant costs or they do not lead to acceptable local air and water quality. For Germany and Holland, however, to apply *uniform* emission standards throughout the EC would have a threefold *economic* advantage. Firstly, the import of pollution from other countries is reduced cost-free for the domestic economies; secondly, industries in Britain and other countries would have to incur additional costs, which should be good for German and Dutch competitivity; thirdly, emission control technologies, well developed in Germany and Holland, find an enlarged market.

In the end, however, the Community has always found a solution to such differences of interest. In the case just cited it is possible to combine uniform emission standards and quality objectives. This possibility was indeed emphasised in the EC's Fourth Environmental Action Programme. The Discharge of Dangerous Substances Directive leaves it to member states to apply emission standards (by reference to quality standards) for the grey list substances but makes emission standards obligatory for the (more toxic) black list substances but with the possibility of exceptions.

The Single Market and Maastricht

EC environmental policy is certainly a successful example of international environmental protection, and it can be reasonably assumed that without the EC there would be less stringent environmental protection in most of the Community area. But it is equally safe to assume that without the EC the strain on the natural environment would also be less in most of its area. This stress is bound to increase with the completion of the Internal Market, normally referred to in Britain as the Single Market.

The Single European Act of 1987 amended the Treaty to include in Article 8A (after Maastricht 7A) the removal at the end of 1992 of all barriers on the movement of people, goods, services and capital. A White Paper (1985) was published, listing some 300 steps necessary for the completion of the Internal Market.

The Council decision on completing the internal market gave new impetus to Europe. Before 1985 there had been much talk of

'Eurosclerosis' comparing the Old Continent unfavourably with the vigorous countries of the Pacific Rim and even the United States. After the Single Market decision the tone became much more optimistic, and the Cecchini Report calculated total economic benefits for the citizens of Europe to the tune of some £130 billion (Cecchini, 1987). These benefits following on completion of the European internal market by 1992 were calculated at £58 billion from dismantling trade restrictions, £48 billion as a result of the enlarged market enabling firms to benefit from economies of scale, a further £38 billion as firms responded to increased competition by clamping down on costs, and finally, some £8 billion with the abolition of customs formalities.

However all this is bound to increase the strain on the environment through an increase in economic activity and in the flow of traffic (see Chapter 6) which means that even more land will be covered by concrete. It means more pollution, more waste and a higher level of energy consumption. Moreover, there is the danger that increased competition will lead to local economic crises which can easily divert public attention from environmental protection. This fear, formulated first in 1987 at a time when it sounded very far-fetched, has become a gruesome reality by 1993.

More threats to the environment come from other Single Market stipulations. Waste may legally be declared as a tradeable good, and is therefore able to cross frontiers without restriction, even though the Council has endorsed the 'proximity principle' under which waste should be disposed of close to the point of production, and the principle that countries should aim to be self-sufficient in disposal facilities.

More troubles may flow from the Single Market through the application of the new Article 100B of the EEC Treaty, under the provisions of which the Council, by majority vote, can decide that member states may, in the case of a particular product, have to accept as equivalent to their own another member state's provisions which may in fact be less stringent.

The doubling of the Regional Fund does not augur well for the environment, as much of this money is used for buildings, installations and transport infrastructure, all of which are putting additional burdens on the environment (Baldock, 1989). It must be said, however, that the European Union has at least undertaken to apply its own Environmental Impact Assessment Directive to projects funded by the Regional Fund. The EU further encourages countries in receipt of these funds to request funding for environmental protection installations.

The Commission is, at least in theory, aware of the new threats to the environment, and pushed for the inclusion of an environment chapter in the Single European Act of 1987 and for further improvements in the new Union Treaty agreed at Maastricht in December 1991. Articles 3K (Maastricht) and 130 R-T (since the Single European Act) provide a fairly solid mandate for far-reaching environmental policies, and the integration of environmental needs into other Community policies now has a sound legal basis (Baldock et al., 1992).

In particular, Article 130R paragraph 2 is potential dynamite. It makes the polluter-pays principle part of the treaty. Why should we not interpret that basic principle much more radically than before? The principle of eliminating the pollution at source can also be carried further to address the input factors and early stages of production rather than end-of-the-pipe pollution control. The integration of environmental protection into other areas of EU policy theoretically gives the EU Environment Commissioner a powerful voice *vis-à-vis* the other EU portfolios.

It will fall to us Europeans wherever possible to translate potentially far-reaching yet abstract legal titles into legal and economic reality. This is where a certain sense of optimism again becomes relevant. Millions of European citizens have become involved in *active* environmental work, mostly in local and national environmental advocacy groups. More than a hundred such groups have founded the European Environmental Bureau (EEB) in Brussels, whose voice is heard in every proposal for a directive.

Public opinion, a strong push from the European Parliament's Environment Committee and the steady pro-environment work by the Environment Commissioner and the Directorate General XI of the Commission have all moved environmental policy ever higher up the political agenda of the Community. One reflection of this is the Fifth Environmental Action Programme adopted in late 1992 (Commission of the EC, 1992b). It can be seen as a turning point in the direction this book is advocating. 'Towards Sustainability', the title of the Programme, means more than just pollution control and habitat protection. Emphasis is now on the integration of environmental aspects into other Community policies, notably energy and transport policies, previously sacred cows of an expansion-oriented Community which are now addressed as sources of environmental degradation. The Community strategy to limit CO_2 emissions through efficient energy use is a very important step in this direction; it will be further discussed in Chapters 5 and 11 (Commission of the EC, 1991). In October 1993, after years of struggle, the location was decided for the newly created European Environmental Agency. It will be established in Lysø near Copenhagen.

The Maastricht Treaty which received such hostile criticism from nationalists, regionalists and environmentalists alike, will, if finally adopted, considerably strengthen the EC's commitment to environmental protection and introduce important changes to the way EC/EU policies are developed and implemented (Verhoeve et al., 1992).

Larger Europe

The European Union is by no means all of Europe. First there are the six remaining members of EFTA (European Free Trade Association), the organisation which was originally Britain's answer to the European Economic Community of the Six, but now consists of Austria, Finland, Iceland, Norway, Sweden and Switzerland (the latter speaking so far also on behalf of tiny Lichtenstein). After the successful negotiations on the European Economic Area (EEA) which ended in 1991, the EFTA countries will (with the exception of Switzerland which voted against the EEA in September 1992) co-operate very closely with the EU; one of the main results of these negotiations was the EFTA countries unrestricted agreement with the 'four freedoms' set out in Article 7A (earlier 8A) of the Union Treaty.

Due to their geographical position, the EFTA countries — except Iceland — are net importers of pollution. This simple fact may have facilitated their early awareness of the environmental problems, but in any case they were all early advocates of a vigorous environmental policy both domestically and internationally. For them the European Community, now Union, is not just a large economic power but also, very annoyingly, an exporter of pollution. In the context of the EEA, the EFTA countries will push for more stringent environmental measures. With the likely accession to the Union of Austria, Sweden, Norway, and later Finland, Iceland and possibly Switzerland, Council majorities are very likely to be shifted towards more stringent environmental policies.

Next in the queue to become associated with, and eventually full members of, the EC are Malta, Cyprus, Poland and Hungary, the Czech and Slovak states; Turkey, Lithuania, Latvia and Estonia; Slovenia, Croatia and whatever Bosnia-Herzegovina may have become; one day, hopefully, Serbia with what may be left of former Yugoslavia; Romania, Bulgaria and Albania; Moldavia (unless it unites with Romania) and, of course, Russia, Byelorussia and Ukraine. Daunting political and economic problems wait to be solved. This book can neither predict what will happen nor make any political proposals for solutions. But all in all, the road seems to be clear for ever more economic integration between East and West.

Both East and West believe that to clean up the almost unbelievable ecological mess and destruction left by the old socialist regimes, the most promising strategy is industrial and administrative modernisation on the Western model. Several bilateral and multilateral programmes were set up to help economic and ecological recovery, one of the earliest being the EC PHARE programme designed to help Poland and Hungary along the path to environmental recovery. Worth mentioning is also the newly established European Bank for Reconstruction and Development (EBRD) in London which lends hundreds of millions of pounds to Eastern Europe and places special emphasis on ecologically sound reconstruction. For a nation-by-nation analysis of the ecological and economic situation in the East and of remedial measures, see the comprehensive book edited by Joseph Alcamo (1992).

One should not be lulled into complacency by the convenient belief that with the advent of the market system and with some pollution control laws, technologies and programmes, Eastern Europe would automatically move along an environmentally sustainable path. In fact, as a direct result of the Westernisation of the East, there will be far more private cars, so there will be more roads, more urban sprawl and more landscape and habitat destruction. More municipal waste, more high-tech associated toxic substances and more pollution from household chemicals should also be expected.

The planned economy has had its day. It did not allow its citizens to know about their economic and ecological situation and therefore misled all concerned. It did not allow prices to tell the economic truth about costs of production or of scarcity and thereby created wastefulness on the one hand and shortages on the other. But if market economies fail to let prices tell the ecological truth (see Chapter 10), the result could be even worse: the damage could be irreversible.

Chapter 4

Global Visions Emerging

From Kennedy to the Club of Rome

'New Frontiers' was the promise in 1960 of the young President John F. Kennedy, both to his compatriots and to the world at large (Kennedy, 1960). The post-war desire for peace had been stifled by the Cold War but, for the first time in many years, in Kennedy, a political leader had emerged, with a credible belief in the interests of the Earth, rather than solely those of his own country. He concluded an 'Alliance for Progress' with Latin America, sincerely hoping for change which would be to the mutual advantage of both North and South America. He sought talks on bilateral as well as global problems with the post-Stalin Soviet Union, which had startled self-confident America by sending the first satellite, Sputnik, into orbit three years earlier.

Kennedy was a pioneer of Earth Politics, albeit without a specifically ecological hue. He wanted to tackle and solve the problems of the modern world with science and technology, and with scientifically-based medium-term planning. Think tanks sprang into being, and a growing number of scientists started to take seriously the problems of the world. Until then, or at least until the 1930s, most scientists had taken pride in having nothing to do with politics (see Chapter 16).

The Cuban missile crisis in 1962, the escalating war in Vietnam and Kennedy's assassination in November 1963 all seemed to presage a sticky end for this brave new beginning, but the spark was kept alive in different places. As far as global environmental co-operation was concerned, there were a number of important developments.

In 1973, after years of preparation, the International Institute for Applied Systems Analysis (IIASA), was established at Laxenburg, near Vienna, following negotiations between Kennedy's adviser, McGeorge Bundy, and the Soviet Academy of Sciences, with the support of ten nations of West and East. Here many useful methods for global environmental analysis were developed, and scientific contacts between East and West have been maintained ever since.

The international Pugwash movement — founded in the 1950s by Cyrus Eaton, a Canadian industrialist, in the village of Pugwash, Nova

Scotia — became a regular meeting place for leading scientists from East and West to discuss and advise on disarmament, reduction in tension and common threats, including those to the environment.

At the International Council of Scientific Unions (ICSU), in Paris, a scientific committee on environmental problems (SCOPE) was instituted, which dealt in particular with world-wide environmental issues.

The Italian industrialist, Aurelio Peccei, together with the then Secretary General of OECD, Alexander King, and a number of others founded the Club of Rome and began to address the 'world problematique'. The club commissioned a report of hugely ambitious scope which studied the dynamic inter-relations between population, food consumption, industrial production, resource consumption and environmental pollution. Using fairly simple mutual relations, the computer model produced catastrophic scenarios ending in resource depletion, total pollution and overpopulation followed by a sharp population decline owing to starvation or other disasters.

The report which was published under the name *The Limits to Growth* (Meadows et al., 1972), was an instantaneous success, and more than twenty million copies were sold worldwide. The Club of Rome and the young team of authors achieved political fame and clout previously unimaginable for scientists.

The report came just in time to influence the final preparations for the United Nations Conference on the Human Environment held at Stockholm, but reaction to it was mixed. Whilst public opinion in the West gave credence to the report and its pessimistic scenarios, the Third World, in so far as it acknowledged the report at all, was indignant. 'First the North gets rich through unfettered growth at the South's expense, then, having gained all the wealth, the North tells us the limits to growth have been reached,' was, in effect, the response of the developing countries at the Stockholm Conference at which Northern concern with the environment were discredited as neocolonialist.

A response from the South to the *Limits to Growth* was the Bariloche Foundation's *Limits to Poverty* (Gallopin et al., 1974) report, a call for growth and equity for the Third World. More ecologically consistent were the Cocoyoc Declaration and the Blueprint for Survival. Both demanded heavy material sacrifices from the North (which rendered them peripheral to political realities in the North). There were also many voices in the North ready to attack the Club of Rome's 'pessimism', countering it with technological optimism (e.g. Maddox, 1973). The club itself followed up with further reports (e.g. Mesarovic and Pestel, 1974) which made regional distinctions and gave greater prominence to technical progress, thus coming closer to the opposing views, but even so the club continued to be criticised as pessimistic.

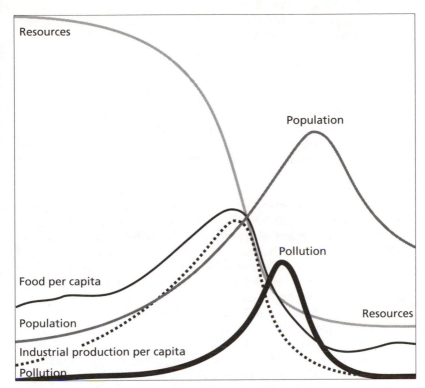

Figure 6: Limits to growth (from Meadows 1972). Computer models linked the five variables — population, pollution, resources, per capita industrial production and food — and projected their development along a time axis from 1980–2100. In the standard model, catastrophe occurs in the first half of the twenty-first century.

The Club of Rome's great merit lay not simply in commissioning and publicising *The Limits to Growth* but in its *Earth vision*. It made the political world irrevocably aware of the interconnections between several well-known global problems which in the past had been seen and tackled in isolation, if at all. It also became undeniably clear that there might be a fundamental problem in using First World standards of living and consumption as the goal of 'development' for some five let alone ten billion people. For a history of the club's influence, see Moll (1991).

This ecopolitical awareness reached another high point in America with the publication in 1980 of the Global 2000 Report to President Jimmy Carter, a much more comprehensive study of the state of the world than the *Limits to Growth* (Barney et al., 1980). A four-page summary essay by Thomas Lovejoy about species extinction made public alarm bells ring. Some ten, twenty or even up to fifty animal or plant species were estimated to be lost every day, a figure that would have been unimaginable until that time (see Chapter 9 for further details).

A Decade Lost

The Limits To Growth debate was exacerbated by the oil crisis. The OPEC countries managed to draw political advantage from the apparent scarcity of one important resource and the world's attention remained focused on our common fate, despite the very slow progress of détente and the disarmament talks.

The basic sentiments of sitting together in one spaceship finally gave way with the invasion of Afghanistan by Soviet troops, the Iranian hostage affair and the ensuing militarisation of American thinking under President Ronald Reagan. Political silence fell over the global ecological themes.

The American psyche had been deeply wounded by Vietnam, Watergate, the OPEC oil price shock and the hostage crisis, and needed to be placated, and people abroad understood that. But the cure turned tragic during the Reagan years. President Reagan sought ever greater confrontation with the Soviet Union, which he called 'the Evil Empire', and followed a path of unparalleled rearmament, calling upon vast financial resources which were not truly available. In America this led to unprecedented budget deficits which in turn pushed up interest rates, first in the USA but soon also on world markets. Foreign debts of developing countries which until then still looked manageable suddenly became a nightmare for the international financial community, for the debtor countries *and for nature conservation*. The destruction of natural resources was accelerated, for only through the sale of raw materials, foodstuffs and agricultural products, produced mostly at the expense of nature and wildlife, could the debts be serviced (see Chapter 8).

Of course, Reagan, his military advisers and the Federal Reserve Bank did not intend to stimulate the massive expansion of forest burning in the Amazon, the Philippines or Ivory Coast, but for nature and the starving in impoverished countries motives count less than facts. And facts and figures tell a grim story about destruction both of nature and of the social fabric in many developing countries. In Latin America and Africa the 1980s are officially called 'the lost decade'.

The end of this dismal period was brought forward by several developments, of which four stand out. Firstly, in the Soviet Union there was a rapid change-over of leaders: Leonid Brezhnev, Yuri Andropov and Konstantin Chernenko died in quick succession. Mikhail Gorbachev, picked and promoted by Andropov, took over the leadership and actively, and ultimately successfully, sought an end to global confrontation. The Reagan camp claims this Soviet development to have been the intended result of the confrontation, but this view fails to explain why the Eisenhower/Dulles period of confrontation had the opposite effect — an apparently blossoming economy in the Soviet Union and Communist expansion worldwide, and why the decay of the Soviet influence in Latin America, Asia and Europe came during the détente years before Reagan.

Secondly, the American physicist Carl Sagan and a group of researchers brought together by SCOPE developed the theory of the nuclear winter. In contemplating Reagan's Strategic Defense Initiative (SDI) and other nuclear war scenarios, and inspired by new theories on the extinction of the dinosaurs 65 million years ago, they demonstrated that a global nuclear war, even if SDI were successfully introduced, would be highly likely to set in train a devastating climatic catastrophe. The theory suggests that the skies would be darkened for months or even years by the huge clouds of dust which would be stirred up, leading to temperatures plummeting by 10, 20 or more degrees and to the widespread destruction of plant life and, consequentially, the harvest. Animals and humans would become the next victims. Ultimately it would make no difference whose nuclear weapons had landed on whom in the first or second strike, nor would it matter who had stayed out of the war (Sagan, 1990). A strong scientific argument against continued military confrontation was thus developed and has been shown to have influenced Gorbachev and the military leaders he appointed.

Thirdly, the Brundtland Report (see Chapters 1, 8 and 14), published in 1987, pungently reminded the international community of the *real* agenda of this world.

Finally, a series of new and worrying reports on the state of the environment were published. The discovery of the hole in the ozone layer, startling confirmations of the greenhouse effect theory and the realisation worldwide of the disaster happening to the world's forests and biodiversity came more or less simultaneously during the second half of the 'Lost Decade'.

Once the political thaw began, it became almost a political necessity that the USA should re-enter the global political arena in a more constructive fashion. The Clinton/Gore campaign, Al Gore's programmatic book (1992) and President Clinton's position on the biodiversity and climate conventions seem to indicate that the USA wants to do exactly that.

The Hole in the Ozone Layer, Greenhouse Effect, Rain Forests

In the mid-1980s, the British Antarctic Survey and American satellites above Antarctica confirmed what academic scientists had feared since the beginning of the 1970s — a thinning of the ozone layer. The culprits were identified with reasonable certainty as chlorofluorocarbons (CFCs) and halons, neither of which occur naturally. These rise over time into the upper layer of the atmosphere, where they remain stable for many years. Should an ozone molecule, O_3, meet a halogen molecule (made available from the CFCs), it is likely to change into normal oxygen, O_2. Ozone has the singular facility to absorb much of the potentially dangerous ultraviolet B radiation, so that a thinning of the ozone layer allows more UV-B radiation to reach the Earth's surface and to cause skin cancer and kill unprotected micro-organisms.

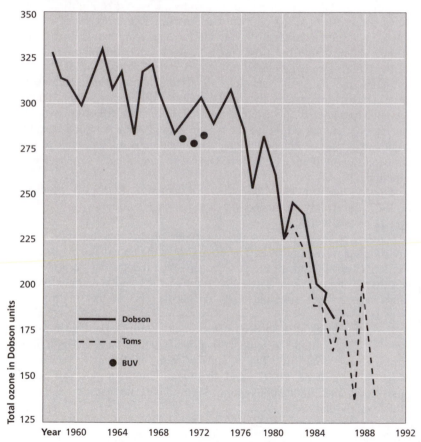

Figure 7: The extent of the ozone hole above the Antarctic during the spring over the years 1979–86. Data from satellite measurements (Bundestag, 1992).

Images of the disappearing ozone in the Antarctic region were seen around the world, and it was clear that this was a global problem. When we come to analyse such global problems, there is no such thing as a German or a Californian (although Germans and Californians contribute disproportionately to the global ozone hole). The global need for the protection of the ozone layer made millions of people aware of the need for a globalised environmental policy or else of '*Earth Politics*'.

There was relatively rapid agreement in Geneva, Vienna and finally Montreal that production of CFCs and halons should be reduced. The outcome of the Montreal conference was, however, considered inadequate by experts and conservationists alike. A much tighter regime on certain CFCs was soon aimed for, and was in effect agreed at the first review conference in London in July 1990, and again at the second review conference in Copenhagen in November 1992. For the story of the ozone diplomacy see Benedick (1991) and, to balance his account of events, also Haigh (1992).

Correlation of CO_2 and Temperature Variation
from 160 000 years before present to 2100

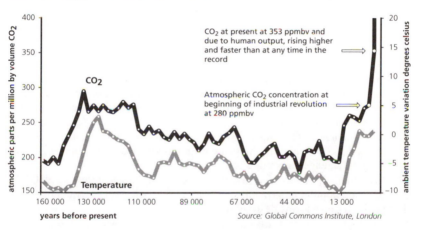

Figure 8: Reconstruction of atmospheric concentration of CO_2 (above) and relative temperature (below).

Ultimately much more alarming than the ozone hole is the prospect of sweeping global climatic change. The theory of the greenhouse effect goes back to the end of the last century when Svante Arrhenius first proposed it. During the 1960s calculations were added suggesting a significant human influence on the effect. The major step forward in our understanding came once again in the mid-1980s from the Antarctic. The chemical analysis of bubbles of air which had been trapped in Antarctic ice for thousands of years allowed researchers of the Soviet and French Vostok expedition to establish that there had been significant variations in CO_2 concentrations

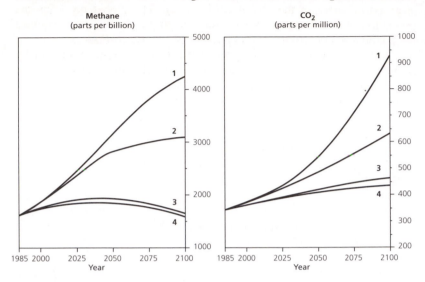

Figure 9: Following the disastrously dry summers of recent years, much thinking has been going on in the USA about the greenhouse effect. The environmental authorities have produced a major study of strategies for reducing greenhouse gases, especially methane and carbon dioxide. The figure shows atmospheric concentrations of CO_2 and methane in the context of four economic scenarios:

1. 'Rapid change'. This scenario envisages the following features: rapid GNP growth, slower population growth, moderate rise in fuel prices, weak technological change, moderate forest destruction.

2. 'Slow change'. This scenario envisages the following features: small GNP growth, rapid population growth, small rise in fuel prices, weak technological change, increasing forest destruction.

3. 'Rapid change/active climate policy'. This scenario envisages the following features: rapid GNP growth, slower population growth, moderate increase in (primary) fuel prices plus energy taxes, very rapid efficiency improvement, rapid market implementation of solar energy and biomass fuels, rapid reafforestation.

4. 'Slow change/active climate policy'. This scenario envisages the following features: small GNP growth, rapid population increase, small increases in (primary) fuel prices plus energy taxes, rapid efficiency improvements, moderate market implementation of solar energy and biomass fuels, rapid reafforestation.

(Source: US Environmental Protection Agency, Policy options for stabilizing global climate, Draft report to congress, Feb 1989, p. 25. See also national Academy of Science, 1991.)

over the millennia. Just as the theory predicted, the periods of high CO_2 concentrations coincided with periods of higher temperatures, which were already known from analysis of vegetation sediments (see, e.g. Gribbin, 1990).

In November 1985 an important meeting took place in Villach, Austria, called by the World Meteorological Organisation (WMO), UNEP and the International Council of Scientific Unions (ICSU). The Villach meeting declared that climatic warming as a result of emissions caused by human activity was, in all probability, a reality and that its effects were potentially threatening for many parts of the Earth. Since then there has been an unbroken series of meetings on the greenhouse effect and its political consequences (Jäger, 1988, see also Schneider, 1989, Oppenheimer and Boyle, 1990, *IPCC*, 1992, Mintzer, 1992).

In 1988 governments agreed to the establishment of an Inter-governmental Panel on Climate Change (IPCC) with three working groups. This international group, led by the Swedish meteorologist, Bert Bolin, delivered its reports in summer 1990 (IPCC, 1990). The scientific report (Houghton et al., 1990) predicts global temperature increase of $0.3°C$ per decade if no counter-measures are taken, but is of the opinion that counter-measures could be taken which would reduce the rate of increase to between $0.2°$ and $0.1°$. There are sharp differences of opinion about the nature of such counter-measures. Basic questions on energy policy (cf. Chapter 5), on North–South disparity (cf. Agarwal and Narain, 1991), and on future environmental policy (cf. Chapter 14) arise. But ultimately, as further described in Chapter 14, it was possible to agree on a United Nations Framework Convention on Climate Change. Recent analysis seems to indicate that the reduction of greenhouse gas emissions does not necessarily imply economic sacrifices (Lovins and Lovins, 1990, Cline, 1992) thus giving us some hope that the Climate Convention will be concretised and implemented speedily despite the sluggish world economy.

Closely linked to the climate debate is the destruction of tropical — and non-tropical — forests. The very existence of the tropical forest is under threat for a number of reasons: the 'jungle' is no longer impenetrable; the age-old search for the Earth's riches has been systematically extended to hitherto untouched forest areas; population pressure in most tropical countries has increased strongly, highly efficient methods of clearance and mechanised logging have been developed and the debt crisis and world trade have increased the pressure for exploitation of rain forest resources. In countries such as Ivory Coast and Madagascar more than 80 per cent of the forest has been destroyed, and in Indonesia, Brazil, Peru, Colombia, Cameroon and Zaire, which had huge swathes of forest, the destruction has increased at a catastrophic rate. Brazil and Indonesia appear to be serious about reducing in part the destruction of tax incentives.

The destruction of the rainforests represents the destruction of the Earth's second biggest air-renewing lung after ocean plankton. It affects us all. Moreover, the tropical forests are home to the Earth's greatest diversity of species (see Chapter 9), and it is here that the loss of species outlined in the first chapter primarily originates (Myers, 1984). The developing countries, however, do not accept that we in the North interfere with their domestic 'use of resources', as they call it, and they feel that it was exactly their present method of resource exploitation which made the North rich. If we in the North are really concerned about the fate of biodiversity and of the rain forests, our policies must go beyond levelling accusations against the tropical countries, as became abundantly clear during the preparations for UNCED (see below).

Earth visions need not wait until international negotiations take place. Much can be done already at a national level. In Germany an important step was taken by parliament through the establishment in 1987 of a Committee of Inquiry on the Protection of the Earth's Atmosphere. The Committee produced three major reports, all available in English (Bundestag, 1990) urging the government to act promptly on global warming and protection of the ozone layer. As one impressive result, the (conservative!) German government pledged to reduce domestic carbon dioxide emissions by 25–30 per cent until the year 2005. The German government position at international environmental conferences steadily became more progressive, more or less in line with the (mostly all-party) conclusions of the parliamentary committee.

The Earth Summit and the Global Forum

With the hole in the ozone layer, global warming and the biodiversity crisis all calling for action, the Brundtland Report providing a policy framework and the end of the Cold War creating opportunities for global accords, the United Nations finally decided to convene a second UN Conference dealing with environmental matters. Twenty years after the Stockholm Conference, the UN Conference for Environment and Development (UNCED) was held in Rio de Janeiro, in June 1992. Several names were coined for UNCED, including ECO 2 (Stockholm being ECO 1) and the 'Earth Summit'. In this book called *Erdpolitik* I prefer to use the name Earth Summit for the Rio Conference.

Already in its preparatory phase, the Earth Summit attracted much more public and political attention than the Stockholm Conference did in its time. Literally hundreds of international and thousands of national meetings were organised claiming to produce 'inputs' for Rio de Janeiro. Eventually more than a hundred heads of state or of government attended, and more than 7,000 accredited journalists made the Earth Summit the media event of the year.

Parallel to the Earth Summit more than a hundred international conferences were organised under the umbrella of the 'Global Forum' at Rio's Flamenco Park and at dozens of other locations throughout the city. High-calibre meetings of representatives of indigenous people, religious groups, scientists, women's groups, youth, business people, parliamentarians and other groups were convened and gave testimony to a common concern for saving the planet and for global justice. For a good account of the role of global NGOs see Ekins (1992) and Finger (1993).

The Global Forum, perhaps more than the Earth Summit itself, was a sign of hope for the emerging earth visions. The Earth Summit and its policy implications will be further discussed in Chapter 14.

PART TWO:

WORLD IN CRISIS — FIVE KEY ISSUES

Part One of this book offered some views on the history of environmental protection and set out the framework for Earth Politics. The need for new models of wealth was postulated and it was argued that Europe should by all means play a pioneering role in developing it.

The new models need to be so designed that they may be extended to the global population of eventually ten or more billion people without thereby causing a disastrous deterioration of the Earth's natural environment. This is the very meaning — applied to Europe — of 'sustainable development' according to the Brundtland Report. Against this postulate present European, Anglo-American and Japanese standards of living clearly appear as unsustainable. Everything that is part and parcel of our present unsustainable lifestyles has now to be seen as part of the global ecological crisis or as a 'field of crisis'.

Part Two of this book makes a selection of five fields of crisis which may deserve special attention on our road to solutions — the subject of the third part of the book. We shall examine energy and matter first, transport second and agriculture third. The fourth chapter (Chapter 8) covers 'the Third World', which is suffering the biggest environmental crisis of our time and is trapped both in unequal international economic relations and in a hopeless desire to emulate the unsustainable Northern models of wealth. The fifth field of crisis is biodiversity, fully understandable only *after* discussing the Third World crisis.

In each chapter first attempts are made to formulate solutions belonging to 'realpolitik', but none the less belonging to a more radical and more comprehensive set of proposals ultimately meant to lead to sustainable development in the North. In each chapter it also becomes apparent that conventional answers of the 'end-of-the-pipe' category fall very far short of what is needed to reach sustainability.

Chapter 5

Energy and Material Resources

Energy — Symbol of Progress

'Energy' as used in modern physics is a surprisingly new concept. William Thomson (Lord Kelvin) first used the term 'kinetic energy' in 1851. From 1853 A. O. Rankine used the concept of energy in the applied science of energy transformation. James Watt, inventor of the steam engine, and Alessandro Volta, who discovered innumerable electrical phenomena and laws, still had to manage without the word 'energy'. Detailed study of the heat engine led the French engineer, Sadi Carnot, in 1824 to a practical understanding of the transformation of temperature differences into 'dynamic power' (kinetic energy) and vice versa. He recognised that heat without temperature differences did not in itself produce power. Developing Carnot's work, Rudolf Clausius in 1850 formulated the law we nowadays call as the Second Law of Thermodynamics: all power is transformed into heat and in the process leads to a rise in 'entropy'. The ultimate state of worldwide high entropy was viewed in those days as a desolate uniform warmth and was called 'heat death'. This concept gave rise to much gloom in nineteenth-century intellectual circles, although physicists gave some assurance that reaching 'heat death' would take thousands of years. They did not dare speculate that it could actually take billions of years or might not happen at all.

Some reassurance could also be drawn from the First Law of Thermodynamics, according to which the total amount of energy is conserved. Eventually the 'principle of the conservation of energy' (formulated by Robert Mayer and Hermann von Helmholtz) brought together all known forms of energy — heat, mechanical energy, chemical energy and electromagnetic energy — and thereby made possible the emergence of a unified concept of energy.

In the nineteenth century, the replacement of human labour by man-made energy became the very symbol of progress. The World Exhibition in Paris of 1889 was a veritable parade of possibilities, demonstrating the extent to which the human mind with the help of man-made energy, in particular electricity, could free the human body from toil, perhaps, even go one better and make it redundant. A symbol of the era is the Palace of Electricity built for the World Exhibition in Paris in 1900. Karl Marx, Henry Ford and Vladimir Ilyich Lenin were all equally convinced of the positive role of energy in the attainment of the social goals they dreamt of.

Around the turn of the century, an economy based on science and technology developed, which established a close correlation between prosperity and energy consumption. After the Second World War, when the horror of the atomic bomb was tempered by the promise that swords would be turned into ploughshares and that atomic energy would be used for peaceful purposes and be available without limit, it seemed that energy was enthroned as the queen of the economy and progress.

The Energy Crisis

In the years after the Second World War, primary energy consumption in Europe grew by between 3 and 10 per cent a year. Coal, which for a hundred years had dominated the energy market, increasingly made way for oil, which ousted it from first place by the end of the 1960s. No upper limit for energy demand was in sight (see Figure 10), but at least it was clear that there were limits to the reserves of fossil fuels. Just as in earlier times before coal was mined, industrial growth had been limited by the dwindling reserves of wood, so finite reserves of coal, oil and gas seemed to set limits to growth in the late twentieth century. The first report to the Club of Rome (see Chapter 4) pointed clearly in this direction without, however, coming up with an alternative to the high levels of energy consumption; so, logically enough, the club had to support nuclear power, possibly nuclear fusion.

Henry Kissinger, when National Security Advisor to President Nixon, was concerned that low oil prices were leading to excessive consumption and imports, thus to a dangerous American dependence on continued oil imports from the Persian Gulf. He wanted to raise oil prices but this rational wish remained unfulfilled. Then in October 1973 came the Yom Kippur War which gave the Arabs the opportunity to take action directed at Israel's friends abroad. OPEC (the Organisation of Petroleum Exporting Countries), which was led by the Arab oil producers decided on a boycott of exports to certain countries and a fourfold increase in world oil prices. The result was a severe shock to the economies of the West, a crisis in some newly industrialising countries and economic collapse to the point of despair in some of the poorest developing countries which depended on oil imports. The terms Fourth World and Least Developed Countries (LDC) were coined in the wake of the oil crisis.

In 1974 the West, that is the OECD countries, founded an International Energy Agency (IEA), as its answer to OPEC. The IEA was set up in

Paris at OECD headquarters and was to help formulate political answers to the new challenges. Its main goal was, however, conventional: to ensure 'adequate' energy supplies (enough to cover every 'demand') at the lowest possible prices. The demand forecasts, which before 1973 had shown a sharp rise throughout the next decades, were revised downwards, but only slightly. The basic assumption, that energy demand would *naturally* continue to rise remained unchallenged (see Figure 10).

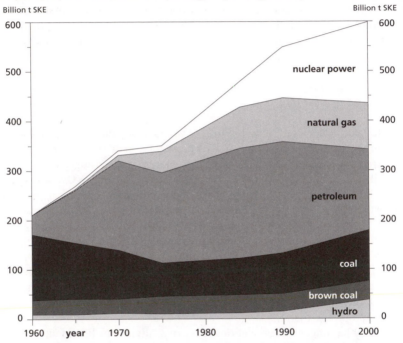

Figure 10: The 'good old times' of energy growth. Empirical energy consumption in West Germany until 1975 and projections from that time until the year 2000 (From the Second Update 1975 of the Federal Energy Programme).

The market, however, reacted exactly as laid down in the economics textbooks: high prices led to a reduction in demand. All of a sudden it was recognised that houses which were not energy-efficient, cars which did fewer than 20 miles to the gallon or domestic appliances which swallowed up electricity had little to do with comfort but were the quasi-rational result of the incredibly low energy prices before 1973. After 1973, industry made a greater effort to reduce the unnecessary consumption of energy both in consumer goods and in the manufacturing process.

Energy conservation became known in Britain as the Fifth Fuel. In Germany the 'rational use of energy' was a somewhat more bureaucratic expression for the same thing. Energy efficiency increased and only very few people in the industrialised countries noticeably needed to tighten their belts. After only a few years of 'energy crisis' it became clear that economic growth could be elegantly decoupled from energy consumption.

During the energy crisis much thought was given to the actual level of world energy demand (see, e.g. Helm (1990), notably Alvin Weinberg's paper therein). A large-scale study carried out by the International Institute for Applied Systems Analysis (IIASA) under the leadership of Wolf Häfele (1981) arrived at an estimate of up to 35 Terawatt years per year (approximately 300 million million kilowatt hours a year). Amory Lovins on the other hand, in *Soft Energy Paths* came up with a figure nearly seven times lower, an amount which could moreover be met by rapidly increasing the contribution of solar energy (Lovins, 1977). He and his wife, Hunter Lovins, were later awarded the 'Alternative Nobel Prize' for their pioneering work on alternative energy futures.

In all studies of worldwide energy policy there was no getting round one obvious and important underlying fact: the per capita energy consumption of the industrialised countries has been around ten times that of the developing countries (with the exception of the OPEC countries) for many years. The IIASA Study, and indeed almost all estimates of governments, IEA or the World Energy Conferences including that in Madrid (September 1992), take as their base the present-day per capita consumption of the industrialised countries, adjust it slightly and then calculate world energy demands on the assumption of growing equity between North and South (see WEC, 1993). In those years it was primarily Amory Lovins who had the courage to demand and forecast sharply falling per capita energy consumption levels in the North.

Fossil? Nuclear? Renewables?

It is, of course, a legitimate question whether or not there is any ecological or other need to reduce Northern energy consumption levels, and the answer is that it is. Every way of providing energy for human use involves potential environmental, political, financial or long-term availability problems. Hardly any environmentally neutral let alone benign use of energy is conceivable.

Using energy produces entropy, although the levels of human energy use so far do not contribute more than one per cent of one per cent to global entropy production, and Jeremy Rifkin's fears in this context seem exaggerated (1990).

Energy produces noise whenever mechanical movement is involved. This is not a fundamental ecological problem, since quieter engines, noise insulation and appropriate spacing and timing can solve most problems. The matter of waste heat may be a more severe environmental problem, as many power plants deposit their waste heat into rivers or lakes. This causes localised lack of oxygen for aquatic life.

More disquieting is the release of pollutants into the atmosphere, in particular nitrous oxides and, depending on the sulphur content of the fuel, sulphur dioxide. Nitrous oxides are seen as primarily responsible for dying forests and acid rain. For a policy analysis of the problems relating to energy and the environment see Byrne and Rich (1992).

In the mid-1980s, Lutz Wicke (1986) estimated *economic* damage caused by energy-related environmental pollution at some 50 billion Marks (£20 billion) annually. Admittedly, that was before German legislation on large combustion plants came into force. On the other hand, Wicke did not even take into account any costs relating to the risks of nuclear energy or to the greenhouse effect (see chapter 4).

When evaluating nuclear power, there has been a worldwide tendency to deal primarily with reactor safety and — with limited success — the disposal or reprocessing of radioactive waste (Lenssen, 1991). The vulnerability of reactors and other nuclear installations to military action or sabotage (and the associated scenarios of terrorist or political blackmail) give rise to immense concern and yet are hardly addressed by the defenders of nuclear energy. and we should not be deceived by the silence surrounding the issue to assume that there are no problems.

One aspect has been dealt with in public, the worldwide stockpiling of plutonium. Paul Leventhal and Milton Hoenig (1986) have projected nuclear reprocessing trends of the mid-1980s until the year 2000 and found that more fissionable material suitable for weapon-making, chiefly plutonium, could enter the *commercial* marketplace than is presently stored in the arsenals of the USA and the former USSR. While much of this plutonium would not be weapons grade, it could still be used to build crude bombs by technically sophisticated terrorists. Is anybody cynical enough not to feel threatened by this prospect, especially if we remember that more than a dozen wars have been fought and billions of dollars accumulated in the pockets of dubious groups since Leventhal and Hoenig published their figures.

In addition, the world has been embarrassingly negligent about the effects of uranium mining. In North America, some of the mining sites were called 'sacrifice areas'. That at least is honest. In the former Soviet Union the country's notorious secrecy prevented the mine workers, the nearby residents and the general public from recognising the damage and protesting. Sacred mountains and other tribal areas in Australia continue to be devastated by uranium mining, while the East German uranium mines at Wismut (where the chemical element Bismutum was first found) constitute the most desperate ecological heritage of the former GDR (World Uranium Hearing, 1993).

One cost factor that has received too little attention for a long time is the decommissioning of reactors and other nuclear installations. The Worldwatch Institute (Pollock, 1986) estimated decommissioning costs in the order of a million dollars for every megawatt installed. German nuclear companies feel that some DM300,000 per megawatt should be enough to cover all costs, though it has yet to be established conclusively that before decommissioned reactors are finally physically removed they do not present a cauldron of ecological dangers. Due to neutron absorption, the structure and machinery of an abandoned nuclear power plant represents a large quantity of moderately radioactive material. In no case have we developed safe ways to deal with or dispose of material which remains radioactive for tens of thousands of years.

Gould and Goldman (1990) present what they consider scientific evidence about health and the genetic effects of low doses of non-natural radiation, notably the significant increases in mortality and morbidity worldwide, often thousands of miles away from the sources, in the wake of atmospheric nuclear testing (until its ban) and of the Chernobyl accident. In addition, high leukemia incidence rates near nuclear installations (Sellafield and Krümmel, Germany) are often quoted. Conversely, few people are aware that there is significant radioactivity in fly ash and bottom ash from burning many coals.

All in all it seems extemely hazardous to rely on nuclear energy as the mainstay of energy supplies. Both politically and ecologically I would feel extremely uncomfortable with any strategy of nuclear expansion based on the existing reactor types. Unlike many people, however, I would not advocate a close-down of properly functioning nuclear reactors and I would not even exclude the long-term possibility of developing a reasonably safe nuclear energy philosophy, for example using 'inherently safe' reactors built well below the surface, and therefore less of a target for terrorist or military action, and isolated from groundwater, with well protected processing facilities for nuclear fuel. But that possibility, if at all feasible, would lead to electricity prices at least twice as high as those from today's reactors — and even they cannot compete under strictly commercial conditions with coal power plants.

Until now the obvious alternative to nuclear energy was burning more fossil fuels, of which greater reserves were discovered as exploration was intensified after the oil crisis. The Earth now appears to have coal stocks sufficient for more than 300 years, even under generous assumptions for our consumption levels. The main problem with fossil fuels is no longer seen as fuel availability but the absorption capacity of our environment. The findings of the Intergovernmental Panel on Climate Change (IPCC, c.f. Chapter 4) make a *drastic reduction* of fossil fuel consumption imperative, and certainly don't allow for further expansion. The Climate Convention of Rio de Janeiro should be read as giving legally binding form to this unavoidable conclusion. It is extremely difficult to judge whether the expansion of nuclear energy or of fossil energy consumption is the bigger evil. The best strategy would clearly be to reduce both (Schipper and Myers, 1992).

Conventional thinking of a 'naturally' given, and rising, energy demand leads us inevitably to renewable forms of energy sources. But they too are far from being environmentally innocent if used at today's consumption levels. One has only to think of the many large hydroelectric projects with their often devastating ecological and social effects in developing countries to appreciate the dangers involved (Goldsmith and Hildyard, 1985–89). Biomass plantations are also an ecological nightmare if designed to feed many power stations of thousands of megawatts or fuel the car fleets of European or North American continents. Tidal and geothermal energy (the only two forms not based upon solar radiation) affect aquatic life or result in large quantities of hazardous brines. Even wind power, generally considered the least environmentally degrading, has turned out to be hazardous to birds.

Biomass (energy from plant material) was the first form of artificial energy used by humans. It certainly makes sense in agriculture and in the lumber and paper industries to use the energy contents of manure, straw, waste wood and the like. As shown by Brazil, it is technically possible to produce motor fuel alcohol from sugar cane. However, in a world where too many people suffer hunger, and too many forests have been destroyed, it is difficult to justify the use of crop or forest land in order to fuel transportation and industry.

Direct solar power (unlike indirect solar energy from wind, hydropower or biomass) requires storage systems since solar radiation is obviously not available at night. When used to generate electricity, the necessary auxiliary storage system dominates the overall design. For example, large-scale solar power gathered in desert areas, turned into electricity and used to produce hydrogen from water is a theoretically attractive idea. Hydrogen is an excellent intermediary energy carrier which can be stored or injected into the growing net of natural gas pipelines. However, if extended to a size of millions of gigawatt-hours, the 'Sahara hydrogen' idea also has nightmarish features: potential weather alterations, transport hazards (hydrogen is highly explosive when mixed with ordinary air) and the environmental impact of the gigantic equipment and operation supply industry are just a few problems that spring to mind. Besides, the system's commercial feasibility lies in the distant future.

I am even less optimistic about some of the more futuristic technological dreams presented as 'renewable' forms of energy. Satellites with huge paddles reflecting and focusing high-intensity solar rays into industrial-size furnaces on earth are one such dream. But who could guarantee that the deadly rays are not accidentally or deliberately redirected onto the cities of Birmingham or Cairo?

And nuclear fusion? This is also a form of 'renewable' energy for all practical purposes. The taming of fusion at the JET laboratories was an admirable scientific and technological breakthrough, but the transition from a laboratory demonstration into a commercial fusion reactor will take at least forty years. In addition, there are serious political and environmental fears with fusion power, just as with nuclear fission, e.g. permanent gigantic flows of neutrons which are bound to make any conceivable wall materials radioactive. Fusion engineers must also solve the containment nightmare for huge quantities of radioactive tritium with a half life of twelve years, easily incorporated by living organisms in place of hydrogen. That, plus unknown and as yet unassessed dangers of terrorist and military abuse, are reasons enough to warn against any premature reliance on a fusion contribution to world energy supplies.

Renewables do nevertheless make a lot of sense in the search for a solution to the world's energy demand problems (Goldemberg et al., 1987, Twiddell and Weir, 1990). Rather than one big solar techno-fix, it is a complex web of numerous small-scale solutions that promise to *really* help. Windmills make sense for limited areas at modest consumption rates, while geothermal energy is good where available, but only a limited option for certain countries. Photovoltaics will help to make homes in sunny regions self-sufficient in electricity during certain hours of the day and solar cookers can help save large quantities of fuel wood. Biogas is a very reasonable alternative resource wherever there are noticeable concentrations of animal (and human) manure, and can also be combined with plant biomass, while biomass, including the use of agricultural and municipal refuse, can play a useful role in providing some fuel for vehicles besides providing boiler fuel for generating electricity and heat. 'Passive' solar energy (direct or diffuse daylight radiation heating rooms or water) could provide much of our housing heat requirements. In many sunny countries, solar hot water systems are standard practice today. But passive solar is economic only where massive efforts have been made to reduce energy waste in buildings.

Generally speaking, renewables only make sense if combined with a clear strategy of energy conservation. Conservation, however, is too conservative an expression which should be turned around and called the increase of *energy productivity*. Increasing energy productivity should be the name for the new game.

Energy Productivity

Economists talk about productivity gains as the real essence of progress and growth. By productivity they almost always mean labour productivity. They also observe that productivity has risen by a factor twenty or more since the early days of industrialisation. Productivity gains and economic growth have paralleled the growth of energy consumption remarkably well throughout the industrial revolution.

Although major gains in energy efficiency of particular processes were achieved, macroeconomic energy productivity, measured in GDP units per unit of energy consumed, did not on average increase until 1973. Only after the recent oil crises did political and industrial leaders begin to consciously think in terms of energy productivity or the rational use of energy (see the section on the energy crisis). For the first time did the wasteful use of energy make a true difference in the quarterly reports, which is perhaps the only reality *all* managers are obliged to take note of. Thus, the oil crisis has induced a much better understanding in all trades and in public planning of what is technologically feasible in energy savings.

To increase macroeconomic energy productivity, the first logical steps are increasing energy efficiency of existing processes. According to Lovins and Lovins (1990), efficiency increases by factors three to four are technically feasible for virtually all sectors of energy consumption without any significant loss of convenience. Motor cars could reach about 100 miles to the gallon. Gas light bulbs can do four times better than the classical incandescent lamps. Household appliances can be made perhaps three times more energy efficient than the average items now in use. Implementing the Swedish building code for heat insulation could save at least 70 per cent of central European (and perhaps 80 per cent of US American) heating fuel consumption. Combined heat and power (CHP) schemes might produce an additional 20 per cent energy savings. All in all, a doubling of energy efficiency at no loss of convenience, i.e. with no change in lifestyles seem like a *very* conservative estimate for what can be achieved. The time span for doing it could be some thirty years, again as a generous estimate (provided, of course, there is a political determination to do it).

Gains would be even higher if we were to move from the conventional emphasis on energy efficiency to the wider notion of energy productivity which also involves stuctural change (Jochem, 1992). The twentyfold rise in labour productivity during the Industrial Revolution, after all, was not the result of labour *efficiency* gains alone (e.g. by having shoemakers and carpenters hammering twenty times as fast as they previously did). Energy productivity gains, just like labour productivity gains, consist primarily of *substitutions* of clumsy by more elegant methods and processes. Aluminium from scrap needs some fifteen times less energy than aluminium from bauxite. Food could easily contain more calories (from the sun) than are invested in farming, processing, transport, cooling and cooking; today much more commercial energy is expended for food than the energy ultimately reaching our stomachs. Our visions of mobility may also change. Bicycles conveniently packed into agreeable buses, tram-ways or suburban railways of new designs would make even villages, small towns and suburbs liveable places with just one family car which is used only for heavy shopping, late evening trips and holidays.

Let us imagine we were living through the early days of *a new industrial revolution*, a revolution in energy productivity. Let us imagine that energy productivity would become a target for engineers, economists and politicians as equally important as labour productivity. And let us allow for an equivalent period of 100 or 150 years to reach a ten- or twentyfold increase of energy productivity. It would be the essence of the *new* progress, the progress towards a sustainable global economy. (Hand in hand with energy productivity we would expect materials productivity to increase by similar or probably even bigger factors, as will be discussed in the concluding section of this chapter.)

So far this new progress is a dream. But looking at today's technological realities and comparing them with the technological realities of labour productivity in 1840, we have to conclude that the dream is based on a very solid rock of technological reality. It is not so daring to assume that the above-mentioned doubling of energy efficiency in thirty years can be supplemented by an additional doubling of energy productivity through technology-based lifestyle changes within a period perhaps ten years longer. We would then experience a fourfold increase in overall energy productivity within some forty years. A further fifty per cent increase in energy productivity — leading to a sixfold factor in total — is conceivable using *today's* scientific, technological, sociological and psychological knowledge. Who would have dared to say anything similar about labour productivity prospects during the early years of Queen Victoria's reign?

Energy Prices Should Tell the Truth

Where does the discrepancy lie between what is technologically plausible and what is seen as politically realistic? In my view, the single most important cause of this discrepancy is a fundamental misunderstanding about energy pricing. According to classical economic theory, energy prices should reflect the meeting point between supply costs and the customer's willingness to pay. But in political reality, whenever it has been convenient to believe that certain consumers, private or industrial, could not pay the real price of supplies, prices were kept artificially low, by the taxpayer. This system of hiding the true costs was almost a doctrine in the former socialist states and most certainly contributed to their economic collapse. Not dissimilar is the present situation in many developing countries which try to stimulate industrial growth and please their people by subsidising energy prices. According to market economics, such subsidies make the economies frailer, not stronger. In also the West there are numerous examples of subsidised energy or at least tax exemptions to protect energy-intensive industries and to facilitate the mechanisation of agriculture.

What is more, there are scarcely any attempts to make energy users pay the real *long-term* price, which would include the external costs. Energy prices throughout the world are much too low to reflect long-term scarcities or to 'tell the ecological truth'. Hence they induce all economies to over-exploit the environment. The highly contentious question of the quantification of environmental externalities will be taken up in Chapter 10. The political answer, a gradually progressing, revenue-neutral ecological tax shift, is the centrepiece of Chapter 11. In the context of the energy discussion I shall restrict myself to a few concluding remarks.

Largely independent of an ecological pricing policy, many smaller measures can already be taken to increase energy productivity and to enlarge the share of renewables in the energy supply pie. Incentives can be given for energy-saving investments. Aluminium and glass recycling can be facilitated or subsidised. The use of public money for this can be legitimated as a means of reducing solid waste. Many rules and standards can be established or modified which govern the use of energy, such as the fuel efficiency of cars and the energy efficiency of homes and appliances, or obligatory CHP schemes under certain circumstances. The marketing of energy efficiency ('negawatts') should be promoted by least cost planning (LCP) which makes the construction of a new power plant dependent on the proof that no cheaper way of meeting the demand exists (see, e.g., Johannson et al. 1989). Sales promotion for energy can be generally restricted. Some rules and regulations will require EC harmonisation, but many could also be adopted at national or even regional level.

All this and more is a popular playing field for environmental politicians wanting to show their competence in areas other than pollution control, but even taken together all such regulatory measures will at best serve to reach the modest 'stabilisation' goals currently under discussion (e.g. the EC's commitment to stabilise CO_2 emissions at 1990 levels by the year 2000). They will not lead to anything like a quadrupling of energy productivity.

That revolutionary increase can only be expected from the strategy of making prices tell the ecological truth. To give an indication of the effects on energy demand and on the share of renewables in the energy pie of a price increase of fossil and nuclear energy, let us imagine a doubling, quadrupling and octupling of the latter (assuming, for a first approximation, that renewables were not to be taxed for environmental reasons). And let the economy take its time to adjust and develop technologies, logistics, infrastructure and usage patterns adapted to the new price levels. Assuming rational market behaviour, the result could look as indicated in Figure 11.

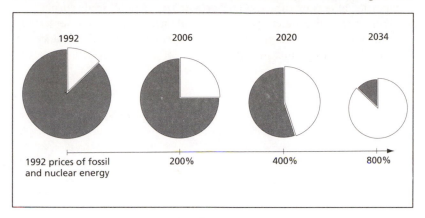

Figure 11: Energy demand and the achievable percentage of solar and other renewable energy are not fixed quantities. They depend heavily on the price for fossil and nuclear fuel. The diagram gives a rough estimate of what will happen to energy demand (size of the pie) and to the proportion of renewable energy (yellow) in the next 20–50 years, if fossil and nuclear fuel prices are increased along the lines indicated.

Economists and politicians do not usually think first of productivity gains when they hear of rising energy prices. In fact, the mere idea of rising energy prices raises many fears and brings back bad memories; after all, the shock of higher energy prices in the 1970s led to a worldwide recession. On a closer look, however, it can be seen that the recession was not caused by the increase in energy prices as such. The problem was in fact that the change came unannounced and thus as a shock; the global economy was unprepared and many investments had to be written off overnight; business leaders and politicians were bewildered and behaved accordingly; and, worst of all, additional tens of billions of pounds were flowing out of the OECD economies to the OPEC countries with almost no immediate domestic multiplier effects.

Significantly, those economies which artificially further enhanced the price signal fared much better economically than those which tried to keep domestic energy prices very low. There was a clear energy price 'hierarchy' among the four biggest economic powers between 1975 and 1990: Japan, the EC, the USA and the USSR. It is well known which of these economies flourished and which stagnated during this period.

I was puzzled by this qualitative observation, which appeared to suggest a positive correlation between energy prices and economic performance, and at my suggestion Rudolf Rechsteiner looked more systematically into energy prices and economic performances of eight comparable OECD countries. Defining (somewhat arbitrarily) economic performance as a composite value consisting of GNP growth (per capita), trade surplus, the number of patents granted (per capita) and energy efficiency, he found a striking positive correlation for two consecutive periods of five years each. The results are presented in Figure 12.

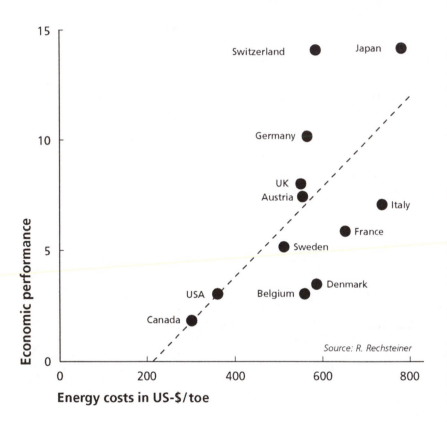

Figure 12: Economic performance and energy prices 1978–90. Economic performance being defined by a composite parameter consisting of rank scores for trade surplus (or deficit), patents per one million inhabitants, GDP growth and energy efficiency. Energy prices are defined by a mix of electricity for industry, petrol and light oil for domestic heating. There seems to be rather a positive than a negative correlation between economic performance and energy prices (from Rechsteiner, 1994).

Some sectors of the economy are obviously more vulnerable than others to energy price increases, metallurgy, bulk chemicals, cement and road traffic being among the most exposed sectors. On average, however, energy costs make no more than 3.5–4 per cent of the industry's running costs in the EC countries. A gradual price increase of fossil and nuclear energy of some 5 per cent annually (see Chapter 11) would therefore produce average cost changes of not more than 0.2 per cent. If all the money thus collected were returned to the economy via tax reductions, one would not expect any macroeconomic damage to be done by a policy of gradually making prices tell the truth.

Material Resources

Energy resources enter our economy by being extracted and they become part of the economy by being processed, refined, transformed, used or wasted in an enormous variety of ways; and they finally leave as unused heat. Things are very similar with material resources. They are extracted from the ground, broken down, purified, chemically changed, incorporated into products and used or wasted in an equally enormous variety of ways, and finally are discarded as waste or as harmful emissions.

Like energy, many material resources are limited by the finite quantity available in the earth. Some materials come from biological sources with the limiting factor being the rate at which the source plants or animals are replenished. In the case of inorganic resources the limiting factor is mostly the financial, energy and ecological cost of concentrating and transforming primary materials into a form suitable for human use.

In the last 40 years enormous progress has been made in geology, mining, transport, processing, chemistry and scientific research and in the use of materials in hundreds of thousands of different products. In journalistic terms, this remarkable progress was perhaps overshadowed by developments in the fields of nuclear energy, space technology, microelectronics and information technology, biotechnology and medicine, but it was of far greater significance both for everyday life and for the environment than all the high-visibility technologies taken together. Figure 13 from Robert Ayres (1991) indicates that the world has actually gone through a long period of exponential growth of human-driven material flows.

As far as nature was concerned, the exponential rise in the use of raw materials was disastrous. Where is nature still untouched? When will the ever-growing mountains of waste be cleared up and by whom? What is the ultimate fate of the manufactured goods which are in use today, not to speak of those which will be produced in the coming decades? Where are we to put the tons of plutonium, the thousands of tons of cadmium and mercury, the hundreds of thousands of tons of lead and copper, the millions of tons of waste generated in the mining of metals? (cf. Young, 1992) and the millions of tons of structures containing an intricate mix of metal wires, glass fibre, and hundreds of different plastics, coated with a thousand different varnishes and paints?

Metal production in 1,000 t (logarithmic increase)

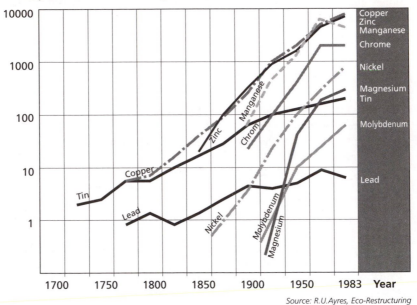

Source: R.U.Ayres, Eco-Restructuring

Figure 13: Selected metals show a near-exponential growth pattern in their 'consumption' by the world economy. Note that the vertical axis is logarithmic. Picture redrawn after Ayres (1991).

In the past, environmental policy concentrated on the unintentional emissions caused by manufacturing industry, but in future it will have to concern itself systematically with products which have been intentionally manufactured and the flood of materials which accompany their path from 'the cradle to the grave'.

Just as with energy, the nub of a rational environmental policy should be the adjustment of prices in accordance with the long-term cost materials cause throughout their life. Material prices at present reflect only mining and transport, refining, synthesising and processing costs — and all of these at energy prices which are far too low. Other costs generally remain hidden — restoring the land after mining (above all in developing countries), the cost of ecological damage caused by transportation and processing, as well as the cost of environmentally-friendly disposal after use. Material prices are always therefore much too low and are far from telling the 'ecological truth'.

Increasing and ultimately high taxes on virgin materials would create a stimulus for intelligent and parsimonious use of them. It would also create a market for 'secondary raw materials' and would work as a powerful 'vacuum cleaner' on the economy. To imagine the effects the reader is invited to reflect on what the fate of used batteries would be if they contained gold instead of cadmium!

From the above logic, four principles can be deduced for a strategy to solve the problem of materials and waste. Firstly, the establishment of artificially high prices for secondary raw materials (bottle refunds are but one approach, taxes on virgin materials another, and there are more). Secondly, the imposition of levies on waste: user fees to cover the operating cost of the disposal service *plus* charges to cover general environmental costs relating to materials, e.g. restoration of mining and old dump sites *plus* revenue-neutral taxes to achieve the needed size of the signal (see further Chapter 11). (It should be noted that taxes on primary materials or on energy are easier to implement and enforce than waste charges; the latter are susceptible to evasion from unscrupulous individuals using the cheaper road of illicit dumping!) Thirdly, the fixing of higher prices for energy, as suggested in the previous section; this makes the mining of materials and their transportation more expensive. It also helps to establish an adequate price signal on materials needing much energy in the early stages of processing, thus further stimulating recycling. Finally, the creation of rules whereby the producer of durable goods such as cars or dishwashers (or even chemicals which are used as catalysts) retain ownership and with it ecological responsibility for the whole period of their use, while the customer pays a leasing price. The producer would have the greatest interest in facilitating the re-use of the raw materials and would adapt product design accordingly. In Chapter 6 the potential of the 'obligatory leasing' idea for solving the dilemma of public transport will be taken up again.

Chapter 6

Transport

Transport Too Is A Symbol of Progress

Like energy, transport plays a central role in economic development. Passenger and freight miles can be used like megawatt hours to indicate economic activity and are seen by many as yardsticks of prosperity.

Christopher Columbus, Vasco da Gama, Gottlieb Daimler, Henry Ford and Charles Lindbergh have all come to symbolise progress because they were transport pioneers. 'Progress', after all, in its Latin roots means moving on. It is notable that transport as a symbol of progress is almost exclusively a male domain, not just among the pioneers but also in politics and business.

Transport brings competing goods and services to the customer or the customer to the goods and services. Without transport the market economy makes no sense. Transport also means mobility for the workforce, including managers. Transport is also a significant part of modern lifestyle, of freedom, leisure and the holiday; it is hardly surprising, then, that transport and the associated infrastructure and industries have elicited the sympathy of politicians of all colours.

Transport and the Environment

At the same time transport is one of the main causes of damage to nature and strain on the environment. In ancient times the Phoenicians sacrificed large tracts of Mediterranean forest to build their ships, in the process bringing ecological ruin to the region in the ensuing centuries, while a few centuries ago large areas of the Black Forest were denuded for shipbuilding in Holland. In order to make rivers navigable countless ecologically unique wetlands have been destroyed. On land, road and railway construction cut criss-cross through the woods and fields that lay in the way. Transport, of course, has always facilitated the exploitation of raw material sources; without modern transport the rain forests would not be in danger — they would be 'inaccessible'.

In Germany transport accounts for almost a quarter of total energy consumption, 60 per cent of nitric oxides pollution and 70 per cent of carbon monoxide pollution. The figure for nitric oxides is expected to rise to 70 per cent, before declining as a result of the EC decision to introduce the catalytic converter for all categories of car in all member states by the end of the century. Road and other transport construction may be responsible for half the area covered by concrete, bitumen etc. and for

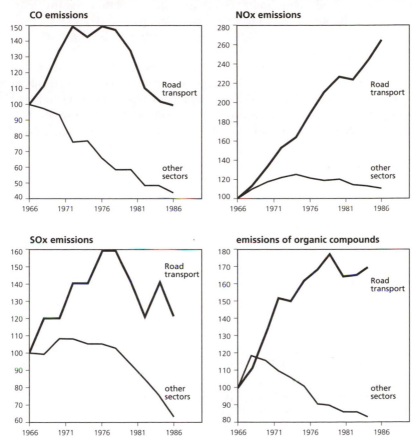

Figure 14: Air pollution (CO, NOx, SOx, VOCs): road transport compared with other sectors. Figures for 1966 defined as 100. Source: IEEP (Institute for European Environmental Policy), Bonn using data from Verkehr in Zahlen, 1988.

some 80 per cent of the cutting through of natural habitats causing biotope shrinking and isolation dangerous to the survival of many species.

Noise pollution is due above all to motor traffic, while pollution from the wear of tyres, ice-melting salt and the use of herbicides on railway and road embankments all cause considerable harm to water and the soil. In all its manifestations transport is one of the most significant sources of damage to the environment.

Many fixed sources of environmental damage, like domestic sewage, the chemical industry and power stations have over the last twenty years either been dealt with quite effectively or a solution is in sight. Unfortunately, this is not so with transport, and particularly so with road traffic where there has been little progress. Figure 14 demonstrates this with four examples.

The steep rise in pollution from road transport naturally reflects the rapid increase in this form of transport compared with rail and inland waterways. Figure 15 shows the steep rise in (private) transport compared with rail in the last twenty years; air transport has increased even more rapidly over the same period.

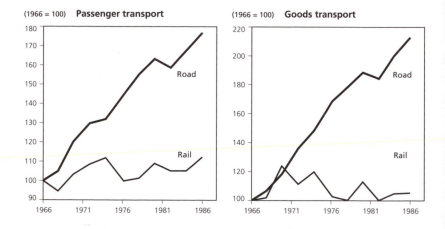

Figure 15: Stagnating rail transport — exploding road transport. Figures for 1966 defined as 100. Source: IEEP, using data from Verkehr in Zahlen, 1988.

Common Market Deregulation Makes Things Worse

Trends of intensifying traffic are bound to continue, and the falling of the Iron Curtain will easily double road traffic in central Europe, while the completion of the Internal Market will lead to at least 40 per cent more lorry traffic across national borders within the EC (Prognos, 1988).

The EEC was from the very beginning considering a Common Transport Policy akin to the Common Agricultural Policy. The mandate for this was laid down in Articles 74–84 (Title IV Transport) of the EEC Treaty of 1957, and it clearly meant systematic and unrestricted expansion of traffic. Somehow the mandate was never legally fulfilled, although the figures cited here demonstrate that this did not prevent traffic from growing. In 1983 the European Parliament woke up to the fact that the Community had not fulfilled its Treaty obligations and it brought an action against the European Council, in effect against its own member states, for failing to introduce the common transport policy. The European Court of Justice, to which the complaint was made, on 22 May 1985 upheld the parliament's view. In its judgment the court held that the principles governing the freedom to provide services must be applied to the Community's transport policy.

The judgment was perfectly timed, coming three weeks before the publication of the EC's White Paper on the completion of the Internal Market (White Paper, 1985): crucial to this are measures relating to what later became Article 7A (8A until 1993) of the Treaty, the four freedoms including the freedom to offer services anywhere within the Community. Some two weeks later, on 28–29 June, the ten heads of state and government of the European Council met in Milan and decided to bring about a completely liberalised (or deregulated) market for freight traffic by 1991.

Much the same happened with air transport: in April 1986 the European Court gave a judgement prohibiting all measures which restrict or distort competition. On 25 June 1987 at the meeting of the Community's Council of Transport Ministers the liberalisation of air transport was adopted. The deregulation of the transport market means that the railways lose all their remaining privileges and road hauliers can now compete with each other for any service anywhere in the Community. This is leading to a price war, which means that freight prices are falling. In turn this will increase still further road's competitive edge over rail. Transport deregulation will inevitably lead to a sharp increase in the environmental problems caused by transport. What can be done about it?

Most importantly, all carriers should bear the full- and long-term costs of their use of human and natural resources including, of course, external costs. As long as external costs are believed to be higher than 'external benefits' (benefits we all have without paying for them), there would not even be a justification for spending a penny of public money on transport infrastructure. If deregulation is meant to allow markets to steer what bureaucrats cannot steer with equal efficiency, it is only logical to make prices tell the full truth, otherwise market forces become destructive.

The polluter-pays principle should be applied in full, and it should be extended also to make landscape destroyers and resource consumers pay.

The German term *Verursacherprinzip* (principle of the responsibility of the causing actor) can easily be understood to be applicable far beyond pollution. In English we should perhaps speak of full-cost pricing rather than of the polluter-pays principle. Deregulation and full-cost pricing should be seen as inseparable twins.

The EEC's Transport 2000 Strategy (Commission of the EC, DG VII, 1991), initiated by Transport Commissioner Karel van Miert, acknowledges all this in principle and seems open to measures which really do make car users pay more for roads and fuel. It also acknowledges that symmetry should be established between road and rail as regards the infrastructure cost (which the railway companies usually have to bear while roads can be used free), but the Strategy remains conventional as far as practical policy measures are concerned.

The question, of course, is what are the full environmental costs, what concrete steps can be taken to allocate the costs to the agent producing the damage and what kind of elasticity to price signals can be expected? This will be discussed in a sub-section on pages 70 to 74 and, more systematically, in Chapters 10 and 11.

Rail or Road?

One thing seems to be certain. External costs per ton or per passenger and kilometre are considerably higher for road than for rail. In a report prepared for the German railways, the Basel-based Prognos AG has drawn up a comparison between road and rail of harmful emissions per passenger kilometre and per freight tonne kilometre (Figures 16 and 17, from Prognos, 1987).

In terms of primary energy consumption per kilometre, the car is less efficient than the train by a factor of 3 or 4 (Figure 17). One passenger kilometre on an inland flight uses 4.2 times more primary energy than the train. Similarly far more land is consumed by road than rail transport, both in relative and absolute terms.

Some crude estimates exist as to the total monetary cost of transport externalities. The Institute for European Environmental Policy (IEEP) in Bonn has compiled data from some existing German studies which are illustrated in Figure 18. Not counting investments (which are not *external* costs), the road traffic externalities added up to more than 80 billion DM (ca 30 billion £St) annually for West Germany in 1985 (when the greenhouse effect was not yet taken into account). More recent studies indicate substantially higher externalities. Similar calculations exist for the USA (MacKenzie et al., 1992). Rail externalities, by comparison, remain at insignificantly low levels.

Consumers hardly feel the huge differences in damage to the environment, which don't show up in the costs. In the daily choice between road or rail, the car invariably looks cheaper. Petrol costs in the EC work out at about 2 to 4 pence per kilometre, whereas the charge for rail travel is 7 to 14 pence per kilometre, though various fare reductions bring this down to an average to about 6 pence. The fixed costs of car use, keeping a car on the road (tax, insurance etc.), in fact raise the average costs to anything between 18 and 40 pence per kilometre, but because owning a car is a must for whoever can afford it, it is realistic both psychologically and economically only to count the 'variable cost' (the price of the *additional* kilometre) of, say, 4 pence when making one's daily transport choice. This effect tends to be exaggerated as commuters and travellers generally receive compensations or tax benefits calculated on the average *total* cost (i.e. 20–25 pence per kilometre); hence every additional kilometre driven actually *pays* for owning the car.

Toxicity of pollution

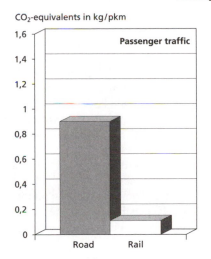

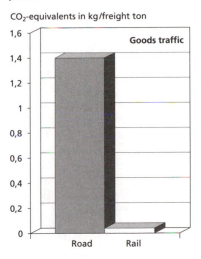

Figure 16: Toxicity of pollution (CO_2 equivalents in kg per passenger kilometre or per freight tonne weighted according to toxicity). Source: Prognos, Basle (Prognos, 1987).

This is the economic dilemma of public transport. Railways and buses cannot win the battle against the car. Under the honest pricing philosophy or under conditions of privatisation they are supposed to charge prices per kilometre that also cover the fixed costs (which are very substantial even if the state were to take over rail infrastructure costs). Otherwise they lose money. So long as there is a political will to let them run even if they lose money (as is the case with the military, the police and schools), they can survive, but with rising budget deficits in most countries this political will is eroding and parliaments and town councils are becoming tired of subsidising rail or local public transport.

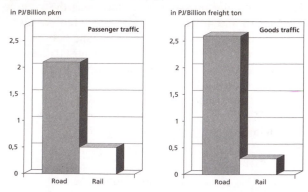

Figure 17: Energy consumption (in megajoules/passenger kilometres or per freight tonne kilometres) in the Federal Republic of Germany, 1985. Left: Passenger transport, right: Freight. Source: Prognos (Prognos, 1987).

The obvious environmental policy answer to the dilemma of public transport is to raise the cost of road transport. Petrol and diesel taxes are a favourite proposal from the environmental camp. I too believe that rising fuel taxes are unavoidable (see the next section), but they are extremely unpopular, especially in the USA, a country which can be said to be organised around the automobile. A similar effect to fuel taxes can be expected from *road pricing* which carries the disadvantage of not influencing fuel efficiency but differentiating between congested and less heavily used roads. This may not be easy to administer, but modern remote sensing and electronics do make it technically feasible. Once the public begins to grasp its implications, road pricing may be no more popular than fuel taxes.

There may be other possibilities of solving the public transport dilemma. If *additional* costs for the car user are so unpopular, a different method should be explored, by 'variabilising' the fixed costs of the car without raising the *total* or annual costs. Had the car owner to pay the full amount of some 18 to 40 pence per kilometre calculated by the automobile clubs to justify high kilometre compensations — for every additional kilometre he or she would think twice before using the car for commuting, shopping or seeing friends. More people would make use of public transport. Local councils — or private entrepreneurs — would hasten to meet the added demand and would thereby make the public or collective transport system more attractive.

But how can the fixed costs be variabilised without increasing the total cost? Several steps — or independent options — are conceivable. The first would be to drop all taxes and charges relating to car ownership and put the same total amount onto existing fuel taxes. The second step, recently introduced in California, is variabilising the insurance premium to become mileage-dependent without rising on average. (Insurance companies would probably not like this idea because it penalises high mileage drivers who tend to be the safest drivers, but there are other ways of rewarding safe driving; for the environment high mileage drivers are a high risk even if they never have an accident.)

Billion DM

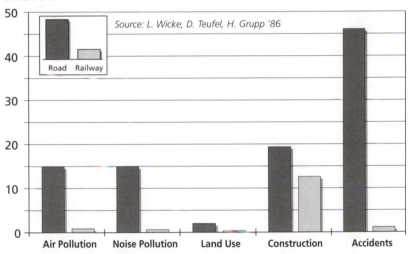

Figure 18: Environmental damage in billion DM caused by the different forms of transport (1985). (Estimates compiled from Wicke, 1986 ; D. Teufel, 1986 UPI-Report Nr 15; Grupp, 1986.)

The third step, 'obligatory leasing' instead of car ownership, may sound rather eccentric in our car-obsessed world but is nevertheless very rational. The idea is that the car user has virtually no fixed costs and that the price he or she pays per kilometre is calculated to cover the fixed costs to the owner, who is *not* the user and could be the manufacturer or any intermediary entrepreneur. A legal stipulation should exclude the charging of major time-dependent flat rates (which would, of course, destroy the intended signal). For poor people cars would become more accessible than today because they need less initial capital and they would have the use of a car for emergencies cases, major shopping expeditions or late night visits. The losers would be frequent drivers, which is the aim of the exercise. But, as we said before, the public transport system can be expected to react and eventually to come up with satisfactory services and prices even for high-mobility groups.

Excessive car use is not the only threat to the environment. Air traffic with its two digits annual growth rates may soon become one of the biggest concerns for environmentalists. Too little is as yet known about the implications of high density air traffic for the weather and climate. The solution may once again lie on the rail. Distances of 500, perhaps as many as 800 kilometres, ought by and large to be covered by rail. 'There and back in a day' is what the business community demands, and at the 200–300 kilometre per hour speeds of the Japanese Bullet Train, the French TGV and the German ICE this is an achievable target for business trips between Paris and Frankfurt, London and Edinburgh, Rome and Zurich, Prague and Berlin.

So far we have dealt almost exclusively with passenger transport. Things are in fact not dissimilar with freight, but the competition situation is not as difficult for rail because not everybody owns a lorry and commercial hauliers have to charge their fixed costs to the customer just as rail does. Rail's disadvantage with goods transport lies elsewhere. Rail is slower and much less flexible in end-distribution than lorries. The Japanese manufacturing philosophy of just-in-time delivery of parts to the factory does not work as a rule with the existing clumsy rail system. But rail, for its part, does not have the commercial freedom to make the necessary investment to speed up rail freight, make it more reliable or to develop the infrastructure for a really effective combination of rail and road. In principle the technologies exist for high-speed cargo trains, for rapid de- and recomposition of cargo trains and for efficient terminals for the switch from rail to road. Investment into these technologies makes sense in macroeconomic (and, of course, ecological) terms, but from a microeconomic perspective the balance is against rail and so nothing changes.

It would be a different world altogether for rail if there were a clear expectation that the costs per kilometre of road use were rising, doubling, tripling or quadrupling. With such expectations railway managers would quickly decide in favour of investing the necessary billions, but even quick decisions would not lead to rapid improvements. After ten years at the earliest, freight customers would begin to enjoy the fruits of the decisions and the breakthrough to a fully working new system should not be expected within less than thirty years. Long-term thinking is necessary when dealing with transport.

Fuel Prices and Taxes

As we have said before, the easiest way of making the polluter pay the full costs of transport is raising fuel taxes. Most countries in the world have long since introduced petrol taxes, whose philosophical origin lies in the taxation of luxuries. Later the idea was added that car users should be made financially responsible for road construction, and in several countries including Italy, Japan and Germany the annual revenues from fuel taxes often exceeded the annual road construction and maintenance costs. In the 1970s after the oil crisis, some countries, notably Japan and Italy, both totally dependent on oil imports, raised fuel taxes further to provide an additional stimulus for fuel efficiency and fuel conservation, but until recently there was no mentioning of the environment as an additional reason for fuel taxes.

This has changed. The greenhouse effect has forced politicians to acknowledge that more needs to be done than adopting laws which control exhaust emissions. The Netherlands introduced an environmental component of about 6 pence per litre on the petrol taxes in 1990, and both Sweden and Norway have followed suit. The EC has also thought of the transport sector when proposing carbon/energy taxes throughout the Community (Commission of the EC, 1991, see Chapter 11).

Expectations about the steering effect fuel taxes will have remain very cautious. It is generally believed that the price elasticity is very low in relation to people's use of their cars and automobile technology. 'People get angry at petrol price increases but they don't change their driving habits,' is what politicians tend to claim. In doing so they usually take into account the *short-term* elasticity only. Long-term elasticities are more difficult to measure, but international comparison among countries with similar levels of prosperity and different fuel price levels can serve as a first approximation to an empirical measurement of long-term price elasticity. Figure 19 shows the striking result.

There are other factors which also influence specific (per capita) fuel consumption, We studied two: population density, which is negatively correlated with specific fuel consumption and per capita GNP, which is positively correlated. Neither of the two, however, has a remotely similar influence on specific fuel consumption (Weizsäcker and Jesinghaus, 1992, pp. 31–42).

Technological breakthroughs can be expected in fuel efficiency of passenger cars. Lighter and technologically advanced cars do 50 miles per gallon or more. Allowing some compromise on size, comfort and speed, even 100 mpg are conceivable. Bureaucratic technology forcing via efficiency standards, however, is less efficient than fuel taxes for reaching the same goal.

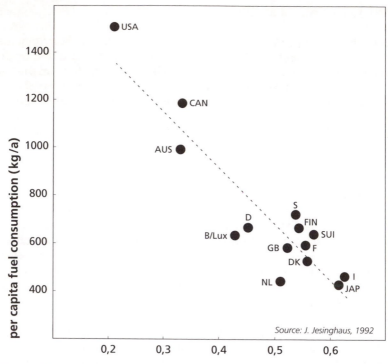

Figure 19: Annual per capita fuel consumption plotted against fuel prices in OECD countries 1988. The graph seems to indicate a very strong, if long-term price elasticity for the use of motor fuels. After von Weizsäcker and Jesinghaus (1992).

An interesting proposal, the 'Eco-bonus', has come from Switzerland. It is proposed that a supplement of around 2 Swiss francs be put on a litre of petrol and the revenue distributed among all adults (VCS, 1989). Those who drive a lot will have to pay more, those who travel little or use public transport will benefit. The increased fuel costs and the bonus received would balance out at around 7,000 kilometres per year. The idea, which is one variety of ecological tax reform, has been widely discussed in Switzerland and has steadily gained support, but is unlikely to be implemented soon.

What Next?

It is clear that raising fuel taxes is not the only conceivable component in an ecological transport policy, and a number of other ways of tackling the problem also exist.

Park-and-ride systems and technologies can be developed much further to keep the commuters' and shoppers' cars out of overcrowded inner cities. Sophisticated pick-up services, collective taxis and special lanes for buses and taxis can also help reduce car traffic. Satellite-based electronic communication technologies are being developed to tell drivers in congested areas which route is the least congested, although this is ecologically rather dubious as it lures still more cars onto the roads. Other technologies are being conceived to better combine individual and mass transport. Chapter 15 (pp. 182–83) discusses various examples of combination or piggy-back technologies (see also Vester, 1991).

Generally speaking, it is possible to increase the attractiveness of environmentally friendly forms of transport, and various cities and regions have explored ideas which are worth pursuing.

In the Netherlands there is the Nationale Strippenkaart, which is valid for public transport in all Dutch cities. These strips of tickets can be purchased in advance at convenient locations and cost around £4 for fifteen units. For most urban journeys two units are cancelled. The average journey costs therefore around 50 pence. The tram system is still being expanded rather than reduced, buses and taxis enjoy the convenience of special lanes on many streets and the national railway system connects virtually all cities and even many villages with frequent trains throughout the day and until late in the evening.

In Zürich, the citizens rejected by referenda proposals both for city motorways and for an underground railway ('Why should the clean commuter be forced to travel in the dark while the dirty cars remain in the daylight?' was a powerful slogan in the fiercely fought campaign). As a result, the city transport department systematically set about making the existing tram system more attractive to the user; in particular all spots which caused delay (badly timed traffic lights, car lanes in front of crossings for traffic turning left) were adjusted to the tram's advantage. In this way the tram network was dramatically speeded up and had to be extended in response to growing demand. In addition, an exemplary local railway system was extended. Other Swiss cities have not dissimilar success stories.

Bologna, and following its example several other Italian cities, have closed their centres to traffic from outside; only permanently resident citizens may obtain access licenses for their cars.

There are other ways of making transport environmentally more friendly. As long as the 'variabilisation' of the fixed costs of cars makes no progress, some other changes can be made in the incentive system. Tax deduction for regular commuting (a popular habit of subsidising workforce mobility) should be calculated by distance not by 'cost' in order to remove the unfair advantage of car commuting over all other modes of transport. Also, pollution rather than cylinder capacity (as is the case in several European countries) should determine the level of vehicle tax. This change has recently taken effect in Germany. This measure, however, only addresses the car make, not its use, energy consumption, CO_2 emission or the landscape destruction.

Road tolls can be levied, above all on entering cities and motorways; the cost and effort involved, however, are considerable and the results — so far as can be seen from the charges levied in the USA and in Europe — negligible.

A ban on lorries can be introduced on certain stretches of road or motorway — forcing freight on to rail; it seems that Austria and Switzerland will do this with the new Brenner and Gotthard tunnels, and of course the Channel Tunnel, is reserved for rail. It remains unsatisfactory, though, that these rail passages are designed to be convenient for lorries and do not act as an incentive for the entire journey to take place by rail.

Roads or bridges can be reserved for cars containing more than one or more than two passengers at certain traffic bottle-necks so as to induce commuters to agree on regular lift-sharing; this idea was first introduced in San Francisco for the Bay Bridge.

The re-introduction of a spartan but cheap third class in trains, to win back those with small budgets who often make the roads unsafe by driving in old and polluting cars, is also a possibility.

Innovation and innovative thinking can solve the horrendous environmental problems caused by transport, but such innovation itself can also put a strain on the environment. Trams, trains and special tracks for high speed trains as well as container terminals for the rail-road-link take up space; any such construction project, however meaningful for an environmentally sound transport system, will automatically come under fire from local campaign groups. One way round the problem might be a bargain struck in which every public developer, for every square metre of land developed has to demonstrate that he has given a square metre back to nature elsewhere. In such circumstances, anyone who continues to protest will be doing so out of local egoism and not for the sake of nature or the greater good. In a free country, everybody has the right to be an egoist and to fight for his or her own local interest, but if such a system were operated support would not flood in as happened with symbolic construction sites such as the new runway at Frankfurt Airport which could only be built with heavy police protection.

Chapter 7

Agriculture

Millenia of Partnership with Nature

From the earliest times human beings developed an ability to make use of the world around them and shape it to their own ends. Until the 'neolithic revolution', which took place around 5000 BC, this did no serious damage to nature. Only with the spread of arable and livestock farming can it be said that humanity encroached on nature to such an extent that it came to dominate the Earth. This domination was commanded to Man in the Story of Creation in the Old Testament, the relevant Genesis passage was written several thousand years *after* the neolithic revolution. The religious emphasis on human domination of the Earth is therefore an *ex post facto* justification for this state of affairs (Liedke, 1972).

Arable and livestock farming changed the face of the Earth. A growing population used primitive methods of cultivation which required great tracts of land. Over thousands of years in Europe, China, India and the Middle East virtually all reasonably fertile or accessible land therefore came under the plough or was used for grazing, but this did not necessarily cause serious damage to biological diversity. Of course, some major animals became extinct or very rare, and the ecological face of the Earth thereby changed fundamentally. But where earlier homogeneous forests were ecologically diversified by local clearings, small-crop fields, pasture, artificial ponds, kitchen gardens, hedges and several other new biotopes, more rather than fewer species were able to survive and further evolve. This species enrichment in parallel to agricultural development certainly occurred in Northern Central Europe (Sukopp and Hampicke, 1985).

As Hermann Priebe (1988) writes, this amazingly harmonious way of life also had a remarkable social side. Priebe portrays the peasantry as the bedrock of advanced civilisations. In its original form — the family farm based on the family working together with the draught animal, the plough and the cart — productivity increased to such an extent that a high level of civilisation was feasible without slavery. The civilisations of the ancient Greeks, the Romans and the Germanic peoples originally drew their strength from a social order based on the peasantry, while the advent of big landowners and slavery often led to their ruin (Priebe, 1988, p. 35).

Or to take another example, the devastating defeat of German peasantry in the Peasant's war of 1525, in which they fought for their ancient rights, essentially their rights to use the commons, can therefore be seen as a tragedy of the first order. It was part of the 'tragedy of the commons' according to Garrett Hardin (Hardin and Baden, 1980).

The Victory of the Large Farms Ideology

The tragedy continued to unfold in those areas where an ideology of large-scale farming succeeded the collapsing feudal structures. In Prussia, the remarkable reforms of Baron von Stein in 1807, which were intended to restore to small farmers their ancient rights, were perverted by Chancellor Hardenberg's decree nine years later restricting the benefits to big farmers. In the eastern part of what was to become Germany, which until then had kept up economically and technically with the West and South, the victory of the large landlords created a landless rural proletariat. Uncounted old villages disappeared and with them their skilled workers. The resulting pauperisation of the East German population contributed to the revolution of 1848, but this barely won them the right to self-support. In the West and the South of the country on the other hand a steady development of agriculture as an organic whole was possible, integrating craft trades and industry with a measure of division of labour; this process has been described as 'progress without structural change' (Priebe, 1988, pp.36–41). The rural population remained steady right up until 1950: only where there was surplus population was there migration to the towns. Even without machines productivity increased by as much as 1.2 per cent per year between 1850 and 1913.

Even though the large-scale farmers in Eastern Germany enjoyed privileged status, for example, by being allowed to employ poorly-paid itinerant, generally Polish workers, they kept getting into economic difficulty. The Nazi concept of the *Reichsnährstand* (food guild of the Reich), meant as a new aristocracy 'of blood and soil', was another attempt to give the large landowners privileges over small farmers. The Hitler regime had plans (which did not take effect due to the war) by which the small farmers should hand their land over to big estates, as had once been the case in the Eastern provinces (Priebe, 1988, p.51).

Priebe's historical account comes to the surprising conclusion that over long periods of time small farmers held their own economically — often selling their produce direct and earning extra non-farming income in a variety of ways. Big farmers meanwhile became increasingly dependent on the state for patronage, privileges like exclusive distilling licences and subsidies, for example the so-called *Osthilfe* (Eastern help) in the 1920s.

Against this background it is not surprising that the enormous kolkhoz or collective farms of Eastern Europe were not a success and that the EEC's agricultural policy which adopted the 'grow or get out' motto of the big farmers depended on rising levels of protection and subsidies. It is ironic that small farmers lost out every time: in the East under the banner of the 'workers' and peasants' state', through the large farms ideology under Prussian and Nazi rulers and also in the EEC through the policy of 'improving' agricultural structures, especially by farm enlargement. In all three cases the rhetoric of the farm lobby pretended to speak also on behalf of the millions of small farmers, but was in reality employed to eradicate them.

In earlier times the logic of big farms had served to validate serfdom, and later acted as a justification for mechanisation. In the 1920s systematic mechanisation of farmwork emerged in the United States. With cheap, flat, fertile land, cheap energy and mass production of tractors it was possible to achieve enormous productivity gains and, before long, big grain surpluses. There was just one ecological sign of warning: the 'Dust Bowl'. In the course of a dry period an area the size of Germany was for a time turned into dusty, infertile land.

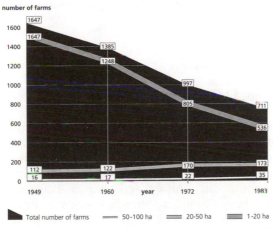

Figure 20: The decline in the number of farms in the Federal Republic of Germany between 1949 and 1983 and the increase in average size. (Priebe, 1988, p. 174.)

After the Second World War mechanisation also triumphed in Europe, proceeding hand in hand with the political push towards big farms and bigger fields to suit big, often American-made, machinery. What used to be the family farm was proudly renamed a 'business' (Betrieb) and the 'agricultural entrepreneur' (Landwirt, as opposed to Bauer) behaved accordingly as might be expected in the Economic Century. Under economic pressure farms were forced to specialise. Some grew and sold only grain, others produced sugar beet, some built factory-like housing for chickens or pigs while yet others concentrated on milk production and cattle. The old crop rotation system was abandoned as fertilisers and pesticides became readily available. Human and animal power was increasingly replaced by commercial energy. Agriculture, previously the chief supplier of energy, now became a major net energy consumer.

All this happened in the name of economic reason, but it turned out to be profoundly illogical from an economic point of view. Eventually, the Common Agricultural Policy (CAP) became one of the greatest financial disasters in history. Unprecedented surpluses were produced, placed in a network of storehouses of massive dimensions and periodically destroyed, given away or dumped on the world markets, thereby often undermining the fragile economic position of farmers in developing countries.

No less important than the economic calamity was the ecological disaster caused by the CAP. Nature and the beauty of the countryside were of no consequence in the new business thinking. Only when the new methods led to a fall in yield through disease or damage to the soil were environmental considerations given much thought. In vain did more traditional farmers warn against sacrificing the old values. They had to make way.

Environmental Problems

For a long period in Germany the farming lobby denied the existence of environmental problems. Unlike in Britain, Denmark, Holland and even Italy, until the mid-1980s German agricultural policy persisted in the view that agriculture as such was not detrimental to nature and the environment so long as farming was pursued in an 'orderly' way. This is the scandalous substance of the agriculture clauses in the German Nature Conservation Law of 1976 which sees 'orderly' agriculture as being in keeping with the goals of the law, although no attempt is made to define the term.

In 1983 the German Council of Experts on Environmental Affairs (SRU) finally addressed the environmental problems of agriculture. Professor Wolfgang Haber co-ordinated this work and put together a comprehensive report, 'Environmental Problems in Agriculture' which shows in matter-of-fact language the degree to which modern agriculture has become one of the most important threats to the environment (SRU, 1985). In 1993 Haber was awarded the first German Environment Prize, a 'green Nobel Prize'.

Top of the list of environmental damage resulting from agriculture is the loss of species and varieties. No other single factor has put at risk or eradicated so many animal and plant species in Germany as agriculture

(Figure 21). The causes of species destruction through agriculture are many. The excessive application of fertilisers to meadows leads to the decline of the 'lean' meadows which are in fact surprisingly rich in plant and animal life because so many plants which thrive on nutrient-poor conditions survive there, unharassed by the few fast-growing plant species found on overfertilised meadows. Pesticides and herbicides cause direct damage to fauna and flora alike; drainage schemes destroy wetlands; land consolidation destroys hedges and other small biotopes; machines and frequent mowing disturb or destroy the habitat of ground-nesting birds. In legal terms, the agriculture clauses of the Conservation Law are here clearly in breach of the EC's Birds Directive (79/409/EEC).

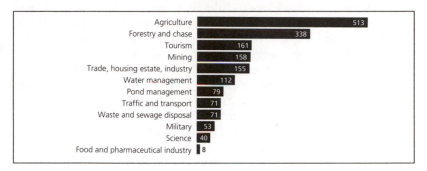

Figure 21: The main causes of the decline in the number of species (land use and branches of industry).

Modern agriculture is the biggest single factor responsible for the decline in the number of species. The figures refer to plant species on the Red List i.e. endangered species. Since some species are named several times where they are exposed to a variety of threats, the figures add up to a total higher than the actual total of species examined (711). Source: Umweltbundesamt, 1989, p. 134.

In other, mostly less industrialised, countries the effect of agriculture in putting species at risk of extinction tends to be even greater. One reason for the destruction of forests by farmers in developing countries is that much of the land is under the economic control of absentee landlords who tend to have a limited interest in the long-term sustainability of land management. The rural poor, on the other hand, often have no choice other than to slash and burn the forest, adopt shifting cultivation patterns or damage the land in other ways (see further Chapters 8 and 9).

In Europe the second major environmental problem caused by agriculture is pollution of ground and surface waters. Nitrates from liquid manure and commercial fertilisers are particularly dangerous for still or slow flowing waters. The run-off of waste nutrients into rivers and lakes can lead to excessive algae growth and ultimately to more or less fatal eutrophication, especially when additional toxic substances kill small animals living off the algae. One of the biggest contemporary dangers to the North, Baltic and Black Seas stems from the excessive influx of nutrients. In areas of intensive agriculture the continuous over-supply of nitrates also causes serious contamination of drinking water.

Pesticides are designed expressly to interfere with the biochemistry of living organisms — small wonder therefore that many are also toxic for humans, animals, crops and soil micro-organisms. Some highly toxic pesticides such as DDT and the 'Drin' family are largely banned in most of the OECD countries, yet they continue to be manufactured for use in developing countries, often without expert knowledge. Not infrequently they find their way back to us in the fruit, wool, flowers or even meat imported by the manufacturing countries. None the less, the World Health Organisation and the UN Food and Agriculture Organisation, together with most developing countries, are still opposed to a worldwide ban on DDT, primarily because it remains the only cheap means of combating the tsetse fly, other carriers of tropical diseases and certain agricultural pests. This situation is worrying from an ecological point of view. In the short term the most realistic approach may be to introduce a minimum requirement that not only importers but also users of these products in the developing countries give their prior informed consent to the choice of these toxic products so that they may be used only if their dangers are fully understood.

Less toxic pesticides continue to be used in the West in vast quantities. In West Germany the figure was around 30,000 tonnes of active ingredients in 1988. The EC's Drinking Water Directive of 1980 permits not more than 0.1 microgrammes of any one pesticide per litre of drinking water and not more than 0.5 microgrammes of combined pesticide. This extremely ambitious standard was adopted in 1980 as a *political* target to become effective in 1985; it was meant to keep all pesticides out of drinking water. There was no compelling *health* reason to treat all pesticides in the same way as the most noxious ones: certain herbicides, even when concentrated a thousandfold, are, so far as one can judge, no danger at all to human health, even when large quantities of water are drunk (Ohnesorge, 1989). From an ecological point of view, however, this extremely high standard may have its merits as it will lead logically to a ban on all pesticides (often herbicides) which do not biodegrade quickly, so that the accumulation of pesticides in soil and water would be avoided. On the other hand, we know little about the harmful ecological effects of the new generation of degradable pesticides which, one should assume, are biochemically more active than the old ones.

There are further examples of environmental damage caused by agriculture. Soil erosion is caused by water and wind, especially where cultivation leaves the soil uncovered for long periods, especially on hillsides. In Germany this is particularly the case with vines, maize, hops, oil seed, rape, wheat and all other cereals. Acid rain is produced by ammonia and nitrous oxides from pig and cattle farming and excessive local concentrations of manure; indeed, in Holland agriculture is considered to be the greatest source of acid rain. Overgrazing and ecologically damaging grazing by goats, and often sheep and cows, especially in developing countries, can cause irreversible damage to the vegetation; in some EU countries, including Germany and Britain, the EU Less Favoured Areas Directive (75/268/EEC), designed to maintain farming partly for environmental reasons, has ironically contributed to overgrazing. Soil compression has resulted from the use of heavy farm machinery. Agriculture has become a major net consumer of energy in contrast with earlier historical times when agriculture was the main producer of energy (see, e.g. Martinez-Alier, 1987 who also covers East European authors otherwise deplorably unknown in Western environmental economics).

Britain, Holland and the European Union

While in Germany the SRU Report drew attention to these problems and for the first time proposed ways of solving them, they were also being addressed in other countries. In Britain, an EC member since 1973, anger at the CAP was mounting year by year. The CAP cut British consumers off from cheap butter from New Zealand and other overseas produce and at the same time led to nonsensical surpluses resulting from the guaranteed prices, the financing of which British taxpayers had unwillingly contributed in large measures.

Soon warnings were heard that the CAP was ruining the environment. Since joining the EC the value of agricultural land in Britain had increased steeply, and in only a few years the area under wheat had increased significantly at the expense of grassland; a great many ponds, marshes and moors had been drained and the effects on birds and other species were increasingly apparent. Politicians, newspapers and environmental organisations all criticised the fact that taxpayers were financing both surpluses and damage to nature because of the EC. For the millions of nature conservationists in Britain, it made no sense at all that Continental agriculture ministers and even nature conservationists, for example the Bund (German Friends of the Earth), or the Greens supported high agricultural prices. In some British eyes, when German Agriculture Minister Ignaz Kiechle vetoed the lowering of grain prices by 1.6 per cent in March 1985, this was clear proof that Germany was not serious about environmental protection. But in Germany there was barely any press coverage of the veto, and certainly no environmentalist outside the Institute for European Environmental Policy was remotely aware that the veto might have any environmental significance. The German grain price veto may in effect have helped to delay by some two to three years British agreement to the EC directives on car emissions and large combustion plants. Why, it was felt, should the British dig deep into their pockets to help save German forests when the Germans wouldn't budge an inch on farm prices which in Britain were considered ecologically and financially important? In German newspapers British hesitations about air pollution control were, however, interpreted as a lack of 'environmental consciousness'.

Holland, too, was earlier than Germany in recognising the environmental problems stemming from agriculture. The disposal of liquid manure in the Netherlands is a problem comparable in scale to the disposal of special waste in Germany, and ground and surface water pollution, smell and acid rain make for formidable environmental problems caused by agriculture.

Quite early on, under British, Dutch and Danish pressure, the EC drew attention to environmental problems connected with agriculture. In the Green Paper on reform of the CAP (Commission of the EC, 1985) some of the major ecological problems were addressed and the validity of the polluter-pays principle confirmed with specific reference to agriculture. Under Regulation 1760/87/EEC annual direct payments of the order of 100 ECU per hectare were for the first time allocated from EC funds to farmers for programmes to maintain environmentally friendly agricultural practices in ecologically sensitive areas. Germany blocked this provision for more than two years. Again, none of this was publicised in Germany, where it was conveniently maintained that nothing good ever came out of Brussels.

More Than Food

Hemmed in by environmental regulations and offended by increasingly vigorous and at times unfair attacks, the farm lobby has reacted defensively to environmental protection. Indeed the industrial society, which has become so critical of agriculture in environmental matters, itself causes pollution on a vast scale which then rains down on the countryside. The cities consume and pollute huge quantities of water and expect it to be regenerated by the land. The cities produce refuse but reject the idea of disposing of it on their own ground, and they produce sewage and want it to be spread on the countryside.

Town and country are ecologically one. It will not be possible to solve the ecological problems of agriculture unless we address the problem as a whole. Urban conurbations have in one sense a parasitic relationship with the rural areas. Clearly it is not only food for the cities that is produced by the countryside. *Ecological* 'production' there is becoming ever more important, but as yet has not been sufficiently recognised. Economically, the countryside is still losing ground against the cities and 'economies of density' are governing the spatial development. Where there is infrastructure, education, culture, technology, industry, government offices, business headquarters and so on, there will be more of the same, and there will be the jobs and hence prosperity. Sicily, Extremadura, the Massif Central, Mecklenburg and Wales are all less favoured areas, and tend to become more so as the Union develops further (see Chapter 13). In sometimes desperate moves to try to catch up, the less favoured areas destroy what could be their last major assets, a healthy environment.

The cities should make an appropriate financial contribution to the ecological functions of the countryside. Regenerating water and air, maintaining biodiversity and the beauty of the landscape are essential services the countryside is or should be providing, but essential services should not be provided free in a fair economy. The big questions are, of course, what is a fair price for such services and how can payment be guaranteed?

Breaking the Vicious Circle

Agriculture and the rural environment both seem caught in a vicious circle. Further rationalisation in the traditional sense may yet be of some financial help to farmers, but only if we are prepared to sacrifice rather more than 70 per cent of the farms remaining on the Continent. Environmental damage would increase apace even if numerous new environmental regulations were adopted, since rationalisation allows only labour-saving, chemical-intensive practices.

On the other hand, radical environmental legislation aimed at reversing or slowing down this process would either reduce agricultural income to an unacceptably low level or, as in Switzerland and Norway, necessitate excessively high guaranteed prices. Given the pressure from low world market prices and US demands to reduce subsidies, this is just not feasible for the enormous EU market with its population of 340 million. Another option might be a strict quota system as was introduced for milk, which helped the butter mountain and the milk lake virtually to disappear, though not without large-scale dumping. But if practically all agricultural products were to be treated in this way, an administrative nightmare would be created, and this would conflict sharply with the principles of the market economy. It would mean massive and comprehensive protectionism and would stoke the trade war with the United States and other large suppliers and would be no less than a continuation of the current mechanisms of the CAP.

There is, it seems, no ideal approach, but it is possible to take some steps in the right direction which together might go a long way towards a reasonable solution (Weizsäcker, 1987; see also Ruttan, 1992). A number of such measures can be identified.

Environmental regulations should be enforced in agriculture. The application and licensing of agrochemicals, the spreading of liquid manure, livestock density per hectare, pasture regulation, soil protection and the establishment of nature reserves will all have to be covered by binding regulations, in so far as these do not already exist. The application of chemicals should become more costly according to the polluter-pays principle (for example, there should be a nitrate tax — see Chapter 11). Some ecological measures actually seem likely to have little impact on farmers' net income. Weinschenck and Werner (1989) estimated average losses of not more than DM250 (£100) per hectare per year for a switch from highly-polluting to environmentally-sensitive crop production. Some ecologically important measures, such as certain types of crop rotation, involve even smaller losses and in a few cases even lead to financial gains. Another type of regulatory measure is the cutting of subsidies for wetland drainage, inappropriate irrigation and counter-productive 'modernisation' (such as the destruction of Spanish oak forests to make way for agricultural production using orthodox modern European farming techniques and the production of even more surplus farm products). Similarly, special tax exemptions for the use of diesel in agriculture should be phased out.

There should be full transparency for the consumer about food production techniques including genetic engineering and the agricultural residues that result, and clear identification of all additives. A wider range of products should be available to give choice to those consumers who for whatever reason reject the use of certain chemicals or specific methods of livestock farming. On the other hand, direct sales of farm produce to consumers through farm shops, markets and so on should not be impeded by bureaucratic obstacles. As far as hygiene is concerned ordinary supervision and legislation concerning civil liability for producers is enough to protect local customers. It is a scandal that for reasons allegedly connected with hygiene it is almost impossible in many villages to buy the produce from the surrounding countryside. Similarly much of the existing legislation on product standardisation — often concerning only the appearance of food — is simply foolish and should be discarded.

Encouraging organic farming is another very important strategy. The EU has taken a useful step forward by adopting a set of rules that define most organic produce; this will greatly facilitate marketing throughout the Union. Many farms are in need of advice and modest financial assistance to make the switch to organic farming and such conversion subsidies would be beneficial in macroeconomic terms because organic farming is most unlikely to lead to costly agricultural surpluses and entails hardly any environmental side-effects. Research into organic farming, which has been seriously neglected by all European academic institutions, should now receive major support.

With or without going in for organic farming in the strict sense, farmers should receive many additional options for voluntary ecological management agreements with attractive compensation. Extensification (if possible 'de-intensification' over the whole area of the farm, not just spatial 'set asides') is but one option. Others are low rates of fertiliser use and no use of certain pesticides in important drinking water catchment areas, for which typical compensation rates in Germany can be around DM300 per hectare per year (the 'water penny' first introduced in Baden-Württemberg); the cultivation and breeding of certain rare plant and animal varieties are worth conserving even if they are not competitive under prevailing conditions; and certain management practices that help to protect wild animal and plant species, as in the wet meadows/bird protection programmes introduced by several German regions; here too a compensation payment of DM300 per hectare per year is a typical figure.

Direct payments can also be given for activities which may be ancillary to farming itself. Remuneration for nature conservation measures (maintaining or planting hedges, returning wetlands to their natural state, and the like) is one possibility. A different approach is to offer remuneration for visible success, e.g. the 'purchasing' of water meeting certain high standards from the farmers in the catchment area or financial awards to farmers on whose land rare species of animal, bird, insect or plant can be studied regularly. Such awards could awaken the considerable biological expertise possessed by many farmers who may know more about the ecological needs of local rare species than university scholars. Payments could be made also for the acceptance of sewage sludge, the absorption of CO_2 and the maintenance of certain vulnerable parts of the landscape.

Direct payments may mean some departure from the concept of full-time farming. Small farms and even some larger farms may find that their viability depends on diversifying their income sources. Additional sources of income both for farmers and other family members should be actively promoted in any modern policy for the rural areas. Examples of gainful activities include food processing, providing bed and breakfast facilities, running a restaurant, providing accommodation for those convalescing from illness, drugs or mental disorders, winter jobs on the roads, teaching and a number of modern activities that require little more than a computer, electronic mail and a fax machine. This is the 'telecottages' idea which originated in Scandinavia in the late 1980s and is now spreading; (contact address: Sixtus Lanner, Brucknerstrasse 6, A1040 Vienna). Interestingly, the German Agricultural Reports show a relative improvement in the income for part-time farmers against full-time farmers since 1988.

Besides such steps to reform agricultural and rural development policy, other measures are necessary. The overall economic system frame should be changed so as to make prices 'tell the ecological truth', which has been the main drift of the two preceding chapters of this book (see also Chapters 10, 11 and 13). Applied to the crisis afflicting the countryside this means that the conurbations may no longer behave as parasites and must pay the correct price for water, air, energy, materials and transport. If the costs of energy and non-renewable raw materials are artificially raised, the time will come for farmers to grow renewable raw materials, including energy crops. Obviously, just as with the cultivation of foodstuffs, these will require the strict observation of ecological rules.

Under political pressure finally to conclude the GATT Uruguay Round and to pave the way for creating a Multilateral Trade Organisation (MTO), the EU has moved away quite a distance from the earlier CAP. Creating a system, however, that satisfied the interests of farmers, free trade and the environment appeared at first to be just about impossible (see Schmidt-Bleek and Wohlmeyer, 1991). But the proposals by Farm Commissioner Ray MacSharry appeared to come astonishingly close to satisfying all needs except those of farmers relying heavily on export subsidies. The MacSharry reform, the first CAP reform since the days of Sicco Mansholt, is a major step forward towards a countryside revival with much less overproduction and less environmental damage. Environmentalists throughout the European Union should join hands with farmers and ministries of agriculture to fully use the potential inherent in this new beginning (assuming, of course, that the French government drops their objections to the Blair House compromise with the USA and allows these proposals to go ahead).

Chapter 8

The Third World

At the Heart of the Destruction

The horrifying figures for worldwide environmental destruction mentioned in the introductory chapter refer for the most part to the countries of the Third World. Perhaps 90 per cent of the extinction of species, soil erosion, forest and wilderness destruction and also desertification are taking place in the developing countries (with Russia and other CIS states rapidly joining the Third World, notably as regards sacrificing nature to world trade). The most devastating individual cases of local air and water pollution are now to be found in developing and newly industrialised countries, for example in Mexico City, Wuhan, Taipeh and Cairo. By comparison, the Ruhr or Pittsburgh look almost like spa towns. Waste disposal, water treatment, even provisions for the removal of animal corpses only exist at a very basic level in many Third World cities.

If we genuinely wish to protect the environment, then we must not ignore the conservation and environmental problems of the developing countries. For this we have to understand the causes of environmental destruction in the South, and the following reasons perhaps summarise the situation.

Firstly, the developing countries lie almost exclusively in climate zones where both wind and water erode unprotected soil with particular ferocity.

Secondly, the majority of animal and plant species are native to the regions classified today as the Third World; the ecological destruction of a square mile in the South is therefore bound to carry with it a significantly greater loss of species than the destruction of a comparable area in the North (Wilson 1992). It should also be said that the North has already simplified its landscapes over the centuries, with the corresponding loss of species this involves.

Thirdly, there is a severe imbalance in trade between the industrialised and the developing countries in goods which have an impact on the environment (e.g. Khor, 1992). According to the Indian scholar Anil Agarwal (personal communication), the total biomass exported today from developing to industrialised countries may be some ten times greater than during the much maligned colonial period. In addition, there is the export of mineral ores, oil and other raw materials, demand for which not only diminishes finite reserves but also often inflicts visible local ecological damage.

Fourthly, dominant élites, frequently in collaboration with Northern industries and agencies, have often pushed for resource mining, industrialisation and the related infrastructure at any cost. These 'modern' structures are often polluting and wasteful in environmental terms as well as inefficient in economic terms. Moreover, pollution control measures tend to be too costly for the economies of less developed countries.

Fifthly, many people in rural areas draw their sustenance directly from forests, soils and waters. As they come under pressure from the official economy to produce cash value they are often forced to use the better land resources for cash crops while pushing subsistence farming ever deeper into areas which cannot sustainably support regular harvesting (see e.g. Durning, 1989).

Finally, population growth and the resulting needs for more intensive use of resources, including land, are primarily found in the developing countries (Ehrlich and Ehrlich, 1990).

Looking more carefully at these six reasons for ecological destruction in the South, we discover that the population of the North plays a considerable role in some of them, notably the trade imbalance (see the sub-section on the international division of labour) which can be seen as having its roots primarily in the North. To a considerable degree, therefore, poverty and other reasons for environmental destruction have their roots in unequal North-South relations.

Development aid from the North has in the past tended to exacerbate the ecological problems of the Third World. 'Development' primarily meant more mining, more roads, more energy and the use of more chemicals in agriculture. Even after the introduction during the mid-1980s of environmental-impact assessments, ecologically harmful projects prevailed; it was, however, mostly the developing countries themselves which were hesitant about environmental restrictions on their development programmes.

Population Pressure

Whenever people in the North debate the environment crisis or the developing countries' economic plight, the first issue which invariably comes to their minds is population growth (e.g. Simon, 1989). The seemingly never-ending increase in population in developing countries is looked on with horror, pity or disgust as the source of all their ills.

Everything would, of course, be much easier if population numbers were soon to stabilise or to fall, but Europeans have precious little right to preach about the population issue. Firstly, because the birthrate is closely connected to the level of poverty in the Third World, a problem which the North is doing little to alleviate. In addition, Western Europe is much more densely populated than most developing countries, although Europe's carrying capacity is admittedly greater than that of the Sahel or the Amazon Basin. We should also recall that the number of children per family in developing countries is declining much more quickly than was ever the case in Europe; from 1965 to 1991 it fell from 6 to 3.9, according to statistics of the United Nations Fund for Population Activities (UNFPA, 1992). It should also be noted that the governments of almost all non-Islamic (and even some Islamic) developing countries are keen to check population expansion, which was never the case in Europe. Finally, owing to unequal consumption rates, the 0.6 per cent annual population growth of OECD countries creates more ecological pressure on the Earth than the current, falling, 2.2 per cent annual population growth of the South.

Rather than preaching, the nations of the North should do something about the situation, and it is certainly not enough simply to issue calls for greater use of various methods of birth control.

One of the most important tasks is to create the social and economic conditions in which parents become genuinely interested in having small families or at least lose interest in having a large number of children. The desire for a big family is related to various factors. A family's health and wealth are often measured, culturally, by its size, and children are frequently the best form of insurance for the parents' old age. In a subsistence economy, children constitute a valuable additional workforce, particularly where the fetching and carrying of wood and water is a major demand on people's time. The tragedy is that, as a result of increased population density, the shortage of wood and water becomes ever more pronounced.

Conversely, the desire for children declines proportionately with improved education for and social standing of women, with secure employment and with improvements in health and hygiene for small children, and so their chances of survival.

The key point in any attempt to remedy the situation should therefore be obvious: securing the livelihoods of the vulnerable groups in society should be the first economic priority. This would include more specific strategies such as welfare for the elderly, the development of possible alternatives to children's work, improvement of women's social and educational status, and with it their ability to make independent decisions and child health care programmes. If, and only if, these social measures lay the ground, the pill, vasectomy and other measures have a realistic chance to work effectively.

Not surprisingly, the most effective measures have a significant financial cost. The Worldwatch Institute (Brown et al., 1990) estimates annual cost of an effective worldwide population control policy to be 30 billion dollars. The authors add, however, that the industrialised nations should foot this bill as a down-payment on a long-term sustainable future.

Subsistence Economy — Not So Outdated

Many people in the developing countries know well that the destruction of the environment could also mean the destruction of their livelihoods. Destruction has often come under the veil of 'development', and those who felt most affected were the first to protest. But where in the North in the 1960s the prime movers of the environmental protest movement were chiefly women and children from well-to-do families, in the developing countries it was, strikingly, often the poorest of the poor, again mostly women, who carried the burden of organising and maintaining the protest and who were desperate to defend their interests against the bulldozers.

Easily the best known example of the poor resisting the destruction of their immediate environment is the Chipko movement in India. Chipko, which means 'tree-hugging', is a peasant protest movement against the commercial felling of their forests which originated in the northern Indian state of Uttar Pradesh in 1973 when a logging company moved into woods belonging to the village of Gopeshwar. The villagers, particularly the women, decided to obstruct the logging by embracing the trees, and the company ultimately had to beat a retreat. The news of this successful action spread rapidly, with many other such Chipko protests taking place (Bandyopadhyay and Shiva, 1987, Shiva, 1989).

The strength of the movements to protect the forests was enhanced by the tragic experience of a catastrophic flood in 1970 which brought home to the subsistence farmers of the region, who were not all from the forests, how vital the forests were to their existence. While the woods were being cleared, mainly to supply markets in the towns, the local poor were left to cope with the consequences: erosion, greater distances to walk for firewood and an increased likelihood of flooding. Material losses were not the only consideration, as Vandana Shiva so vividly explains: the destruction of beauty also hurt the local women and made them all the more determined to save their environment.

It had long been the declared aim of 'development' to overcome and supersede the subsistence economy. The success story of industrialisation serves as proof and paradigm for this view which places subsistence on a level with poverty and backwardness.

In line with mainstream economic thinking, national development plans in developing countries, as well as the supporting aid programmes from the North and from the international lending institutions, have aimed at overcoming the subsistence economy in all its forms. Industrialisation, technical education, energy supply and transport infrastructure have been the favourite targets of development. The integration into the world market was and continues to be a prime objective of development strategies and of the more recent restructuring efforts by the International Monetary Fund and the World Bank. All this is done in a spirit of crusading for a good cause. Successful examples are the Asian 'Four Tigers' which have 'taken off', as well as Chile, Mexico and even Ghana which all show signs of recovery after the 'lost decade' of the 1980s. But at what price? The environment is mined and the subsistence economy is destroyed.

Only recently have some non-Marxist and non-Dependency Theory economists, and especially female economists and economists from developing countries, begun to cast doubt on the validity of current economic development theory (Mitter, 1989, Arizpe 1989, Bello, 1989, Shiva, 1989, Khor, 1992, Goodland et al., 1991, Sachs, 1992). They point out that many people not only derive no benefit from 'development' of their country, but are often massively disadvantaged by it. To the losers the promise by mainstream economists of an eventual economic take-off has no more credibility than the promises of a classless society had to the people in Eastern Europe. And if the immediate threat by development projects is the destruction of their daily support system, one would not expect them to remain passive and indulgent.

In addition, the issue of democracy needs to be considered. Early democratic theory was based on people who enjoyed their independence, meaning that they were not susceptible to blackmailing with regard to their basic needs. In Switzerland the economically independent citizen, ideally the free (if poor) farmer, plays a central role also ideologically in the country's centuries old democracy.

In today's real world it does not seem feasible to have everyone enjoying the wealth of today's Swiss citizens (nor of British landlords, for that matter). But the advantage of not being vulnerable to political or economic blackmailing can theoretically be assured — if a minimum level of subsistence economy can be safeguarded. It would seem ironic if the American zeal for democratisation of the world was using mostly an instrument — world market integration — which has as one of its side-effects the erosion of the very basis of functioning democracies.

International Division of Labour

According to traditional economics, efficient world markets serve to benefit all. World markets are based on the division of labour on a world scale, but this division of labour is not symmetrical. The North, owing to its technological superiority stemming from colonial times, was assured of all the high-value, economically interesting tasks, while the developing countries were rather confirmed in their role as providers of raw materials, a role they neither wanted nor particularly valued. As Eduardo Galeano, the Uruguayan historian, said, 'The international division of labour consists of some specialising in winning and some in losing.' (quotation from Brown et al., 1990, p. 140)

One example from colonial times (i.e. long before development aid) is described by the Indian historian, R. Mukerjee: the overtaking of India by Great Britain as the world's major cotton and textile supplier as a result of the industrial revolution. Even as far back as 1786, India (Bengal) was finding that its hand-made but technically superior cotton could no longer compete with the British article, which was becoming ever cheaper. For a while the export market for Indian muslin, which British machinery was not yet capable of producing, held up, but soon India was beaten at that game as well. If India was, until about 1800, the technological workshop of the world, writes Mukerjee, with a hint of sadness, it had now become one of the (as yet) richest sources of raw materials. 'A phase of de-industrialisation now commenced for India.' 150 years later, the rich supplies of raw materials had either been exported or exhausted, and India had sunk to being one of the poorest countries in the world. The very same process is, of course, portrayed in British economic history as 'progress'.

The export of those rich supplies of raw materials has accelerated in recent times, thanks in no small part to improved methods of transport. Improvements in transport infrastructure, classed without cynicism as 'development aid', typically had a negative effect on the environment and were of doubtful benefit to the process of development. Their effect was firstly, to facilitate exploitation and transportation of mineral and other natural resources, and so in effect to accelerate environmental destruction and secondly, because this was happening all over the world, to cause a glut of these products on the international market and hence a fall in prices. Fröbel et al. (1977, 1986) were able to show how improvements in transport resulted in Third World production becoming divisions of global factories, whose nerve centres were of course located in the industrialised countries. The limbs of such global factory bodies are extremely vulnerable to small cost differentials originating from any other part of the planet and to sudden decisions taken by the brains to sever the limbs. Mass unemployment often came overnight.

Despite clearly being the losers in all of this, the developing countries managed for a long time to put a brave face on their position in the world labour market. Until around 1970 it appeared to them that their poverty and dependence were transitory consequences of colonialism and that with de-colonisation things would change for the better. They placed considerable hopes in the UN, where they were in the majority, but the UN was losing influence at the very time when it was coming to be dominated by the developing countries.

When in 1973 the price of oil was suddenly trebled by OPEC, politicians and intellectuals in the Third World thought that maybe the role of supplying raw materials was not so bad after all. With its hunger for raw materials, the North might well become more and more dependent on the South. Copper exporting countries dreamt of a 'copper OPEC', the cotton producers hoped for a 'cotton OPEC', and bauxite mines, banana plantations and cattle ranches were suddenly seen in a much brighter light than before.

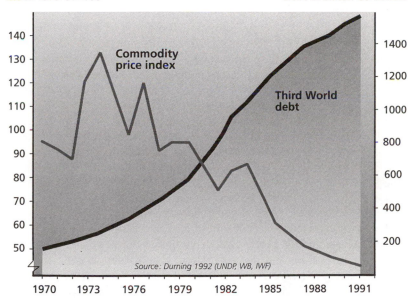

Figure 22: Commodity prices and Third World debt between 1970 and 1989. From Lester Brown et al., (1990), p. 144.

Moreover, the banks, which were gradually filled up with recycled petro-dollars, were keen to put much of that money into commodity investments which appeared very safe. Interest rates were low and there was no question of any failure of repayment. Only the Least Developed Countries (whose economies were severely hit by the oil price shock) needed official development aid funds or (soft) loans for financing investments into developing the exploitation of their natural resources.

One did not need to be an economist to predict that such massive investments into resource exploitation on a global scale would eventually lead to falling commodity prices, and this is what happened. Simultaneously, the financial burden of all those loans increased. This dual trend continued throughout the late 1970s until the present, as can be seen (until 1988) in Figure 22. The debt crisis started as early as 1978 when interest rates began to go up steeply, and it became a debt disaster during the Reagan years (see p. 40).

The debt crisis can be said to originate in the industrialised countries, but is gradually turning into a dangerous 'debt boomerang' for the North, as Susan George puts it (S. George, 1990; see also Sabet, 1992). The indebted countries have no choice but to 'sell' their nature on the world markets, and precisely the same is now happening with debt-laden Russia and other CIS states.

All in all, it seems that the international division of labour is far from producing benefits for all parties. It certainly raises average labour productivity, but this effect does not by itself create international equity and almost by definition leads to the plundering of nature. The debt crisis adds to this general effect. Sometimes indebted countries even 'sell' their air, their water and their land to the North, as for example, when Japanese, European or North American polluting industries relocate in the Third World. Cases in point are imports of feedstuffs from the tropics, because Europeans consider our own land as too valuable to be used for such purposes, or when our special waste is shipped direct to the Third World. The latter is at last coming under some form of control through the Basel Convention on the Transboundary Transportation of Waste.

In many cases the links between the international division of labour and ecological tragedies are not so visible. The clearing of forests to make room for farmland for export cash crops quite often resulted in rapid soil degradation, erosion and desertification. Heavy rains occurring at this stage are likely to lead to floods in low-lying land, while in the dry season springs dry up and whole areas can turn to dust. Whereas in the 1960s approximately 5.2 million people were affected annually by flood disasters, in the 1970s the number had risen to 18.5 million. The ratio for those affected by drought is similar. Neither weather nor population increase nor improved statistical measurement can explain a factor of 3.5 within a decade. According to Lloyd Timberlake of the International Institute for

Environment and Development in London, these have clearly been for the most part man-made disasters (Timberlake, 1984).

The term 'environmental refugee' is a new one in the almanac of horrors (UNEP, 1985). The Henri Dunant Institute in Geneva (the research institute of the Red Cross) estimates the number of environmental refugees to be in the region of 500 million. Whereas the Chipko women were able to defend the forests to some degree against the march of 'development' because the danger was localised and visible, most environmental refugees are helpless victims of events that have happened hundreds of miles away.

Despite all this being well recognised, the international division of labour and 'development' forge ahead on all fronts. The International Monetary Fund, the World Bank and GATT, the General Agreement on Tariffs and Trade, all seek to remedy today's economic troubles with ever more international division of labour. If the environment features at all in the considerations of these Bretton Woods institutions, it is used in the conventional sense of some pollution-control measures and perhaps an occasional environmental impact assessment, but no attempts are made to seek the origin of the ecological degradation in the prevailing division of labour (see e.g. Khor, 1992).

Some pioneers in the business community have recently begun to acknowledge that certain ecological problems are rooted in world trade (Schmidheiny, 1992; see also Anderson and Blackhurst, 1992, Verbruggen, 1991). The greening of GATT is long overdue, yet nowhere are there sufficient instruments for this major task which is so central to Earth politics (see further Chapter 14).

The Brundtland Report and Agenda 21

In 1983, the Norwegian government, recognising the galloping rate of environmental destruction, particularly in the developing countries, decided to take action and suggested to the UN that a new commission should be set up to assess the state of the world's environment and to examine the efficiency of the UN system in dealing with the ecological situation. With Norwegian and other OECD money, the commission was established and was given the name World Commission for Environment and Development (WCED), to express the concern of the developing countries that their first priority, development, should not be neglected. The Norwegian opposition leader (from 1985–89 and again since 1991, Prime Minister), Dr Gro Harlem Brundtland, was elected to chair the commission.

After three years of intensive work and countless hearings in practically every corner of the globe, the commission published its report, *Our Common Future*, which must rank as one of the most important documents of the decade (World Commission, 1987; see also Starke, 1990; for a critical assessment see De la Court, 1990). A new term was used to help bridge the gap between environmental and developmental aspirations: *sustainable development*. The term remained somewhat open in its meaning, but it certainly helped to give the development discussion a new direction.

One of the most important issues which, although not new, was put into context and made public by the Brundtland report, is the movement of vast resources — worth around 40 billion dollars net per year since about 1985 — from the developing countries to the North. Most of this has been for the servicing of debts, above all for paying interest rather than capital repayment. The Brundtland report analysed *net* flows, i.e. after the deduction of the entire capital transfer from the North to the South including all development aid. As we emphasised earlier, these amounts are realised mostly through the sale of natural resources and minerals, i.e. through the sale of nature itself.

The Brundtland Report was presented to the General Assembly of the United Nations and was the key factor leading to the decision to convene a United Nations Conference on Environment and Development (UNCED). The conference, convened in Rio de Janeiro in 1992, was given the central mandate to prepare a Programme of Action on Environment and Development. From its early drafts onwards, the Programme was called Agenda 21, referring to the twenty-first century, which we have termed the Century of the Environment.

Agenda 21, a huge document of more than 800 pages, was at the centre of the negotiations before and at Rio. It covers all conceivable topics from overcoming poverty to solving all kinds of pollution problems. Pollution, poverty, biotechnology, technology transfer, urban renewal and financial means to implement all this gave enough food for the diplomats and their expert advisers to fill the conference with lively debates. In the end, the Agenda 21 was adopted in a somewhat modified form. The total cost for implementing Agenda 21 was estimated at some 600 billion dollars annually, of which 100 billions should come from the North. 100 billion dollars happens to be 0.7 per cent of the GDP of all OECD countries taken together, an important symbolic coincidence which makes it perhaps more understandable why reaching the old target of 0.7 per cent of GDP for Official Development Aid was the biggest contentious issue at Rio de Janeiro. In the end, the Northern countries, except the USA, agreed to stick to this target, albeit with a somewhat vague formula concerning the date by which the target should be reached.

The newly established Commission for Sustainable Development was given the mandate to monitor progress on the implementation of Agenda 21, but the commission will not have funds of its own. The North also agreed to enlarge its commitment for funding the World Bank's Global Environmental Facility, GEF.

In line with my sceptical comments about conventional economics and international trade, I would be bold enough to declare that the vagueness of the financial commitment by the North regarding Agenda 21 is *not* a disaster. Agenda 21, after all, is a fairly conventional bag of growth wishes, although with some relation to environmental protection, but in no way does it address the paramount global problem, the unsustainable lifestyles prevailing in the North.

The Northern Model Remains Unattainable

The Western (and Japanese) development model fascinates people in the developing countries. Wealth and infrastructure that works (from the telephone to the sewage system), a functioning administration, mobility, education, technology, social services *and* environmental protection are all things which the Third World would love to obtain. And who can blame them? In the introductory chapter I have already pointed out that the straightforward adoption of this development model by (today) 5.6 billion, (soon) 6 billion or (one day) 10–12 billion people would be both quantitatively and ecologically impossible, indeed ruinous. If per capita consumption rates for water, energy, minerals and land did not diminish drastically, the Earth would suffer irreversible and disastrous damage within five to ten years. The North in particular, which presently has it so good, can hardly wish for this ecological hell. For the South it would be just as ghastly, but for the South, especially Africa, the situation already seems as though it could hardly become any worse.

Yet deteriorate it will. Many developing countries are threatened with political upheaval similar to that in Eastern Europe. The central role of the state in economic affairs, state planning and a very small ruling élite, sometimes a one party system, are features which many nations in the South have in common with the defunct regimes of Eastern Europe. Mismanagement is correspondingly widespread, but the West demonstrates day-by-day to the developing countries the standard of consumption available to those in power. It is this which closes the vicious circle of mismanagement. In order to bring the developing countries back to health, not only is it necessary to correct unfair trade structures but also to wean them from their vision of the North's throwaway society.

Goodland and Daly (1992) give ten reasons why Northern income growth is not the solution to Southern poverty. All their reasons are also arguments for why the Northern model of wealth remains unattainable for the masses of the South and why attempts to spread the model will lead to further environmental destruction.

What Can Be Done?

First and foremost the North itself needs to search for different models of prosperity as thoroughly and quickly as is possible, but without giving rise to serious crises or disruption.

New models of wealth should be sufficiently attractive to achieve popularity in their own right, even in the democratic countries of the North. For the South, more indigenous patterns of prosperity should be more easily attainable, both technically and economically, than the present Northern throwaway model. From an ecological standpoint the new models in the North must drastically limit pollution and the consumption of non-renewable resources. Then — and only then — will we have the right in North-South negotiations to demand similar standards of the South. New models of wealth and ways in which to achieve them will be dealt with in Parts Three and Four of this book. But we ought not simply to let the matter rest with 'work on new models of wealth'. There are ways in which we can help the Third World directly to rid itself of its ever more pressing environmental crisis.

Let us first address a matter of terminology; activities which open up areas for mineral extraction, from prospecting to the expansion of related transport routes, or activities which transform primary forest into farmland, should cease to be defined as 'development aid' by any OECD country or any development agency using Northern funds. They are accomplices of exploitation. This sort of project cannot be legislated against, yet taxpayers should not be induced to believe that they are financing something worthwhile. There will be borderline cases, of course, such as a railway from a country's interior to a harbour, which might not only transport ore but also be one step further towards an environmentally sustainable transport system. The term 'development aid' might also apply to the development of an ecologically acceptable system of agroforestry enriching, and perhaps saving, a natural forest dying from drought and fire.

What we positively can do, is to promote, as foreseen in Agenda 21, the adoption of environmental technology in various practical ways. Modern combined coal and gas power stations offering significant improvements in energy efficiency, in greenhouse gas reduction and in effects on the immediate environment should be constructed in place of outdated coal-fired power stations. The use of waste recycling techniques and, in exceptional cases, modern waste incinerators would help relieve Third World conurbations of a considerable burden. Modern sewage treatment works would be the best form of immediate aid for the Yangtse, the Nile or the Ganges.

Care would naturally have to be taken that the technologies could be serviced, and also, as soon as possible, actually produced in the developing countries, although this, of course, runs counter to the interests of our export-based economy. The fact that much of the necessary fieldwork is best carried out *in situ* means that research and development for ecologically sustainable but productive forms of agriculture and small-scale technology should be carried out locally and with OECD assistance. Some of the most recent technologies are particularly suited to being integrated with, rather than replacements for, traditional technologies (Weizsäcker, Swaminathan and Lemma, eds., 1983).

Further possibilities might be help with the setting up of efficient administrative structures (e.g. to supervise the environment, forestry and agriculture, town planning etc.) with appropriately qualified staff; assisting structural adjustment, in order to create internal incentives towards the protection of resources; specific aid to strengthen the informal sector, e.g. by supporting the small scale recycling of waste which goes on in almost all centres of population.

Agenda 21 is full of useful examples of where available money can be usefully employed. However, it need not always be *aid* that helps. In my view it is more 'sustainable' to find business opportunities for sustainable development. The book by Stephan Schmidheiny (1992) and his Business Council for Sustainable Development referred to above provides dozens of impressive examples of profitable activities which may be labelled sustainable development.

Unprofitable sustainable development is not attractive for business, nor for the country of operation. Ecologists should bear this in mind when criticising Schmidheiny and his co-authors for what they may still fail to do in protecting the environment.

Chapter 9

Biodiversity and Genetic Engineering

Endangered Biodiversity

Sometimes the world needs a new catch-phrase to draw attention to an aspect of contemporary reality. 'Biodiversity' was just such a term. In 1986 one of America's most prominent biologists, Professor Edward O. Wilson of Harvard University, famous as the originator of the concept of sociobiology, called members of the scientific community to a conference in Washington on the subject of Biodiversity. The conference became an impressive rallying cry to save the biological diversity of the planet (see Wilson, 1992). Wilson declared that the destruction of biological diversity was the environmental sin for which future generations would forgive us least, and he compared the biological community faced with present ecological destruction with art lovers seeing the Louvre and other museums in flames but unable to stop the fire.

A good five years before this dramatic appeal, Thomas Lovejoy had already published four alarming pages on this very subject in the Global 2000 Report prepared during the late 1970s for President Jimmy Carter, but without using the word 'biodiversity' (Lovejoy, 1980). He wrote that, by the year 2000, which was then less than 25 years away, about half a million plant and animal species could have been eradicated.

How could he make such a shocking and scientifically astonishing assertion? Only about 1.5 million plant and animal species had thus far been scientifically identified. Lovejoy used, *inter alia*, a discovery made by a research team of the Smithsonian Institute, where he now works. The Institute had sent an expedition to the Amazonian rainforest and one of its tasks was to identify the variety of species in one family of flies. Fifty-five species were identified, of which only two were known before. This and similar experiences with living organisms allow us to estimate the percentage of known species out of all the species in existence. In this way, if we add the estimated number of unknown species to the 1.5 million already identified we arrive at a figure of some ten million, and possibly as many as sixty million.

The majority of the unknown species is believed to live in tropical forests, often in limited habitats at risk of destruction by human infringement, or else they live in sparsely distributed but none the less interdependent populations, with their gene pools being highly vulnerable to habitat alteration or destruction. Estimates of the rate at which the rainforests and other species-rich habitats are being destroyed have led Lovejoy and other authors to estimate that some 50 species face extinction every day. Because of the increasing rate of forest destruction since the mid-1970s, some writers put the daily figure at 100 species (see, for example, Ryan, 1992).

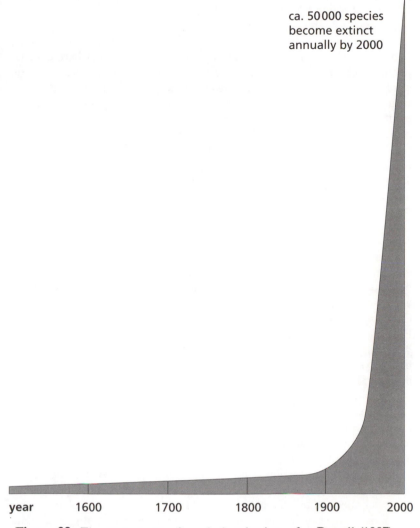

ca. 50 000 species
become extinct
annually by 2000

Figure 23: The steep curve of species' extinction, after Durrell (1987).

Many species, of course, have become extinct in the past. In fact, over 99 per cent of all species ever in existence are assumed to have died out before our time, principally, however, in the course of gradual species succession, to make room for their own progeny. However, extinction was for the most part a very slow process. If today at least 5,000, maybe even 50,000, species are dying out annually, this means that the extinction of species may be proceeding at a thousand times the 'natural' rate. Clearly this situation is cause for deepest ecological concern. Moreover, the greenhouse effect is feared to dramatically accelerate the dynamics of species extinction (Peters and Lovejoy, 1992).

Especially high rates of species loss are found in all areas of primary rainforest decimated by forest burning and intensive logging. The situation is particularly bad in Madagascar, with its unique fauna, where over 90 per cent of the original vegetation has been destroyed; the monsoon rainforests at the foot of the Himalayas, which are under intense pressure from over-population; New Caledonia, which has 83 per cent endemic plant species (that is to say, species which occur nowhere else); the remaining forests of East Africa, where Jane Goodall conducted her famous observations of wild chimpanzees; the West African primary forest, the majority of which has already been given over to cattle-ranching and peanut, cocoa and vegetable plantations; the Malay peninsula, where merciless logging operations have been in progress for the past 20 years (partly in support of a strategy for tracking down guerrillas); South-West China, partly as a result of acid rain; Sumatra, Kalimantan (Borneo) and Sulawesi (Celebes), where one of many problems has been Transmigrasi, a massive resettlement programme of people from overpopulated Java; the Philippines, where the vegetation of many of the 7,000 islands has been destroyed; Central America, mostly through the spreading of export-oriented plantations; North-East Australia, which is not unlike New Caledonia in being very rich in endemic species; the Atlantic forests of Brazil which are reduced to about 4 per cent of their original area.

Clearly, it is not just forest habitats that are threatened. River systems, mangrove swamps, mountain and desert ecosystems are equally under threat and their biodiversity is constantly being reduced.

The situation in Europe, it can be argued, is somewhat better for the simple reason that the original species diversity in that region was much lower than in the tropics. The process of destruction also started earlier and proceeded more slowly. As we observed in Chapter 7, however, agricultural practices in particular have brought a large number of species to the verge of extinction over the last thirty years. According to the German Red List of Endangered Animals and Plants over 50 per cent of all vertebrates and over 30 per cent of all ferns and flowering plant species are either extinct or in danger of becoming so, including almost all wild species of amphibians, reptiles, fowl and orchids (SRU, 1985, pp.

162–178). In addition, the population sizes of countless wild species, and thereby the diversity within them, have been drastically reduced.

Beauty Versus Utility

It is normal for people to react with great concern towards a specific and well-defined threat. In the case of biodiversity, however, mankind is not directly threatened; the danger is indirect and invisible. What is visible, though, is the aesthetic loss. Most likely, our sense of beauty serves as a kind of early-warning system, alerting us to long-term threats to humanity (e.g. Markl, 1989, C.F. von Weizsäcker, 1977).

Hubert Markl, a leading biologist and a former President of the German Research Council, aptly expressed the connection thus:

> Certainly we are not yet familiar with the carrying capacities and stability requirements of most natural habitats, but it would be catastrophic if we trampled them underfoot in getting to know them and destroyed them in ascertaining what should be preserved. Whether we really need the moorhen or the black woodpecker, the fire salamander or the fence lizard, the swallowtail, club moss or orchids is not really the question. All these species are of irreplaceable value in themselves — for their beauty and as a unique form of life which mankind can never recreate. Mankind should therefore restrain its arrogance in presuming to destroy them. After all, this very wealth of species was the breeding ground from which our own species evolved. What sacrilege then, to wipe out the evidence of such a magnificent biological story! How can we instil a profound respect for human life, if we lack respect for the living fabric from which it stems? Yet aside from all philosophical considerations, one practical aspect overrides all others: in an environment in which the moorhen and black woodpecker cannot survive, nor indeed the field hare, fire salamander, fence lizard, swallowtail, club moss or the orchids, mankind will not only be vastly the poorer in beauty, but such life threatening forces will equally endanger our own lives. (Markl, 1989)

Such statements are reinforced by utilitarian considerations, such as those voiced by Dr Daniel Janzen of the University of Pennsylvania, who considers that our best hopes of finding a cure for AIDS lies with substances contained within rainforest plants. He adds, 'It's as if all the countries of the earth had decided to burn down their libraries without bothering to see what books they contain.' (Janzen, 1989)

Markl also points to the fact that the wealth of biological species represents an almost inexhaustible supply of useful raw materials and other chemical resources.

> Four billion people feed themselves — and their domestic animals — on barely a dozen plant species, and these animals themselves amount to only a tiny proportion of the earth's reservoir of animal species. Equally we should remember that in a very short time mankind would suffocate under mountains of refuse and waste if it were not for the thousands of micro-organism species which busily dispose of them for us. We should therefore be just as grateful to these decomposers in cesspools and waste heaps as to the food producing species.

He rightly labels these as 'masters of chemical decomposition and environmental purification' (Markl, 1989, written in the early 1970s, as can be seen from the reference to the figure of four billion people).

Very similar statements can be found in the international literature, e.g. Swanson and Barbier (1992), Tisdell (1991) or Repetto et al. (1987). The general line of thinking is that in the long term, biodiversity losses represent an enormous economic loss and that there is a remarkable willingness to pay for the conservation of biodiversity and natural beauty.

The extinction of a species and the diminution of biological diversity does not occur only when the last few examples of that species perish. The very decline of a species, and therefore of its gene pool, reduces diversity as well as that species' chances of survival. As a rule of thumb, a reproductive community of at least a thousand individuals is necessary in order for a species to survive in the long term. Presumably even higher numbers are necessary to maintain a species' variety and ability to adapt to new ecological challenges. Many species are already so decimated that, even given the maximum amount of protection, there is little hope of them surviving.

A further worry concerns the biological diversity of our stock of domestic animals and seeds (Fowler and Mooney, 1990). As a result of many years of consistent breeding with a particular aim, such as increases in milk yields or bushels per hectare, agriculture now has a large number of individual animals but extremely little genetic variance within them. The damage is not immediately apparent, but climate change or an epidemic could bring the problem suddenly and catastrophically to light. The famous case of the very destructive Southern Corn Blight in the USA springs to mind; this was finally defeated by the discovery in Ethiopia of a blight-resistant corn strain (or gene). The place was so remote that it had not been reached by the monoculture ideology of the Green Revolution.

The Biodiversity Convention of Rio de Janeiro

Remarkably little time elapsed until the efforts by Edward Wilson, Thomas Lovejoy and hundreds of other biologists bore political fruit. WWF, IUCN (the World Conservation Union) and many other non-governmental organisations together with UNEP helped to create an atmosphere of political urgency for the theme of rescuing biodiversity. Pharmaceutical and (agro-) chemical companies joined in, recognising that for them biodiversity was an essential raw material. When the UN decision to hold UNCED was taken, preparations for an international agreement on biodiversity were already so advanced that the plan matured to have a Biodiversity Convention ready for signature at Rio de Janeiro. And indeed negotiators, meeting mostly at UNEP's headquarters in Nairobi, managed to agree on a draft in May 1992 which was ready for signature at the Rio conference.

The Convention on Biological Diversity was signed by some 150 states during the Earth Summit. Collor Fernando, then President of Brazil, proudly provided the first signature. Brazil was not only the host country but is probably also the country with the richest treasures of biodiversity on Earth. The convention, which has to be ratified by at least 30 countries to enter into force, for the first time in history makes the conservation of biological diversity a general political objective. Clear preference is given (in Article 8) to *in situ* conservation (protected areas) over *ex situ* conservation (Article 9, meaning e.g. botanical gardens or gene banks). To win the developing countries' support, the convention reaffirms the sovereign rights of states over their own biological resources (but stipulates that they are responsible for its conservation and *sustainable* use; see also Chapter 14). Furthermore, the convention states that the benefits of biotechnological use of biodiversity should be shared on a fair and equitable basis (Article 19) and that the North should provide new and additional financial resources to enable the South to meet the cost of implementing the agreed obligations (Article 20).

Commercial value is attributed to biodiversity as the users of genetic material are to pay compensations to the country of origin. Some industrialised countries, including the USA, Britain and Australia, would not accept this principle for genetic resources already stored in gene banks or botanical gardens. The South gave in on this point. Participants were all the more astonished to learn at the Rio conference that the White House (under the then President George Bush) declared that the USA was not going to sign the convention. The reason given was an 'unsatisfactory' protection of intellectual property, meaning the patenting of biotechnologically developed life forms. Few observers of the Rio conference were impressed by the US reasoning. President Bush's 'no' to the Convention was probably the single most important factor isolating the USA at the Earth Summit, but in the light of history, George Bush's attitude was perhaps fortuitous for the protection of global biodiversity as it made it psychologically much easier for many developing countries to arrive at a positive attitude to the convention. Initially, most of them were rather negative about Northern talk of biodiversity (e.g. Juma, 1990). In April 1993, President Bill Clinton finally announced the USA's willingness to reconsider its attitude and sign the convention.

Genetic Engineering

Genetic engineering is sometimes presented as a hope for the future, especially in relation to the restoration of biological diversity, but I fear that this will never be anything other than an illusion. Genetic engineering to date consists mostly of implanting *existing* genes into other organisms. New genes can theoretically be created within narrow limits, but not with any prospect of helping ecological biodiversity. The combined research and production capacity of all the genetic laboratories and gene banks in the world would hardly be able to reproduce or even store the biological diversity of one hectare of virgin forest. Moreover, it is highly questionable whether human successes in the field of genetic invention and manipulation are ever likely to approach the ecological wisdom enshrined in any small area of virgin forest.

Meanwhile, the real and far more significant connection between biodiversity and genetic engineering is of a quite different kind. Modern agriculture, oriented towards intensive production, shows a disturbing tendency towards uniformity, monoculture and the depletion of genetic variance. To this tendency, which is not an invention of modern biotechnology, the new techniques of tissue culture breeding and genetic engineering are adding yet more momentum and speed.

If we assume that genetically engineered species may have considerable economic advantages over traditionally bred species, we would expect a greatly accelerated replacement of the traditional strains by the new ones. Imagine, for example, a genetically engineered and completely pest-resistant apple tree which would save the fruit farmer thousands of pounds in pesticide bills and enjoy additional advantages over all present varieties of apple tree in respect of environmental laws. Within ten years such a tree would dominate all the fruit-producing areas of the world. Which farmers would be so romantic and so financially stable that they would entertain the notion of continuing to cultivate those hundreds of varieties of apples that can still be found today? That super-resistant apple tree is, of course, just a dream, and breeders would certainly try and investigate more than one solution. It is a good example because at first glance it looks highly attractive even from an ecological point of view because it greatly reduces the spraying of pesticides. That very fact, however, would make the super-tree absolutely monstrous in terms of the destruction of biodiversity.

Who are we to know where the long-term advantages lie? The Southern Corn Blight story seems to tell us that short-term economic rationality may well be fallacious. I fundamentally doubt that breeders or agricultural strategists will ever really know which genes are to be conserved in the long run. The best long-term insurance is a vast variety, not any 'optimal' set of strains. Conservation in gene banks is no equivalent to *in situ* conservation under real-life conditions. It is poorer both in terms of biological variance and in terms of the cultural knowledge that may be indispensable for preserving certain strains.

This highlights a danger which, despite the regulations concerning genetic engineering, has so far not been addressed. Until now legislation has limited itself to controlling the dangers of abuse and accidents. Present legislation, whether the EU Directive on the deliberate release of genetically modified organisms or, for example, the German Genetic Engineering Law, is inadequate in this respect. The greatest long-term danger, that of the possible epidemic *success* of a genetically modified organism, has not been addressed by the legislators at all. At best, the problem of biodiversity losses from agricultural breeding and practices has been dealt with indirectly, either under the heading of legislation to protect the countryside or nature protection.

Realistically, we have to assume that agricultural genetic engineering will spread throughout the world fairly quickly, whether we consider it morally desirable or not. In the context of increasing eco-political responsibility, well thought out criteria and legal norms for this phase of biotechnological development are well overdue (Fox, 1992).

Criteria for the Application of Biotechnology

I shall now attempt to formulate certain criteria and conditions which should be fulfilled when genetically engineered organisms are to be released into the environment.

The first criterion is that licensing procedures should be open to public scrutiny. Even though industry's wish for secrecy on matters of high technology is understandable, decision-making on applications for production and release permits should not be carried out exclusively by a small circle of experts. In this respect the EU directive is unsatisfactory. The openness of proceedings is left to the discretion of the member state, and those in charge of the proceedings are mostly those very scientists who should themselves be under scrutiny.

It is self-evident that the granting of permission for a release should be dependent on an environmental impact assessment (EIA), and this is provided for in the EU directive. Too much, however, should not be expected from an EIA; the possible effects of a new product or process can often only be guessed at, and what is environmentally tolerable is very much a matter of debate.

Arrangements for the acceptance of liability in the case of accidents must be clear; in particular, liability for the risks involved in releasing new organisms should remain with those responsible for the release. The displacement of wild species by the unintentional spread of new breeds should be heavily penalised and fines could be made payable to biodiversity funds. The individual or firm responsible for the release should be insured, and insurance companies would therefore have a strong interest in minimising risks.

The release of new organisms should be permitted only where the biodiversity of cultivated plants and domestic animals will be thereby increased and that of wild species in no way diminished. Spatial limitation, compulsory crop rotation and ecological criteria for field banks and hedges could become conditions for any permits to be granted.

Where genes from wild plants or animals are used, the compensation payment according to the Biodiversity Convention should be used effectively to enhance the protection of biological diversity.

The practice of gene technology should have as one of its basic aims a lessening of our dependence on chemicals. Other ecological aims should also be considered. These could include the detoxification of waste by appropriate strains of micro-organisms, the cultivation of sites and areas which are not (or not any more) hospitable to ordinary crops (e.g. very dry or very salty places) and the production of self-regenerating raw materials as a substitute for non-renewable resources.

Certain ethical criteria need to be properly defined, such as 'no manipulation of human heredity' and 'no deviation from a biological genus or natural order'.

There should be public funding of research into ways of achieving certain aims without employing the techniques of genetic engineering. This is of particular importance as regards the use of genetically engineered plants in the Third World, where the declared aim is the conquest of hunger but where conventional methods are likely to be rather more effective and less costly (see, for example, Sasson, 1991).

If, and only if, genetic engineering were to fulfil the above criteria in every respect and become part of a credible ecological policy, and if the release of new organisms were to become so expensive, for instance, through insurance premiums, that it would only be used where truly necessary, then genetic engineering could earn itself an entirely respectable place as one of the modern technologies of the Century of the Environment (cf. Chapter 15).

Finally, and this is a question of our *cultural* self-understanding, we should recognise that biodiversity is *not* just a commodity like oil. It is a unique gift to humanity and it should be seen as a value its own right (see Christine von Weizsäcker, 1993).

PART THREE:

TOWARDS COHERENT SOLUTIONS

In the second part of this book five problem areas were outlined in which environmental policies have not been sufficiently effective to date. In each of the five chapters suggestions were given on the first steps towards solutions which could be implemented in the context of today's environmental politics.

In keeping with the basic premiss of this book, the scale of these steps is modest and pragmatic. Even where some of the suggested steps go beyond what has been feasible to date, they do not presume that people will change their values beforehand. The ticking of the ecological clock makes this success-oriented pragmatism mandatory.

Wherever environmental protection clashes with fundamental preferences, people worldwide tend to opt for a standstill in environmental policy rather than sacrificing their value system. The West German situation of 1975 (p. 19), the Reagan years (p. 40) and the present situation in Eastern Europe (p. 36) should all serve as lesson in this regard. In the Economic Century (cf. Chapter 1) one should not expect the majority of the population in any country to abandon its preoccupation with economic well-being. Yet the environmental crisis makes fundamental change inescapable. In Part Three we attempt to outline a coherent strategy based on fundamentally economic assumptions while also making use of the partial solutions offered in Part Two.

Several times we have emphasised in Part Two the need for prices to tell the truth in order for them to play the positive co-ordinating role attributed to them by classical economic theory. Prices should in particular tell the ecological truth as closely as possible (Chapter 10). The suggestion is not to let scientists and bureaucrats sit together and determine the ecological truth and allow the police to become an Orwellian truth enforcement army. On the contrary, our preference is for an instrument that builds firmly on individual freedom and democratic institutions, a rupture-free, gently progressing ecological tax reform (Chapter 11).

Through this tax reform, prices for the use of nature's scarce treasures will be gradually and predictably adjusted until technology, and indeed our civilisation, applies itself to an 'efficiency revolution' in the use of these scarce resources. Benefits, not costs, should be expected to result from this strategy. This is quite different from costly environmental policies which only the rich can afford. 'Economy-friendly' environmental policies are our goal (Chapter 12).

Chapter 13 discusses 'Town and Country'. Worldwide people flock into the conurbations, but these very conurbations are becoming nightmarishly congested, unsafe and unpleasant to live in, and they continue to destroy natural resources and the countryside. Prices don't reveal the true ecological costs of the relations between town and country and within urban systems themselves. Urban environmental problems have been the trigger for modern environmental policies. How will these problems change if the economic framework is changing?

Solutions, however, must not remain on a parochial scale as Earth Politics is about global solutions too. The Earth Summit that took place in Rio de Janeiro opened new horizons for Earth Politics and these are explored in Chapter 14.

Chapter 10

Prices Should Tell the Truth

Greening the Market, Greening the Culprit?

From the time of Adam Smith, the market has been viewed as the generator of increases in wealth. In the early days of the environmental movement, however, it looked as if environmental degradation went strictly hand-in-hand with increased 'wealth' so conservationists tended to see the market as the environment's main enemy and the state as the most plausible agent for protecting the environment from the market. This approach has led to environmental legislation, the idea being to shackle Gulliver, the monstrous market, with as many legal ties as possible. This is a misconceived and outdated idea.

Even strong states have not really been able to prevent continuing environmental destruction, and the socialist countries performed the worst. Their weakness was neither a lack of environmental legislation nor of a powerful state. Western democracies performed better by allowing private industry to work on innovative solutions within a legislative framework, but even this has not helped the environment sufficiently. It has been a costly process both for the state (i.e. for taxpayers) and for business, it did not prevent Gulliver from emigrating. Put simply, why should multinational corporations do ecologically harmful things in countries where they felt harassed by environmental legislation?

According to mainstream economic theory, with its market orientation, detailed regulation does not lead to optimal results. Innovation is not encouraged by bureaucrats and lawyers constantly chasing every potential polluter. In theory it should be possible to utilise market forces and the innovative capacities of the private sector much more efficiently; for this to happen, the government should provide a simple, clearly defined framework but should refrain from going into too many details (see Chapter 12). This framework should consist of a set of simple rules and mechanism which makes prices and costs tell the true ecological cost. When this condition is met, the decisions and choices made by consumers and producers will in theory come close to the ecological optimum.

The system of bureaucratic socialism can be said to have collapsed because it did not allow prices to tell the *economic* truth. This led to gigantic waste on the one hand and corresponding shortages on the other. In countries with a market economy, prices theoretically tell the economic truth unless they are distorted by monopolistic power, subsidies or other state intervention, but market prices are a long way from telling the ecological truth. In this respect world markets are even worse than domestic markets because there is no functioning environmental legislation or mechanism that can direct prices towards reflecting ecological damage or long-term scarcities (see Verbruggen, 1991, and Chapter 14).

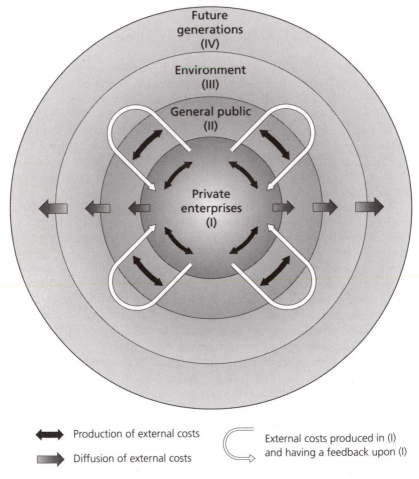

Figure 24: Diffusion of external effects (after Gerhard Maier-Rigaud, 1988, p. 88, with kind permission of the Publishers). The arrows indicate that firms do bear a certain proportion of the 'external costs' themselves, but the greater share of the remaining costs are borne by the general public, the environment (at home and abroad) and future generations.

When prices do not tell the ecological truth manufacturers and consumers are able to divert a goodly proportion of the real cost burden elsewhere. This diversion is known in economics as 'externalising' and results in external costs. Figure 24 is a diagrammatic representation of the routes taken by these costs.

The 'ecological truth', of course, will never be precisely quantifiable in any scientific manner and we must remain aware of this basic fact in the discussion which follows.

Lutz Wicke (1985), a renowned author in environmental economics (and also deputy environment minister of the city state of Berlin), estimated the external costs arising from environmental degradation in West Germany approximately DM 100 billion based on 1985 prices, which represented over 5 per cent of that year's GDP.

Wicke studied only the domestic economic effects on air, water, soil contamination and noise. If we add external costs arising from accidents and environmentally caused illness, soil erosion, climate change, biodiversity losses and for damage exported or imposed on future generations, it does not seem difficult to justify a total of external costs caused by the West German economy in the order of DM 200 billion or some 10 per cent of GDP. In fact, Prognos (1992), the Brazil-based research institute, in a study for the German ministry of economic affairs, assessed external costs of energy use alone at some DM 500 billion (this time including East Germany). On a global scale, Barbir et al. (1990) believe that external effects from burning fossil fuels alone may be in the vicinity of 14 per cent of the global GDP, an unimaginably high amount.

Christian Leipert (1989) using a different method arrives at DM 196 billion for West Germany in what he refers to as 'defensive expenditures'. He defines this as spending on repair measures for environment and health as well as structural and safety measures which become necessary to fend off unwanted damage as conditions deteriorate for both the environment and society.

Such estimates of externalities of between 5 and 10 per cent of GDP can be compared with annual expenditure on environmental protection measures. Taking West Germany as an example, the governments (federal, regional and local) paid out some DM 13 billion, and manufacturing industry some DM 19 billion, making a total of well over DM 30 billion or some 1.5 per cent of GDP. This is a generous estimate; usually estimates mention a figure in the order of 1.1–1.2 per cent only.

The DM 19 billion paid out by manufacturers represents an 'internalisation' of external costs. The same applies to those governments that are financed through taxes and special charges (a total of approximately DM 7.5 billion). Even assuming that costs of between DM 20 and DM 30 billion are met by producers, there remains a four- to tenfold discrepancy between those payments and the external costs, as shown in Figure 25.

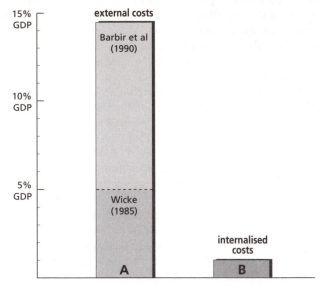

Figure 25: Crude estimates of external costs arising from environmental damage
A. Various guesses about annual external costs as per cent of GDP.
B. Estimates of international costs in Germany as per cent of GDP.

As stated earlier, prices are a long way from telling the ecological truth. We are now in a position to give this assertion some quantitative meaning, bearing in mind that value judgments are involved in the figures. Today's costs, and therefore also today's prices, represent between only a quarter and a tenth of the 'ecological truth'. Put in a different way, if the costs of resource use and environmental pollution were increased by a total amount of approximately 5 to 10 per cent of GDP, then market forces could be assumed to work reasonably well to protect the environment. The market, the old culprit according to the early conservationists, would become their ally.

Limits to the Command and Control Approach

It is clear from the above that environmental policy to date has, despite all efforts, not been able adequately to internalise the external costs as demanded by economic theory. Nor is it easy to devise a policy of setting environmental standards which could do this adequately. The promotion of environmental policies beyond a policy of commanding and controlling standards is needed for at least three powerful reasons.

Firstly, in major areas of environmental policy, such as those outlined in Part Two, standards appear to be systematically incapable of preventing even the most obvious damage. The ecological (long-term) costs of energy use, transport, land use, the global division of labour and the destruction of biological diversity can hardly be influenced by setting any standards, be they emission standards or quality objectives. Moreover, the control of standards implies enormous efforts on the part of the state which are unlikely to be affordable in less affluent countries.

Secondly, standards are always defined in such a way that they enable manufacturers to produce more cleanly than is prescribed by the standards, but in a policy based on standards the producer has no incentive to do so. (A producer may nevertheless do so in expectation of a future tightening of standards, or out of idealism or because he considers such behaviour to be a marketing instrument.)

Thirdly, there are reasonable doubts as to whether a command and control policy is an economically sensible form of environmental policy. Holger Bonus (1984) considers economic instruments of environmental policy to be twice as efficient as command and control instruments, which means that each pound buys twice as much environmental protection when it is applied as economic instrument; the lost money in the command and control system probably fills the pockets only of bureaucrats and environmental lawyers.

Precaution and Minimisation

It is theoretically possible to close the gap in Figure 24 within the context of command and control policies by tightening all standards substantially. As Figure 26 indicates, pollution prevention costs then rise sharply and can reach 5 or 10 per cent of GDP.

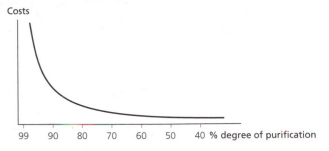

Figure 26: Typical curve for costs of conforming to standards in relation to the level of threshold values (cf. Wicke, 1986, p. 361).

The precautionary principle, one of the pillars of German environmental policy, the strategy of truly minimising emissions of pollutants, appears at a first glance to be both plausible and feasible. There is virtually no level of concentration of pollutants at which one can sit back and argue that all conceivable damage was avoided. The principle of minimising emissions is often applied to suspected carcinogens. In the United States the EPA usually applies extremely low standards in such cases, e.g. 0.0000000008 grams of dioxin per kilogram of bodyweight. Similar precautionary levels are set in the EC Drinking Water Directive of 1980, which sets a limit of 0.0000001 grams per litre of drinking water for both toxic and relatively harmless pesticides. Conforming to these standards costs billions, while the point of zero risk is still hardly reached.

On the other hand, concentrating all efforts on minimising any particular risk makes it almost inevitable that for economic reasons protection against other risks will be neglected. Using available means to minimise the emissions of a handful of substances will exhaust the financial resources available for environmental protection, leaving none for all the remaining problems. The result: an environmental disaster.

An apparently cheap but deceptive alternative way of achieving zero emissions is an outright ban on the use and production of these substances. Consider, for example, the economic effects of a hypothetical ban on the use of copper, a relatively toxic metal. From electric wires to pharmaceuticals, from construction to computers, the economic damage would be horrendous, yet the world's oceans would still contain many millions of tons of copper. A total ban on PVC or non-degradable herbicides would probably bring about economic and social costs far in excess of the costs to the economy of the environmental damage caused by these substances. Of course, it is sometimes the case that environmental damage is so important that a ban which seems economically unreasonable may nevertheless be justified. Certain pharmaceuticals which represent huge economic markets may well be a case in point.

The precautionary principle is in danger of being ideologically overvalued. The apparently sensible saying 'an ounce of prevention is cheaper than a pound of cure' is usually correct, but in some cases can be downright wrong. It is, for example, particularly wrong to attempt to avoid all eventualities at any price. The synergy of chemicals within a reaction process under all imaginable weather conditions cannot be foreseen, so the damaging effects of such synergy cannot be foreseen and cannot be ruled out. A radical precautionary principle would remove all 70,000 existing chemicals from the market, but such a 'cure' would impoverish millions of people, and cause deaths from starvation in a very short time even in Western Europe and North America.

Of course nobody demands such an exaggerated form of the precautionary principle which runs counter to accepted legal principles and would not be tenable in law. The environmental debate is, however, still haunted by the demand for zero emissions and the assertion that prevention is in every case better than cure.

The concepts of minimisation and precaution will not allow us to escape the fundamental problems of environmental politics; priorities need to be set, advantages and disadvantages weighed against one another, and the alternatives should be made sufficiently clear for a rational democratic majority decision to become possible. Minimisation and precaution in themselves are not solutions to any problem.

Of course, the *goal* of keeping risks to a minimum remains a sensible one, and the precautionary principle will remain a cornerstone of environmental policy, but I would argue that the risk minimisation goal and strategies to prevent ecological disasters could be equally well satisfied within a strategy of making prices tell the ecological truth.

The Polluter-Pays Principle: A New Lease of Life?

The polluter-pays principle (which dates back to Plato: Nomoi H 845), is also one of the cornerstones of environmental policy. Like the precautionary principle, it was formalised in the first German environmental programme and in the first EC Environmental Action Programme. It has been progressively strengthened ever since; through the Single European Act it has even become part of the EEC Treaty, now the Maastricht Union Treaty. The principle states that the producer of environmental damage should meet the financial costs of that damage, but because the 'damage cost' approach appeared inoperable, an 'avoidance cost' approach was chosen as a pragmatic solution for the polluter-pays principle. This approach means that standards are set by the state and the compliance cost should be borne by the polluter. Whenever this is held to be unreasonable out of social considerations, the community-pays principle comes into play and the general public meets the costs of prevention or, indeed, restitution.

Right from the start, the polluter-pays principle was meant to make prices more or less tell the ecological truth. Following the reasoning above, the existing command-and-control policy has failed to make price tell the truth. The polluter-pays principle should therefore be extended beyond the narrow confines of the command-and-control policy (see also Pearce et al., 1989). For this to be translated into action we need to remind ourselves of the three inadequacies we have identified in the present policy. Firstly, the polluter-pays principle should be made increasingly valid in energy, distribution, transport, agriculture and other sectors. Chapter 11 covers this aim in detail. Secondly, polluters should be subject to financial burdens (e.g. special charges) even when they remain below the permitted levels. Thirdly, market-based economic instruments must be given substantially more weight in environmental protection. The second and third points are discussed in the section on economic instruments.

Only when all three points are realised will the polluter-pays principle receive a new lease of life. It will receive a new image and become far more comprehensible. Of the cornerstones of environmental policy, the polluter-pays principle is that most suited to market economies and should be welcomed by all those who celebrated the victory of the market system over bureaucratic socialism.

Economic Instruments

The EC and the OECD have since the mid-1980s declared that they would give more prominence to economic instruments of environmental policy. In June 1985 the OECD environment ministers declared that they would strive towards the extensive use of the polluter-pays principle and agreed the introduction of economic instruments in addition to regulatory instruments. The OECD commissioned Professor Johannes Opschoor, then at the University of Amsterdam, and Hans Vos to present an overview of the use of economic instruments in OECD countries. There were comprehensive responses from France, Germany, Italy, the Netherlands, the Scandinavian countries and the USA. Over 150 instances of use of economic instruments were distinguished and analysed systematically. Figure 27 gives an overview of the instruments which are applied in different OECD countries.

The principal instruments included the following. *Emission charges* or directional charges, particularly for waste water and aircraft noise, and a variety of waste taxes (in Australia, Belgium, Denmark, France, Italy, the Netherlands and the USA; and in Sweden and Norway for scrap cars as well). *User charges*, widely used for municipal waste disposal, and strictly speaking not intended as an instrument for ecological purposes. *Product charges*, for instance for non-returnable bottles in Scandinavia, for mercury and cadmium batteries in Norway and Sweden, for sulphur content in fuels in the Netherlands and Norway, or for lubricants, as in the German used-oil charge. *Administrative charges*, for instance for the registration of new chemicals, or, in Sweden, to cover the costs of an environmental impact assessment. *Tradeable permits* for emissions, now well established in the USA for air quality and more recently introduced into water laws. *Extended environmental liability*, e.g. a duty to prove the existence of contingency funds or liability insurance. *Deposits*, akin to those already applicable to bottles, and in the USA, to drinks cans; they possibly become likewise applicable to batteries or entire motor cars. *Tax breaks* for environmentally friendly products, e.g. lead-free petrol, or cars fitted with catalytic converters.

Country	Air	Water	Waste	Noise	Consumer tax	Product tax	Admin charges	Tax breaks
Australia	+	+			+		+	
Belgium	+				+		+	
Canada					+			
Germany	+			+	+	+	+	
Denmark					+	+	+	+
Finland					+	+	+	+
France	+	+		+	+	+		
Italy	+				+	+		
Japan	+			+				
Netherlands	+	+	+	+	+	+	+	+
Norway					+	+	+	+
Sweden					+	+	+	+
Switzerland				+	+			+
UK				+	+	+		
USA			+	+	+		+	

Figure 27: Charging mechanisms in OECD countries (Opschoor and Vos, 1989, p. 34).

Additionally, there are other instruments which were either not identified by the OECD study, or which were identified as only peripheral. These include: a combination of *charges* on hazardous substances and *subsidies* for preventative technologies; *tax exemptions* for environmental investments; *fines* for infringements of standards, a system which has been widespread in Eastern Europe, where, however, they had limited effect because fines imposed on state undertakings simply meant a shifting of funds without any significant steering effect; *user advantages*, e.g. permits to use only cars fitted with catalytic converters when smog is forecast; (this type of instrument has been most frequently used in aircraft noise control policies); public procurement can take a further influential 'economical' role in adopting government purchasing practice; *voluntary agreements* between the state and certain groups of manufacturers; *environmental taxes*; the OECD team found, however, that only in the Netherlands could an expressively environmental portion be found in the petrol taxes, while a plastic bag tax in Italy has only been implemented locally, with limited effect and Japan's electricity tax, which was not directly motivated by ecological concern, was sacrificed on the introduction of VAT in 1988.

Of particular significance has been Japan's high charge on sulphur dioxide emissions, which was abolished — because it was no longer necessary — in 1989. The charge paid for a fund for payment of compensation to victims (or their dependants) of pulmonary diseases. Japan also has emission standards for power stations, which, however, were rendered meaningless by the SO_2 charge. It simply would not have occurred to a power station operator to exhaust the potential allowed by the standards, because of the expense. Jochen Jesinghaus (1988) has calculated that if the new German power station at Buschhaus near Hanover were located in Osaka and continued to churn out the level of emissions permitted in Germany, it would be required to pay DM 1.6 billion a year in SO_2 charges, that is about 80 times the annual expenditure on its flue gas desulphurisation plant.

This sort of calculation gives us hope that, one day, for at least some environmental problems, we will be able to avoid them without recourse to a policy of command and control which is always somewhat arbitrary. Rigid emission standards combined with the 'best available technology' philosophy work as an invitation to delay the availability of better environmental technology. Command and control therefore act as a disincentive to technological progress. The reverse is true for charges and taxes; in these instances the financial managers of firms have a strong interest in pushing for improvements in technology in order to reduce the burden of charges. In sum, the authors and the OECD believe that economic instruments should come into their own.

Important and welcome as these economic instruments are, they are still not adequate to deal effectively with the crisis areas covered in Part Two. Indeed, few of them have been introduced with any radical, preventive purpose in mind. Rather they are, as in the OECD's 1985 declaration and a similar declaration by the German government, modestly designated as 'complementary' to normal regulatory policies.

Detailed data about the revenues generated by emission and product charges are not provided in the Opschoor/Vos report, but it appears to be likely that special charges will not amount to more than a thousandth part of GDP, except perhaps in the Netherlands, Sweden and Norway, where they may be somewhat higher. Communal waste disposal charges are similarly in the region of one thousandth of GNP, although, as noted earlier, they are not intended to be directional and have been unable to halt the growth of mountains of waste.

There is also a good legal reason for the failure of charges to match the potential damage to the environment. The revenues raised may only be used for abatement of the pollution caused, and the costs of pollution have, until now, been defined only in terms of concretely proven expenses.

If we assume, as we did in Figure 25, that the true damage is substantially higher, then existing charges fall far short of being able to fulfil the polluter-pays principle in its more ambitious form. For an updated overview of economic instruments in the context of environmental economics see Cropper and Oates, 1992 and Huppes et al., 1992.

Value Judgments Are Unavoidable

Because most 'classical' economic instruments are only capable of allocating to the producer those costs which are real, or scientifically demonstrable, they are basically incapable of 'internalising' the costs of long-term and other less measurable damage. It is precisely these which are barely quantifiable, but none the less very threatening damage which cause the massive discrepancy in Figure 25 between the polluters' expenditure and the estimated external costs.

Only the introduction of instruments which allow a normative valuation will help reduce that discrepancy in a meaningful way. On economic grounds, a value-loaded emissions minimisation principle can be dangerous and should be discarded. Of the instruments which appear economically *efficient*, only two allow a valuation of external costs beyond scientifically demonstrable costs.

Through tradeable permits and ecological tax reform the state can use a normative valuation steadily to reduce to a very low level the permissible total output of waste and air pollutants. The monetary value of the permits will then rise sharply, which makes for a strong incentive to avoid emissions. Polluting products and processes would become correspondingly more expensive. For a systematic treatment of tradeable permits see, e.g. Pearce and Turner, 1990, pp. 70–77 (relations to the Coase theorem and property rights) and pp. 110–119.

The trouble with these pollution permits is that, attractive as they are from the point of view of theoretical economics, they tend to require a high level of measurement and control. The measuring and control task is not simply, as with standards, to determine whether the standard was exceeded but to produce permanent emission data with a precision that satisfies both the government and the holder of the permit. The high costs of permanent emission measurements are probably far beyond the available resources of most developing countries. Moreover, whilst permits for emissions are a relatively familiar concept, permits for energy use, material flows, transport, agriculture or biological diversity are not.

The second instrument is ecological tax reform. Government and parliament can also determine the level of environmental taxation (just as with other taxes) through valuation. Ecological tax reform will probably emerge as the most realistic instrument for approximating economic costs to the 'ecological truth'. This holds for the EU and Eastern Europe as well as for less developed countries. The next chapter is dedicated wholly to this subject.

Chapter 11

Ecological Tax Reform

Taxes Versus Charges

The traditional purpose of taxes is to raise fiscal revenue, but, environmental taxes have a directional purpose in addition to that. Where environmental taxes are intended merely as a replacement for other taxes, rather than increasing state income, that directional purpose becomes dominant and we can talk of *ecological tax reform*. The revenue from environmental taxation is *not* controlled by the environment minister but by the finance minister, who is likely to veto any hypothecation. Not to veto it would be to limit the fiscal autonomy of parliament. It follows that environmentalists and environment ministers, seeing the need for ever greater funding for their multifarious activities, typically are not interested in environmental taxes, but rather in hypothecated charges or trust fund taxes the revenues of which are 'theirs'.

That may well be the reason why it took so long for an ecological tax shift to be introduced, for who, other than environmentalists, would be in favour? One could hardly count on Treasury politicians, for they are unlikely to espouse a tax whose express intent is to narrow the basis of tax revenue.

Not until environmental politicians are convinced that ecological tax reform would produce decisive, additional and directional effects will environmental taxes be adopted in addition to special charges or trust fund taxes. Assuming that they are targeted correctly, the steering effect of both charges and taxes chiefly depends on the *level* at which they are set.

The highest attainable level, or maximum extent of the directional effect, is where the decisive difference between hypothecated charges and ecological tax reform comes in. We established in the last chapter that the level at which charges can be set almost unavoidably remains very limited. Even during a period of high political acceptance of charges, their total amount barely reached a tenth of 1 per cent of GDP. There are other, economic-political grounds for this constraint on charges. For the economy, every special charge or additional trust fund is an additional burden. The business world is extremely suspicious of instruments which increase the fiscal burden and create new bureaucracies (as is intended in the case of special charges or hypothecated taxes). It is very unlikely that any government will ever get away with special charges at anything approaching the 5–10 per cent of GDP which we considered to be the external cost of resource use and environmental degradation. Let us assume, very optimistically, that the total revenue from special charges can attain five times its present maximum size, i.e. 0.5 per cent of GDP. This is the assumption underlying Figure 28.

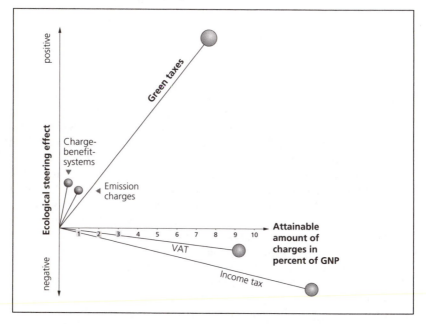

Figure 28: The ecological steering effect of green charges (or hypothecated taxes) and ecological tax reform. The directional or steering effect follows the upward axis, and the precision of that effect (the specific effect per $ or £ of charge) is shown by the steepness of the gradient between zero and the respective instrument. Hypothecation is assumed to produce a high directional precision, ecological tax reform a comparatively low one. However, the total steering effect of environmental taxes within the tax reform will outstrip that of special charges provided taxes are raised in a revenue neutral way and thus achieve a substantially higher level than special charges. The positive steering effect of environmental taxes is reinforced if taxes with a negative ecological steering effect are reduced.

Environmental taxes within an ecological tax reform, by contrast, can grow to at least fifty times the order of magnitude of present special charges. Even a factor of 100 is legally possible and economically justifiable. A fifty- to one-hundredfold-increase in the weight of the signal would surely bring about a disproportionately faster and deeper reorientation of the whole economy; Figure 28 illustrates the relationships in a semi-quantitative way. The figure also shows two current taxes which are assumed to exert a negative ecological directional effect. Both VAT and income taxes work as an added, macro-economically undesired incentive to replace human labour by machines and energy, thus increasing pressure on the environment. The positive effect of environmental taxes is therefore strengthened by the concurrent reduction of these taxes.

There are two principal reasons for allowing green taxes to reach a much higher level than special charges.

Firstly, the rate and level of taxes, unlike special charges, may be *politically* determined and are not tied to calculations of the costs associated with environmental damage or its restitution. The finance minister is under no obligation whatsoever to prove a quantitative relationship between the tax and damage to the environment. (Imagine a finance minister working under the obligation to first prove damages done by professional labour before being entitled to collect income taxes....)

Secondly, because environmental taxes within an ecological tax reform flow directly to the Treasury (and *not* to a trust fund), parliament can (and should) decide to reduce other taxes proportionately. There is then no increase in the average fiscal burden. Revenue neutrality is of crucial political importance and distinguishes ecological tax reform from the introduction of additional green taxes.

From Pigou to the EC Carbon/Energy Tax Proposal

As early as 1920, the British economist, Arthur Cecil Pigou suggested the use of taxes as an instrument for steering the economy in the direction of common welfare (which would, of course, include environmental quality). A decade later, Harold Hotelling (1931) developed the idea that the state should influence prices artificially to achieve the best possible balance between the use of resources and their long-term availability. K. William Kapp (1950) in his consideration of the attribution of external effects to the producer also includes state influence on prices. This influence is best achieved by the use of simple taxes (or tradeable permits, where feasible) and avoiding detailed bureaucratic price regimes.

Environmental taxes re-emerged in the 1970s in the context of the pollution crisis. Foremost among its proponents were William Baumol and Wallace E. Oates (1979, 1988) who introduced the concept of pollution taxes, the amount or the 'price' of which was to be determined by the cost of meeting certain standards. This standards/price approach was meant to induce polluters to avoid the tax by preventing the pollution. Other authors proposing environmental taxes included Bruno S. Frey (1971),

Hans Christoph Binswanger (1983), Malcolm Slesser (1972) and David Pearce et al. (1989). An extreme position is held by Farel Bradbury (1989) with his Unitax proposal which essentially does away with all existing taxes by replacing them with energy taxes.

During the 1970s many proponents of green taxes linked them with their hopes and dreams of financing aid to the Third World or ecological employment programmes, but as the tide of Keynesian political thinking faded, these ideas too disappeared from the public arena.

Baumol and Oates' standards/price approach was clearly a child of the pollution-abatement period. It tacitly assumes, as all environmental economics of that period does, that protection of the environment always means add-on *costs*, economically speaking. All the more remarkable is it that Oates (1988), referring to Edgar Browning, says that environmental taxes may work as an economic *benefit* to society, since they would tend to replace or reduce income taxes which Browning saw as damaging to the economy.

In Europe, environmental tax ideas were revived independently in at least half a dozen countries in the late 1980s. In the Scandinavian countries, the Netherlands, Germany, Luxembourg, Austria and Switzerland green taxes first moved from academia to the political arena. The common trigger was probably the Chernobyl disaster of 1986, coinciding with the greenhouse debate after the Villach Conference of November 1985 (see Chapters 4 and 5) and the despair about traffic congestion and ever-increasing transport volumes which has grown since the mid-1980s. The conviction was simultaneously spreading that fuel switches were not a satisfactory solution to global energy problems and that cheap road use was probably leading to more costs than benefits. The favourite targets for green taxes in the European debate were therefore not pollutants but energy and road use.

At EC level it was certainly the greenhouse discussion, combined with the anti-nuclear positions of Denmark, Greece, Italy and Luxembourg, which led to the insight that a combined carbon/energy tax was inescapable if the target of carbon dioxide emission stabilisation, let alone reduction, was to be achieved (Commission of the EC, 1991). The Commission's proposal is to raise a combined carbon/energy tax of an amount equivalent to $3 per barrel of oil. This means a higher tax per energy unit of coal, a lower one for natural gas, because half of the tax would be modulated according to the different carbon contents per energy unit. Accordingly, nuclear and hydro-electric energy equivalents would be charged half the rate. The tax is meant to rise by one dollar per barrel annually and to reach $10 per barrel by the year 2000.

This tax proposal is an integrated part of a package of measures intended to improve energy efficiency in the Community so that energy consumers making use of old and new opportunities to improve their energy efficiency would barely feel the effect of the tax. Those few industries which for technical reasons could not proportionately reduce their energy consumption would enjoy an exemption from the tax. Finally, the Commission firmly requests member states to reduce other taxes by equivalent amounts. It is hard to imagine a package of environmental policy measures that is less onerous for industry.

Nevertheless it is a commonly held view, primarily among industrialists, that energy taxes, however packaged, would lead to economic losses (see e.g. International Chamber of Commerce, 1992). The British government blocked all attempts at a Council agreement on the tax package by plainly declaring that the tax matters were none of Brussels' business.

President Bill Clinton in the USA was not luckier with his energy tax proposal of 1993. His opponents, as expected, came from coal, oil, metal and car-dependent stakes. A coast-to-coast campaign riding on anti tax feelings among the American public ultimately defeated the proposal.

A Gradualist Approach

The opponent's well-founded mistrust of any new tax and their not so well-founded belief that ecological tax reform would lead to economic losses has made acceptance of the strategy of ecological tax reform difficult. This chapter sets out to persuade some of the sceptics. I happen to believe that, in face of the ecological crisis, an ecological tax reform is both imperative and can be economically and politically attractive, but for this reform to be seen as attractive, certain criteria should be formulated and observed.

Environmental taxes should be raised on goods or services which are generally agreed to place the greatest burden on the environment. Ecological tax reform must be worthy of its name and not simply be a means of financing additional state activities. An attractive way of ensuring revenue neutrality is to start the tax reform with a systematic cutting of unreasonable tax privileges and subsidies. In times of high unemployment, however, priority should be given to the reduction of taxes and charges on labour, e.g. pension contributions. Ecological tax reform must be just; if social hardship ensues, this should, in some measure at least, be compensated. Environmental taxes should be simple, transparent and easy to administer. They should be introduced gradually so the change of the cost structure is in line with the capacity of private households, business and technology to adjust. Environmental taxes should increase predictably over a very long time-scale, e.g. over 40 years, in order to encourage the private sector, public research and development institutions and state offices to invest in long-term solutions for sustainable development.

Ecological tax reform should be internationally harmonised, but if the assumption is correct that ecological tax reform produces macro-economic benefits rather than losses, the need for harmonisation is much less than with costly pollution control measures. Ecological tax reform should not be misappropriated to serve undeclared controversial aims, such as redistribution of wealth or implementation of nuclear power programmes; it may of course serve other consensual aims like administrative simplification.

Using these criteria as a guideline, the following gradualist approach may be offered for an attractive ecological tax reform (see also Chapter 5, where parts of this proposal have already been outlined).

Prices of ecologically less desirable input factors such as energy and primary resources are increased annually by 5 per cent in real terms first by cutting all subsidies and tax exemptions and later raising taxes on these factors. This annual increase is agreed for a minimum period of 20 years, preferably for a period of 40 years. A doubling of the relevant prices is reached after 14 years, a quadrupling after 28 years, an octupling after 42 years. Other taxes are reduced by the same total amount. Preference should be given to the reduction of indirect labour costs. It should gradually become more profitable to 'lay off kilowatt hours and barrels of oil' than to lay off people.

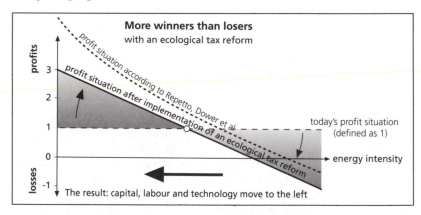

Figure 29: Profitability shift resulting from ecological tax reform. Current levels of profit are defined as unity over an axis of energy or pollution intensity. Gradual introduction of environmental tax reform will lead to a gradual decline into the red for bulky, energy intensive or polluting operations, whilst profits for relatively clean activities will improve. As a result, investment capital and technology and labour will move from right to left.

Candidates for taxation are: fossil fuels, based on carbon content, i.e. carbon dioxide emissions; nuclear energy, possibly differentiated according to safety criteria; large-scale hydro-electricity; water, possibly only above a certain (small) minimum consumption; commercial fertiliser (so as to encourage nitrate recycling on the farm); land used for building purposes; metals and other raw materials (including harmless ones to create an incentive for recycling and other ways of waste reduction); chlorine and other halogens; toxic compounds (which may not be input factors); and solvents, with a provision of tax-exemption for their re-use and recovery.

If certain substances or factors need to be phased out quickly, increases higher than 5 per cent may be considered, or else classical command and control measures may be taken.

If, on average, no money is removed from the private sector, the amount available for distribution as profit should remain constant. Bulky, polluting and energy-intensive production could suffer losses, but at the same time, profits will rise for clean and sophisticated production. Figure 29 illustrates this relationship.

Another effect of ecological tax reform can be studied by looking at product substitution. The example of petrol for cars is certainly of major

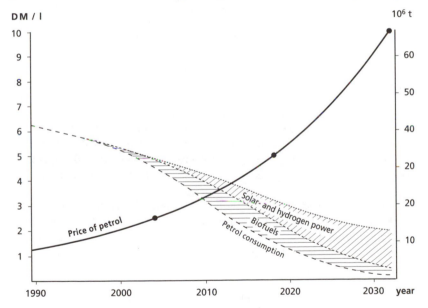

Figure 30: The approximate (speculative) development of fuel sales and the success of solar and hydrogen powered cars under the assumption of an annual 5 per cent increase of petrol prices as well as an annual 2.5 per cent increase in the price of biofuels (the latter commencing in the second period of doubling petrol prices). From Weizsäcker and Jesinghaus (1992), p. 54.

political and scientific interest. We assume an ecological tax reform leading to an annual price increase of 5 per cent for petrol. After a while we shall also assume some taxation, perhaps at half the rate, for biofuels (which also cause environmental problems). Using existing knowledge about costs of fuel efficiency, alternative fuels and infrastructural measures to reduce fuel consumption, we arrive at a rough forecast of the dynamics of substitution which is shown in Figure 30. After 40 years hardly a gallon of mineral fuel could be sold, but it can be expected that overall mobility has not suffered due to the gradual introduction of highly fuel efficient solar and hydrogen vehicles and new technologies combining individual and collective transport (see also Chapter 6).

Figure 30 in particular indicates that the effect of ecological tax reform can be very dramatic with regard to certain products, despite the fact that the annual changes are so moderate that at no time can any losses in mobility or other problems be expected.

Some Objections Answered

Every new political idea invites criticism. That is one of the advantages of democracy. Let us now have a look at the principal arguments marshalled against ecological tax reform. (A fuller elaboration of both objections and answers is given in Weizsäcker/Jesinghaus (1992), pp. 57–70.)

There is the fiscal policy objection that there is a conflict of aims between the directional effect of environmental taxes and their yield (Hansmeyer/Schneider, 1989). For financial experts it is hardly conceivable that the yield of taxes should fail to grow in keeping with the growth of the economy, never mind decreasing over time. But this latter point is the declared aim, indeed a performance indicator for environmental taxes.

To this we answer that the gradualist strategy is arranged to allow for both an increase in revenue and a large directional effect, so the argument that there would be a revenue loss does not hold water, at least for the first period of some 20 years. Even after this period, the yield can be stabilised, if it is so desired, by adding new taxable factors. In any event, the factors I have quoted — energy, water, material resources and land — are of a type which simply does not 'tend towards zero', such as Hansmeyer/Schneider impute to 'every effective directional tax'. Reading their very influential study carefully, one feels reminded of the early days of environmental economics when everything was pollution, which can indeed tend towards zero. For pollution control, as mentioned above, a special charge is preferable to taxes.

There is a social policy objection that environmental taxes hit the poor harder than the rich (Taylor, 1992, Bergmann/Ewringmann, 1989). We agree that most indirect taxes — and environmental taxes are indirect taxes — affect the socially disadvantaged relatively harder. But if the new fiscal burden on human labour is reduced and hence unemployment recedes, it would be rather the disadvantaged who benefit. Moreover, consider the following calculation: energy costs in poorer households lie at around 6 per cent. If energy becomes 5 per cent dearer, the cost differential for the non-adjusting household would be +0.3 per cent. From this we may subtract average energy efficiency gains in cars, machines, heating etc. of some 3 per cent annually, reducing the cost differential to an average (5–3 per cent) x 6 per cent = 0.12 per cent. Income gains or other benefits from the tax reduction side of the reform could even over-compensate this negative effect, leaving people on average slightly better off as a result of energy productivity gains. Finally, there is always the possibility of lump sum transfer to poorer households should any injustice remain.

There is an economic policy objection that environmental taxes are a burden on the economy (Bergmann/Ewringmann, 1989, Foerster 1990, ICC, 1992). There are different versions of this objection, one of which comes from those firms which find themselves at the right hand end of the scale in Figure 29. It is true that these firms suffer under environmental taxation, just as the environment suffers at their hand, but these firms are not 'the economy'. The slow pace of the gradualist approach, plus perhaps some transitory tax exemptions, will, in all likelihood, suffice to avoid capital destruction and ensuing job losses.

A second argument, put forward by Bergmann and Ewringmann, is that investment aimed at reducing liability for environmental taxes costs money at the same time as reducing revenue from those taxes, leaving less available for compensatory tax relief. They argue that there is no getting away from the fact that environmental protection costs money which society has to find from somewhere.

The second of these arguments is valid in the case of pollution control but probably false at least for the first big steps in resource efficiency, and resource efficiency is at the heart of the strategy outlined above. Investments in efficiency, or rather productivity gains, from scarce resources should be economically realistic. The macro-economic return on investments in energy-productivity gains should be compared with the macro-economic return on investments in labour productivity, especially those investments which are induced by the fiscal burden on labour. So long as the environmental taxes are still below the external costs, macro-economic *benefits* from ecological tax reform should indeed be expected. Repetto et al. (1992, p. 11, quoting Ballard and Medema, 1992) feel that 'the total possible gain from shifting to environmental charges could easily be $0.45 to $0.80 per dollar of tax shifted from "goods" to "bads" — with no loss of revenues;' (see also next section).

The unpopularity of environmental taxes is a frequently voiced objection. Opinion polls, however, refute this. A German poll in August 1989 is a case in point (see Figure 31). What is more, the history of democracy throws up many instances of the right course of action being initially unpopular, but with the public being eventually persuaded to accept it.

Question: What do you think of the proposal, to tax environmental pollution like waste, sewage, land use etc, with a proportional reduction of other taxes at the same time ?

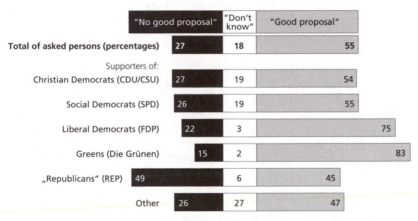

	"No good proposal"	"Don't know"	"Good proposal"
Total of asked persons (percentages)	27	18	55
Supporters of:			
Christian Democrats (CDU/CSU)	27	19	54
Social Democrats (SPD)	26	19	55
Liberal Democrats (FDP)	22	3	75
Greens (Die Grünen)	15	2	83
„Republicans" (REP)	49	6	45
Other	26	27	47

Poll took place in 1989, week 31/32

Figure 31: People in Germany seem to think it would be right to introduce environmental taxes if other taxes are reduced by equivalent amounts, according to the results of a survey held in August 1989. More recent polls confirm these findings.
(Source: infas, September 1989).

Then there is the objection that ecological tax reform is unreliable. Is there really any guarantee that any such reform will be maintained over a period of more than twenty years? After all, ecological tax reform does not make much sense if it is not a reliable, long-term project.

To this we respond that all major political parties and all major social groups can theoretically agree on a long-term strategy, as is typically the case with infrastructural decisions, the basics of social security, the agreement that primary schools and the police should be paid from public funds etc. If it becomes widely known that ecological tax reform may be the most cost-effective way out of the ecological crisis and might even lead to economic benefits (see the next section), an all-party agreement does not seem to be impossible to reach. As regards the EU, there is even the convenient possibility of a decision being taken now that is binding for successor governments regardless of their political creed. (See also the remarks under 'Consensus Again, At Last?' at the end of Chapter 12.)

Some ecologists ask whether we really have got 20 or 40 years to put the environment in order? Young people often ask how such a long-term strategy can be proposed when nature is already in such dire straits.

To this our response is simple. If a quicker strategy can be developed, I shall promptly subscribe to it, but there is no sign of such a strategy. Moreover, as Figure 30 seems to suggest, the strategy of raising the prices of problem-factors by 'only' 5 per cent per annum can mean an unprecedented 'green gallop' of product and system substitution. It is not, of course, a guarantee that we have enough time.

Benefits Expected

The most exciting thing about ecological tax reform, ultimately, seems to be that it is likely to produce macro-economic gains, not losses.

Starting from the experience depicted in Figure 12 in Chapter 5, we can assume that in the past high energy prices have not prevented countries from prospering and becoming *more* competitive on world markets. This is as yet a very cautious interpretation of a positive correlation between energy prices and economic performance. But there may be more in it. We should assume that energy consumption is too high, that none the less the demand for energy services is going to increase and that energy productivity increases are therefore highly desirable economically. We should also recognise that unemployment is a world-wide phenomenon, although in some countries much unemployment is not statistically visible and that at any time only the five or ten most economically successful countries of the world (such as Germany during the 1950s and 60s and Japan until 1992) are or have been spared mass unemployment. In view of this it seems likely that on a world scale new increases in labour productivity bring fewer economic benefits than increases in resource productivity; they may, nevertheless, momentarily remain the decisive factor in determining micro-economic competitiveness.

In this situation a measure which gradually increases the incentive for enhancing resource productivity and slowly depenalises productive human labour and takes some pressure off the need to increase labour productivity seems likely to produce overall economic benefits.

The conjecture seems to be corroborated by the following consideration. If gradually rising fuel prices for cars and lorries lead to a new generation of high-efficiency automobiles and lorries and a renewed infrastructure allowing the same degree of mobility as today at half the fuel consumption, the economy would have to produce or import only half as much petroleum without any loss of convenience. It is of course possible to achieve the same efficiency gains through direct regulation. But is it realistic to assume that bureaucrats will arrive at and prescribe precisely the optimum path of technology substitution? Our view is that it is much more likely that market forces would find the optimum path.

There may be other, more indirect economic benefits (Weizsäcker and Jesinghaus, 1992, pp. 80–83). These relate mostly to advantages for industry and trade from the long-term reliability of the price signal. Investment in new processes and technologies for a sustainable economy then becomes much more reasonable for both industry and public institutions. New sustainable infrastructure (e.g. modern interface technologies between road and rail, see Chapter 6) also requires long-term predictability about cost trends and the resulting shifts in demand.

It is probably not promising too much to say that once ecological tax reform has begun to change technology and industrial planning, the state could begin to dismantle the annoying thicket of command and control regulation. The example of the Japanese SO_2 charge rendering the existing emission standards meaningless is a case in point (see p. 125). This too is likely to produce indirect economic benefits.

Finally, there is hope even of using the ecological tax shift for escaping from the recession of the early nineties. A new and reliable price signal is likely to create a new sense of orientation for the economy. This implies a slightly accelerated obsolescence for the existing stock of durable goods, buildings and infrastructures. An avalanche of new order is likely to follow — just what has been missing during the recession

Chapter 12

Co-operation, Not Harassment

Why Care For Business?

The environmental movement arose out of conflict with business; indeed, some might go so far as to say from that it was a crusade against greed and profit. Business is still often regarded as the all-powerful force from which all environmental degradation derives. In the Economic Century business and economic reasoning have indeed come to overshadow all other factors in our society, and for a long time some business leaders behaved rather foolishly, claiming that environmentalists were seeking a return to the stone age. Now, however, such attitudes belong to the past.

Representatives of industry, on the other hand, especially those from the chemical industry, feel uneasy with the environmental movement, the press and the environment ministry. The environmental camp is, or was, seen as harassing industry with ever new restrictions, controls and generally creating an atmosphere of suspicion, if not hatred.

Who has the upper hand? Curiously, perceptions on both sides are a mirror image of the other: in the conflict between business and the environment both sides see themselves as endangered or powerless and the opponent as incomprehensible, dangerous, even malicious. This was the initial experience we had at the Institute for European Environmental Policy when we began, on the initiative of Procter & Gamble, Germany, to bring the two camps together in talks about detergents, water protection and municipal waste. After six years of fruitful talks involving different individuals from both sides (but also including experts, regulators, consumer groups and labour representatives), all those involved had gained mutual respect and discovered much of common interest (Weizsäcker, 1987, 1989, 1991; see also Svedin, 1991).

One of the essentials of common interest between environmental groups and far-sighted business leaders is structural change towards a sustainable economy. Structural change happens regularly and continuously even without environmental protection, mostly in the wake of technological progress or changes in the international competitive situation. What business and labour (and the state) find difficult to cope with is a steep rise in business failures to crisis level. When this happens the alarm bells ring. Should environment policy be broadly perceived to be the cause, there will be clamour by the majority of the population, not just from the business camp, for a U-turn, or at least a stand-still, in environmental policy. In Germany, where environmental concern was an undisputed top priority in public perception from 1982 until the Earth Summit, June 1992, the situation changed dramatically a few months later when the first massive signs of recession became visible. Ecologically, this public neglect is the last thing we can afford. This is the principal reason why caring for business and opting for 'economy-friendly' policies can under certain conditions be a very sensible attitude for environmentalists.

Consensus helps the environment

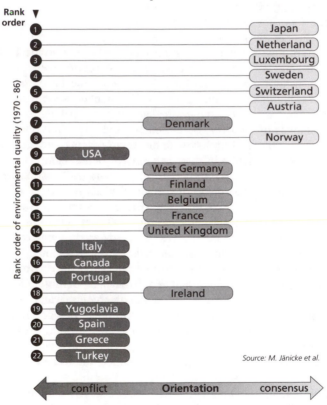

Figure 32: In the early days of the environmental movement conflict was indispensable, but as soon as the problem is recognised in principle, the cause of environmental protection is more likely to be furthered if a consensus is sought, as may be seen by comparing various countries (Jänicke, 1989).

Experience has shown that countries in which political conflict is normally resolved through consensus come off better ecologically than those in which antagonisms are played up. The relationship is shown in Figure 32.

If, in the face of the present global environmental crisis, environmental policy needs to move into the fast lane, it is clear that the principle of economic sustainability and the search for consensus are central to the process. They must be priorities for the environment lobby.

In order for environmental policy to enjoy broad political acceptance and continuity it ought to be economically sustainable, and both state and business have to understand that economic sustainability implies something quite different from the maintenance and protection of outdated structures. It is nearly the reverse.

Five Criteria for Economy-Friendly Environmental Policy

If economic sustainability does not mean preserving outdated structures, what does it mean? Perhaps the following five criteria may help towards a definition of an economically sustainable environmental policy.

First and foremost, all important changes to the terms of reference should be discussed beforehand with industry. If there is to be rapid progress as proposed in this book, industry must be assured that its interests and its constraints are being taken seriously into account. This lies at the heart of the principle of co-operation, which since its inception has been the third axiom of German environmental policy alongside with the polluter-pays principle and the precautionary principle. The discussion beforehand would benefit from active participation by environmental groups so as to make surprising public reactions afterwards less likely. The development of a 'new model of prosperity' demands or causes rapid structural change and will mean bankruptcy for businesses which do not or cannot adapt. But the business world, which is familiar with the dynamics of structural change, will accept this if it is given a hand in determining the direction and the pace of change and in the instruments for its implementation. On the other hand, the term of reference finally arrived at should give the public a sense of assurance that environmentally damaging activities will be phased out. In such circumstances of mutual trust it is less likely that consumers will panic and over-react to certain relatively harmless products.

Secondly, the state should apply strict self-restraint and limit itself to the setting of the terms of reference rather than intervene in many details. Where things go wrong it is a matter for the courts and not the environment minister. (For American firms this is of little comfort because in the US it is generally the legal practice in court which makes business so risky when any hypothetical damages are involved.)

Thirdly, environment policy should as far as is possible be harmonised internationally. For the wealthier countries (which can afford costly environmental administration, control or litigation), intelligent harmonisation also means acknowledging the different situation in less affluent countries. The development forward from command and control to economic instruments (cf. Chapter 10) has also to do with the need for harmonisation, in as much as economic instruments lend themselves to being effectively enforced in less prosperous countries. Aside from this, being the pioneer in environmental protection has in the past strengthened rather than weakened the international competitiveness of different countries.

Fourthly, environmental policy should be planned in a long-term and reliable manner. It should, of course, remain open to new discoveries demanding immediate reaction (e.g. the ozone hole, the greenhouse effect, dying forests and maritime eutrophication). In general, however, the timescale of environmental policy should be roughly in line with the time-scale of investment decisions, i.e. ten or more years; Japanese environmental policy is observing this principle very successfully. By contrast the 'best available technology' principle for pollution abatement can be quite counter-productive. It tends to foster a short-term approach and a lack of business interest in the advance of environmental technology.

Finally, environmental policy should accept the criterion of economic efficiency. One measure is twice as 'efficient' as another if twice as much environmental protection can be 'purchased' for the same money (regardless of who puts the money up). Holger Bonus (1984) has already been quoted as calling market-based instruments twice as efficient as command and control measures. The present German licensing procedures which take from 6 to 22 months are particularly inefficient from an economic point of view (BDI, 1990). As long as environment policy was a relatively small-scale activity it could afford a low level of efficiency, but as the goals become more ambitious, as suggested in this book, this will have to change.

Of course it would please the business world even more if these criteria were observed without forcing the pace of change. Clearly this is not what we are proposing, but there is scope for a deal: environmental policy adopts these criteria and the business world becomes supportive rather than hostile.

In closing this section on economy-friendly environmental policy a word is in place on three of the favourite terms in today's business language — voluntary agreements, compensation arrangements and tradeable permits.

Voluntary agreements can be helpful in phasing out certain toxic substances and in achieving certain objectives in waste reduction. The experience of German environmental policy, however, is that major voluntary agreements simply do not happen unless and until the state has shown determination to solve the problem rapidly. I find it completely unimaginable that the kind of objectives I consider essential for a sustainable model of prosperity in the North can be reached by voluntary agreements. Too much change will be necessary in everyday life, which can hardly be influenced by some agreements between business and government in a few countries. Moreover, shareholders are not going to accept management decisions which systematically lead to losses. It will be unavoidable to change the overall framework so that investment in environmental protection and resource savings becomes truly profitable. The next section on 'greening' the company is also relevant in this context.

Compensation arrangements mean that certain obligations can be met by a 'trading' agreement at a geographically distant place. US and Dutch power stations have committed themselves to afforesting areas in developing countries to make good for the carbon combustion at home. President Clinton strongly supports the idea that multinational companies do their CO_2 abatement wherever it is most cost-effective. And the first Conference of Contracting Parties of the Climate Convention, to be convened in Berlin, March 1995, will focus on 'joint implementation', i.e. compensation arrangements. The obvious danger in this strategy is that the rich countries may remain inactive regarding their homework.

Tradeable permits are based on a quantitative limitation goal and sold or freely distributed at the outset of the programme. After this, pollution or resource consumption is legitimated and quantitatively limited by the number of permits in the possession of a given firm. To reach the quantitative goal defined, tradeable permits are superior at least in theory to an instrument such as ecological tax reform steering the market via prices (Pearce and Turner, 1990). Tradeable permits also have a fairness appeal: everybody knows what he or she is paying for. Most attractive for the South, tradeable CO_2 emission permits would be an instrument for providing international equity. If these permits were initially granted on a per capita basis, the OECD countries (and OPEC and former Eastern block countries) would have to go shopping in India, China, Bangladesh and other populous, low consumption countries. The annual bill could easily exceed annual development aid payments. For further discussion see Grubb (1992).

There are, however, also serious drawbacks. In the case of emission permits, the monitoring and control procedures are bound to be more complicated, more susceptible to cheating and more inviting for endless litigation than is the case even with the unpleasant emission standards of the existing bureaucratic command-and-control policies. Knowing that command and control is already too onerous on environmental administrations of most countries in the world, I suggest that serious scrutiny be given to this practical point about tradeable emission permits and the social costs involved. And nobody should expect Northern industry to favour a worldwide CO_2 permit regime for exactly the reasons that make the scheme attractive for the South.

Moreover, business people should be aware that in times of high demand, permit prices may explode rather unpredictably, and on the ecological side it should be admitted that the quantitative goal defined at the outset could well be based on problematic guesswork. Any adjustment (based on updated guesswork) could again lead to unpredictable price jumps for permits. The promise in ecological tax reform of a steady and predictable price development seems to compare quite favourably from a business point of view.

To sum up, I have considerable theoretical sympathy with industry's favourite approaches, but seeing their limitations would not like them to be treated as an alternative to the ecological tax reform and other measures advocated in this book.

Greening the Company

The aim of an economy-friendly environmental policy is an environmentally sustainable economy. Twenty years of environmental policy and ever increasing environmental consciousness on the part of the consumer have already brought about a considerable shift in industry. Frances Cairncross (1991) tells the history very well. The best known example of the shift is perhaps that of the American office machinery and equipment company, 3M of Minneapolis. One day 3M announced that 'Pollution Prevention Pays'. It marketed this slogan as the new meaning of '3P'. Until then '3P' had always been taken to mean the polluter-pays principle. Indeed by systematically pursuing a policy of pollution prevention and the re-use of chemicals, 3M managed to save $300 million in ten years. In reality, the company gained more than that through their 'clean' policy because it rose visibly in public esteem.

Hundreds of companies worldwide have understood the new message. To behave in a 'green' way and to look 'green' became an important factor in competition, notably for firms directly dependent on end consumers whose daily shopping choices became more and more influenced by environmental considerations. John Elkington and Tom Burke (1988) give a lucid account of the newly emerged 'green capitalism'. As a contribution to the European Year of the Environment (1987–88), Georg Winter, chairman of a Hamburg-based medium sized tools manufacturer published *The Environment Conscious Firm* (Winter, 1987), in English, French and German. He presented 22 checklists for environmental management, covering all aspects from top decision-making down to the vehicle pool. Managers, notably of small- and medium-sized companies, can check their plans against these 22 handy items of Winter's manual.

It did not take long for official business associations to follow the lead of the pioneers. The International Chamber of Commerce followed with a concise brochure on 'Environmental Auditing' (ICC, 1989) calling for an environmental approach to book-keeping. In preparation for the (second) World Industry Conference for Environmental Management in Rotterdam, April 1991, the ICC published a draft Business Charter for Sustainable Development (ICC, 1991) comprising twelve commitments which subscribing companies should observe. Some 500 major firms had signed the Charter prior to the Earth Summit, among them virtually all major Dutch, German, Scandinavian and Swiss companies. It remains to be seen, of course, whether the subscribing firms will live up to the formulated standards.

Perhaps the most encouraging move so far in the direction of greening the corporate world was achieved by the Business Council for Sustainable Development. After the Bergen Conference of May 1990 the UNCED preparatory conference countries of the ECE (ECE, Economic Commission for Europe, the UN body consisting of all European countries together with the USA and Canada and the Asian parts of the USSR /CIS), Maurice Strong, Secretary General of UNCED, asked the Swiss industrialist, Stephan Schmidheiny to prepare industry inputs for UNCED. Strong made his choice fully aware of the continuing work on environmental management from the side of the ICC and other bodies. But, being a businessman himself, he seems to have felt that official associations were not free enough for the extraordinary kind of business contribution he wanted. Schmidheiny was no small fish in his pond. He was put in charge of an enormous family conglomerate at the age of 28 where he had immediately taken daring decisions, namely to get out of asbestos-related businesses at a time when scientific evidence against asbestos was still scarce and when the decision meant a huge financial risk for the company.

Schmidheiny, meanwhile 42, accepted, and he interpreted the mandate rather generously. He brought together almost 50 outstanding business leaders from all continents to form the Business Council for Sustainable Development (BCSD). Among them were Frank Popoff of Dow, Edgar Woolard of Du Pont, Carl Hahn of Volkswagen, Alex Krauer of Ciba-Geigy, Shinroku Morohashi of Mitsubishi and Eliezer Batista of Rio Doce, the biggest Latin American mining company. Schmidheiny also financed a sizeable Secretariat in Geneva which co-operated closely with the BCSD (mostly through the high ranking 'sherpas' designated by each council member). A major report was prepared and finally adopted by the Council, *Changing Course* (Schmidheiny, 1992). The book, which was presented simultaneously in six languages in May 1992, is not only a collection of encouraging examples of environmental excellence under the given circumstances. *Changing Course* also outlines what should be done to change these very circumstances and in particular the book stressed that ecologically false price levels should be corrected to make sustainable development commercially feasible. There are also many other companies outside those which participated in the BCSD which are actively greening their operations beyond mere compliance with the law (Smart, 1992).

Consumer information is another important instrument in addition to the price mechanism. Millions of consumers want to be green consumers, and to be so they need the relevant information readily available; very useful guides to help them in their shopping choices have been published in most OECD countries (see, for example, Elkington, 1990, 1991).

Not every family will buy green shopping guides, however, and information should also be made available to less active consumers. For this purpose, various countries have developed symbols indicating to consumers at a glance that the product is ecologically recommendable, and the EC has developed and introduced its own ecological symbol which became effective in January 1993 (see Figure 33).

Figure 33: The European environmental product label.

There are, of course, other ways and means available for greening the corporate world. There is environmental impact assessment and other regulation. Gradually, regulation will creep deeper into the production processes eventually to exclude the production of any product that is not easily recyclable. (I personally remain rather hesitant about this 'regulate everything' attitude.)

Other approaches are ecological auditing, no longer a demand raised only by environmentalists but also by the ICC (1989) and by the EU; ecological consumer advice; environmental education at schools and universities (for engineers and others); funding for research into environmentally friendly technologies; protests against and boycotts of products, firms and indeed whole countries. Each individual act of this kind will nudge the juggernaut of the economy a little further in the direction of the Century of the Environment.

Structural Change

In addition to measures of this kind, even just long-term thinking on the part of management can lead to decisions which are helpful to the environment. The most important aspect, as already mentioned, is structural change. It goes without saying that every business aims to be on the sunrise side of the economy, a concern shared by the state which has little interest in declining industries. What is commonplace to Japanese business leaders and to Schmidheiny and the BCSD is the awareness that industries and businesses which destroy the environment are inevitably sunset activities.

This means that investment capital should be attracted by elegant, high-technology, resource-efficient, non-polluting, knowledge-based production and services, which was represented by the left-hand side in Figure 29. This fact underscores the assumption expressed in Chapter 11 that ecological tax reform actually helps the economy by guiding investment capital towards reliable sunrise sectors.

Structural ecological change has been there in the past. Martin Jänicke et al. (1989) have carried out an empirical survey into the question of environmentally friendly structural change in various industrial countries. They found that, though in the years since 1970 the more prosperous countries experienced a rapid increase in wealth, the more per capita consumption of energy, cement, steel and freight transport — perhaps the most easily measured indicators of environmentally damaging industries — declined (see Figure 34). The picture would look very similar if these indicators were replaced by the traditional measurements of air and water pollution. In many other countries, on the other hand, the increase in wealth over the same period was matched as in previous periods by the usual increase in environmental degradation.

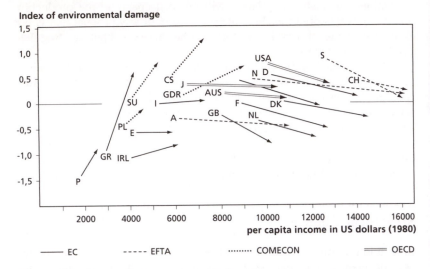

Index of environmental damage

Figure 34: Martin Jänicke et al. (1989) have taken four factors (cement, energy, crude steel and freight transport by road) to form an index of environmental damage. The illustration shows how the technologically advanced EFTA countries and certain EC countries and Japan have achieved a reduction in factors causing environmental damage together with a marked rise in prosperity, while Portugal, Greece and the then COMECON countries combined low rates of growth with greatly increased levels of environmental burden.

It would certainly be a mistake to assume that, in itself, progress leads to greater environmental friendliness. The sharp rise in pollution in the Eastern European countries — in spite of their indisputable technological progress — undoubtedly results from their policy of keeping prices for energy and pollution artificially low. Conversely, an active environmental policy together with an artificial increase in the cost of natural resources can speed up the kind of radical structural change which is ecologically desirable. In cases where environmental damage is not reflected in the price, for example the destruction of habitats by road construction, it cannot be assumed that the logic of the market points automatically to a positive outcome from structural change. As the BCSD has said, it is essential to use prices as a powerful additional message, and this is especially the case with those countries which are at the top of the table in Figure 32.

If we are serious about Earth Politics and long-term sustainability, the curve drawn by Jänicke et al. is still not satisfactory as the excessive per capita use of land, water, wood or other raw materials is not taken into account in the picture. The extinction of species and varieties, the threat to the climate or the soil, the chemical and genetic risks and the negative environmental effects that wealthy countries still manage to export to the less fortunate do not feature either. If these factors were taken into account, the favourable downward trend shown for Germany, Japan and other countries would be invalid: the trend of the last fifteen years in these countries would still be 'upwards' to further environmental deterioration.

Ecological structural change cannot stop with increased energy or steel efficiency and the reduction of certain emissions, it will have to involve the whole infrastructure. Transport, supply and disposal systems, the construction philosophy, repair services, the crafts, vocational training, information systems, in short all of our civilisation's infrastructural achievements are faced with inevitable change. It will take time. The greening of the infrastructure will take more than the 20 to 40 years reckoned for ecological tax reform, but once the message is clear the new infrastructure will evolve almost of its own accord.

Even if ecologically-oriented structural change is still in its early days, and we are a long way from a renewed state of harmony with nature, Jänicke's findings give grounds for optimism: they suggest there are ways out of the present excessive exploitation of nature, away from bulky, resource-devouring, environmentally-damaging industries and technologies towards a system for the future which is environmentally friendly.

Consensus Again, At Last?

If a large section of the public is convinced that environmental sustainability is the only way forward for economic development in the coming decades, then industry gains something it has long been lacking — a clear sense of direction. For more than a century progress has meant a kind of technical progress, which meant putting nature to the use and service of humankind. As this began to cause social disruption and environmental destruction, doubts arose as to the direction this progress was taking. As a result, public acceptance of technological progress has been fading, in Germany perhaps more than in other countries, and panicky reactions and related regulation became a very unpleasant regular experience for company managers.

In the business world and among engineers there are many who believe that the present situation derives from an irrational unwillingness by an under-educated public to accept technological progress. Large sums are therefore spent on advertising the blessings of technology. This alone won't work; the direction technology is taking at present is no longer capable of producing consensus. Nor should it be. Even the convenient comparison between the 'clean' West and the 'dirty' socialism which has now collapsed in the East cannot disguise the global damage (see Chapters 1, 8 and 9) caused by our wasteful 'clean' prosperity. In five years, at the very most, the euphoria at the victory of the market economy will be gone. The market economy will have to stand the test of social acceptability and environmental sustainability.

For the business world to seek consensus — and it has no choice — it will need to identify itself with ecologically-sustainable structural change. It is largely up to business to bring about a new form of consensus in our rudderless society; by helping to shape and support a European consensus for a sustainable model of prosperity, it will help bring an end to the present lack of direction. In this model there will without doubt be room for the entrepreneur and the investor, for profit and modern technology.

In the long term, however, a much deeper cultural transformation is conceivable, as in what we are able to imagine today as a sustainable model of prosperity, will be seen later as a temporary solution fraught with problems. However the long-term perspective is not the main purpose of this book, though it is addressed again in Chapter 18.

Chapter 13

Town and Country

The Urban-Rural Crisis

Lewis Mumford, one of the pioneers of the environmental movement, was developing his critiques of technology and culture as early as the 1930s. Following the publication in 1938 of his book *The Culture of Cities*, he appeared on the cover of *Time*, an unusual honour for an author. A good twenty years later he published his second, larger work, *The City in History*. His diagnosis of the city and its life-cycle makes for gloomy reading.

In his early work he had already identified six stages in the life of a city, from its village beginnings to a terrible and dismal end, which he calls Necropolis, in which the buildings crumble and vandalism flourishes.

Mumford's extreme view could come as a useful shock to the naïve reader living in a well-run Western city. The fact is that the majority of those who live in cities today live in poverty, filth and danger. And it is by no means clear whether our cities can be revived and reclaimed to become, once more, models of urban prosperity, or whether, in reality, vandalism and slums will become the dominant features of cities in the future. The odds are on the latter, a depressing prospect. If the world's population is to redouble in the coming century, and most of the additional 5,000 million come to live in cities, we will need at least a further hundred cities the size of today's Mexico City (20 million inhabitants) or a thousand cities the size of Naples (2 million).

It is highly unlikely that these giant cities will, in the foreseeable future, be able to free themselves from grinding mass poverty, from street gangs and drug epidemics, from traffic chaos or the chronic threats to health due to poor hygiene. Such cities as Florence, Orléans, Brno, Oxford or Karlsruhe which are at present slum-free stand out as the exceptions, almost as museum pieces. And who can guarantee that they will remain slum-free in the long term? This question covers explosive issues, including the heated debates in Europe about refugees from the former Yugoslavia, Africa or Asia and similar divisiveness in North America regarding refugees from Mexico, Haiti and El Salvador, for example. If we fail to raise substantially the living conditions of people in the South and the East, and to put the brakes on population growth, we can expect a dramatic increase in the pressure from refugees on Europe, the USA and other oases of wealth. We should, so it seems, be wary of any rosier definition of 'city' than that of Lewis Mumford.

But why are so many people attracted to the cities even where they are so threatening and inhospitable? Quite simply because, in most cases, the countryside is even less hospitable. The land does not belong to the poor, their families are too large to be sustained by a small plot, and the countryside is boring — there is little or no entertainment, no good education, no modern employment.

Economic power, disposable wealth and cultural life are concentrated in the city. The prosperity which is produced by industry and commerce, even in the poorest countries, provides incomes for millions of workers and employees, trickling down gradually from the well-off quarters into the poorer areas and eventually to the most abject slums. Few are without any means of obtaining at least some income, however meagre it may be, even here. Operating a mobile grill; running messages for firms, the state or wealthy families; selling straw hats, newspapers or stolen watches; cleaning and repairing — such work brings in just enough cash, and for the rest there is a functioning system of self-help in dwelling, food and clothing. In Third World cities, slum clearance is the worst thing that can happen to the poor because it destroys their newly won and reasonably stable existence on the fringes of the modern world.

In spite of the slums, the conurbations are the real winners in the transition from earlier times to the Economic Century. The prevalence of economic thinking made density a real advantage. Economies of density may be more important today than economies of scale. Who would have thought, 50 years ago, when there was talk of 'people without space', that it was *not* to be the large fertile lands, rich in raw materials — like Brazil, Argentina, Canada, Zaire or Siberia — which would become wealthy? Instead, overpopulated countries and areas poor in natural resources, like Japan, Hong Kong, Singapore, London, Paris, the Lower Rhine area, the Po valley, the Swiss lowlands, the East and West coasts of the USA have prospered. Within Brazil, Sao Paulo and Rio de Janeiro have become rich; or, to take one other example, within Canada, Toronto and Montreal.

But what kind of economic success is it that allows the cities to become prosperous and impoverishes the lands which were believed to be rich? This is essentially the success of parasites. Water, air, food, space for dumping rubbish and for recreation, raw materials and biological diversity are all products of the land from which the city benefits, and for which it pays practically nothing. Urban populations pay something for their food, of course, but farmers in both rich and poor countries are well aware of how desperately little of the price paid by the urban consumer actually reaches the farm. Cities pay for their water, but they pay for it to the urban waterworks company. Cities pay nothing for fresh air, which they pollute, and declare themselves generous if they reduce emissions a little, which they do mostly for themselves. In most cities air has the chance to regenerate only if it happens to be blown out into the country. Urban industries use genetic resources from forests and meadows to develop in their laboratories expensive stocks for resale in the country. For recreation and the beauty of nature, the city-dweller pays only as much as the market demands and often enjoys them free of cost; most of the money spent on tourism flows straight back to the city where the tycoons of tourism reside and where the factories making machines used in tourism are located.

For the official economy it is a fair give and take. The city provides, at costs reasonable to those who are well employed within that economy, industrial goods, machines, roads, schools, administration and telecommunications, and pays the wages of many of those employed in the countryside; but these efforts have done little to halt rural decline, and some urban services have even accelerated the process. The worldwide expansion of the transport infrastructure means that foodstuffs can find their way into the city much more easily. Foodstuffs from all corners of the Earth may now compete in the urban marketplace and often make it pointless for local agriculture to ask the fair prices which reflect their costs of production. The consequence is a drop in prices which will, in a *laissez-faire* economy, only come to an end through worldwide food scarcity and when the soil itself shows even further signs of exhaustion. If and when such a stage were reached it would probably be too late to restore the countryside.

Rural decline was certainly not planned or intended, least of all by the rural areas when they asked for the improved roads, and in the short term it would have made things worse for them if they had been left out of the road construction boom at local and regional level.

Another ironic programme guided by mainstream economics was land consolidation. Labour productivity (in a narrow sense) increased, 'excess' people had to leave, making rural life even more boring, and the environment was systematically ruined. Of course, the means of production for this 'consolidated' farm economy are produced in the cities: machinery, chemicals, packaging and vehicles.

The large-scale division of labour, already identified in Chapter 8 as a major problem for the Third World, also poses dangers for rural space and rural life. And the crisis of the cities, so starkly described by Lewis Mumford, is also a crisis for rural society. Let us call it the 'urban-rural' crisis, or the crisis of hidden diseconomies of density.

This book can address only peripherally the ecological and social problems of Third World cities, but it may be of indirect benefit to them if the North manages to make rural life attractive in a new way and if this rural renewal is linked politically to ecological urban renewal.

The Parasite Should Pay

How do we go about finding practical solutions to the urban-rural crisis? With the relationship as it now stands, the principle of the division of labour will continue in effect, since both town and country would be worse off if the rationale of efficient industry and agriculture were to be sacrificed or radically altered under existing conditions.

However, extending the 'full cost pricing' principle (Chapter 10) to the spatial inconsistencies outlined above would require the city to foot the bill not only for continuing pollution but even to pay the countryside cash for restoration and conservation. Before further exploring this contentious proposition, we should perhaps find out if the gradual ecological tax reform (Chapter 11) would already solve much of the problem or possibly aggravate it. A few preliminary observations must suffice for the moment.

Increasing the cost of petrol and removing farmers' tax advantages for diesel fuel would increase the cost of agricultural production and the cost of living in the country. An increase in transport costs would curtail the opportunity for non-local foodstuffs to compete on local markets (see above). Reducing damaging emissions from conurbations would lessen the toxic burden on the land. The introduction of taxation on ground coverage, and on energy and materials, would put intensive (stable-based) husbandry and chemical-based farming at a disadvantage as compared to free-range and organic farming. Taxation of fossil fuels would gradually open up market opportunities for biofuels, wood and other renewable raw materials, as long as these are not themselves damaging the environment. Making long distance tourism more costly and reducing the import of machinery and chemicals would make the countryside more attractive again as a recreational resource.

All in all, it can be assumed that as a net result of the above actions, today's chemical-intensive agriculture would come under economic pressure, but on the other hand, ecological agriculture would definitely have better prospects. A general increase in food prices would come into the equation, against which there would need to be protection against imports of ecologically unsound agricultural produce from abroad (cf. the arguments on GATT, p. 99). The related increases in net profit by weight would not necessarily mean higher net profit per land area. It is likely that under environmental taxation, rural areas would still be at a disadvantage because existing tax advantages for farmers leave comparatively little room for improvement.

Such a series of conjectures should lead us to consider seriously a system of compensation for the countryside's powers of regeneration. In this context, the controversial 'water penny' first introduced by Baden-Württemberg becomes politically justifiable, if in a different legal reasoning. Instead of seeing water as a cost-free commodity and compensating farmers for using less chemicals (as the 'water penny' does), good clean water should come to be regarded as a valuable raw material which consumers should purchase from landowners and tenants in the catchment area. But then consumers have a right to ask for good quality water, creating a 'market' for catchment areas using fewer farm chemicals. Farmers, foresters and dwellers in the catchment area could then get together voluntarily, or be forced to do so by the catchment area's local authorities, to prevent any pollution that puts at risk their income from water.

Paying 'true' water prices also means paying more during the dry season. This could work as a powerful incentive to landowners in drought-stricken areas to afforest barren hills as forests have a much better water-retention capacity than sheep pastures or, of course, bare soil.

More incentives for the maintenance and planting of forests could come from choosing the production of oxygen as a measure of air regeneration. Water and air economies could be of particular significance to landowners in Mediterranean countries, who regularly come under suspicion of deliberately starting forest fires for financial reasons. Special premiums for conservation measures and for species and landscape diversity should ensure that forestry monocultures were not more lucrative than ecologically sound mixed woodlands with clearings and expanses of water.

Payment of a nature conservation premium out of the revenue from a land coverage tax, which would in effect become a nature conservation *charge*, is a proposition put forward by German Environment Minister Klaus Töpfer, and appears thoroughly logical. Like so many other good proposals, however, this one is still waiting to be adopted.

Through payments of this sort the cost of living in towns and cities will come closer to reflecting ecological reality. Some may cut down on unnecessary personal spending and comforts achieved at the expense of nature; some may consider moving or returning to the countryside where the balance will be correspondingly more favourable. And perhaps most useful of all, some may develop viable eco-neighbourhoods and eco-communities within the conurbations, thus reducing travel to, and further 'development' of, the countryside.

The spatial changes intended here may also facilitate a cultural transformation associated with the 'new models of wealth' (Chapter 18). We may become more aware than before that our lifestyle of individual and private gratification, with its associated high rates of consumption and waste and the associated decline in public amenities, has been, both ecologically and socially, a misguided development. Environmental policy should not concentrate solely on waste, water, air, noise and so on, but should help to improve the quality of life, socially and ecologically, in both the conurbations and in the countryside.

Urban Environmental Policy

The environmental crisis first became visible through the decline in the quality of the urban environment. Local campaigns to preserve trees against road construction, to protect local waters against factory effluents, household chemicals and rubbish dumps or to improve air quality by strict clean air legislation were the beginning of the environmental movement. Initially, the NIMBY (not in my backyard) syndrome dominated the local initiatives, but as these grew broader in scope and came to influence decisions at regional and national level, their demands inevitably came to extend to wider horizons. The motto became 'neither here, nor anywhere', 'think globally, act locally' and 'not in *anybody's* backyard'.

Acting locally of course means much more than simply protesting locally. The long-standing and understandable confrontation between conservationists and municipal or regional planners has broadened out, or at any rate changed greatly in character. In many countries the democratic process has swept hundreds of former protesters into municipal administrations.

Scarcely any decisions on local political issues are now made in which there is no environmental dimension. The siting of new industry, proposals for new roads, the operation of public transport, the supply of energy and, of course, waste disposal, sewage and green spaces are all classic themes of local politics which these days the public as well as local government consider to have an environmental impact, either negative or positive.

In Japan in the early 1970s, communities probably played the most important role, alongside the courts, in persuading industry to change to more environmentally acceptable methods of production (cf. p. 16). In 1989, Japan reopened the debate on the relationship between cities and the environment; the title of the annual report on the state of Japan's environment was 'Towards Ecopolis — the City in which Man Lives in Harmony with Nature'.

Denmark, Holland, Britain, Sweden, Switzerland, Germany, Italy and the USA have all witnessed a greening of local politics since the early 1980s. In Denmark energy supply emerged as the most important issue; the rejection of nuclear power and the availability of wind power led to a rapidly growing number of communities aiming for a local supply of electricity, backed up by strict energy conservation measures. In Sweden one of the most significant instruments of environmental policy, the requirement for highly efficient heat insulation in house-building, was decided at the national level. In Britain concern was focused on the degraded quality of life in big cities. In Switzerland traffic was the top issue, while in the USA (as in many other countries), waste disposal became the chief environmental question. In Italy the lack of sewage treatment was a major problem, and is now threatening Adriatic tourism.

The environment is back at the centre of the stage, not only as it relates to global issues but also as it relates to local ones.

Urban Energy Supply

In Germany, the Öko-Institut, based in Freiburg and Darmstadt, played a special role in the greening of urban politics. Following the publication of a first volume about an 'energy revolution' (Krause et al., 1980), which presented ideas on the transition to low power consumption and renewable energy sources, the Öko-Institut followed up with a new book (Hennicke et al., 1985) arguing that the energy revolution is possible. The latter suggested returning to energy generation at local level. The case of a few towns, for example Rottweil, Saarbrücken and Flensburg, demonstrated the economic savings which would be possible through the use of combined heat and power units, along with smaller power stations and tariffs to encourage conservation. That, however, required cities to regain control of the electricity supply. Long-term contracts with the large utilities prevent cities from even installing combined heat and power. Many of these contracts could be terminated in the 1990s, however, so there is the likelihood of a sizeable number of cities regaining control of energy supply.

The German concession contracts are based on the 1935 Energy Act, which was intended by the Nazi regime to put energy supply on a steady footing and, in return, allowed the utilities immense privileges. They are, for instance, not obliged to supply electricity to the operators of small energy units — such as wind or water powered producers — to make up any shortfall in their output. Such provisions led to the demise of many earlier small electricity generators and forced the owners into the big grid all the more that low payments made it unattractive for small producers to put energy into the grid. And, last but not least, the centralised utilities were allowed to cover most of their fixed costs through standing charges, making the added kilowatt hour cheap and the gross price high. This state of affairs is unfavourable for the small-scale consumer, and positively encourages over-consumption. Under strong public pressure some changes were achieved in recent years, for example, concerning payment for small deliveries into the grid, but under the economic pressure since 1993 from the liberalisation of the energy markets (i.e. with the expected massive influx of French nuclear power) the big utilities were able to fend off any radical reform that might lead to an electricity-saving regime.

Waste, Water, Traffic, Buildings and Development

There is a need for local political involvement in countless other areas of environmental policy. We can at best sketch out a few aspects of these spheres and refer to further reading (e.g. Stren, White and Whitney, 1992; Button and Pearce, 1989).

Waste is today perhaps the favourite theme for urban environmental policy (e.g. Kharbanda and Stallworthy, 1990). The majority of waste is still disposed of in landfill sites, which store up burdens for the future. Incineration meets with growing resistance, and recycling and waste avoidance are still in their infancy. Many environmentalists have adopted a strategy of plainly obstructing the throw-away society's traditional disposal routes in order to create pressure for waste minimisation and avoidance. Intellectually attractive as this strategy may be, it is far from solving the problem in the short term. If new disposal installations, which at least avoid some of the environmental damage caused by the old methods, are blocked, the result in many countries is likely to be illicit dumping, false declarations and the internal re-use of unsuitable substances. Waste incineration is the most popular target, yet, when equipped with the latest technology, this system is definitely less dangerous than similarly large, ordinary industrial complexes. Dioxin emissions and human exposure to them are much larger from party grills than from modern waste incinerators.

Nevertheless, waste incinerators are an environmental danger in that they maintain the illusion of sustainability of the throw-away society. Clearly, waste avoidance and material reuse should come to the top of the agenda, as stipulated both in a new EU directive and in German waste disposal laws. Avoidance and re-use are certainly preferable to incineration from an energy use point of view, but, merely by appealing to the public they are unlikely to come about. It will clearly be a difficult problem to deal with in a legal framework. Minister Töpfer has taken bold steps to enforce packaging avoidance and re-use. But the system, symbolised by the 'green point' on recyclable packaging, involves very substantial costs and has in its initial phase led to a flooding with collected packaging waste of several neighbouring countries.

Remembering all that economists say about the macro-economic efficiency of different instruments of environmental policy, I cannot help thinking that waste policies conceived bureaucratically from the end of the life-cycle are going to cost too much to be feasible for less affluent countries. A gradually increasing price tag on the use of energy and primary raw materials is much more likely to produce solutions optimising the entire life-cycle of products and will be much cheaper for the consumer.

Water purification at first glance looks like a problem of the past in countries like Germany, but an avalanche of repair work for upgrading and restoring the sewer network is unavoidable. Estimates speak of DM 100 billion for West Germany alone, and possibly even more than that for East Germany.

Drinking water is a high-profile issue. Should local wells be closed down because of nitrate and pesticide contents outlawed by the EU Drinking Water Directive? Many villages in Southern Europe have in effect to choose between being without running drinking water supply or breaking the EU directive. Should we opt for active carbon filtration if we are unable to eradicate pollution at source? This measure might cost German communities another DM 30 billion. As explained in Chapter 8, I consider some of the EU limits unnecessarily ambitious from the point of view of human health and therefore have very mixed feelings about the closure of small local springs under the pressure of the directive. If the MacSharry reform of the Common Agricultural Policy, taxes on energy and nitrates and the European label for organic food combine to lead to a greening of agriculture, many of the problems which led to the directive would disappear. But by then the centralised water supply structure would make it virtually impossible to re-open local wells, giving rise to further disadvantage for rural areas. High levels of water use and centralisation of water supply should in general be reversed by, among other methods, the simplification and promotion of a decentralised supply of water, notably in regard to non-drinking purposes, e.g. for industrial use, the flush toilet, the washing machine and the garden.

Traffic and transport are crucial issues for the quality of life in cities. Congestion has become a nightmare for European agglomerations, let alone Bangkok, Lagos or Sao Paulo. New roads, such as the six-lane highway the city of Rio de Janeiro built for the Earth Summit to connect the international airport with the city, seem to help for a short time. But more roads attract more cars and hence tend to create new congestion somewhere else. Pedestrian zones are a rather better cure; they help to make car use superfluous and to make cities attractive once again. But that is only a beginning. Other steps are a policy of no public subsidies for parking space, not even requirements for builders to offer a certain number of parking lots; the building of goods distribution centres near railway stations to keep big lorries out of the cities; redesigning buses and urban railways to accommodate bicycles; park and ride systems and other similar ideas (see also Chapter 6).

Buildings are a neglected domain of urban environmental policy on which municipalities have only an indirect influence. Cities can work at their architectural image through public contracts, planning, zoning standards and the protection of historic buildings and monuments. New ecological standards or incentives may relate to energy efficiency, decentralised water use, green facades, solar energy use, conservatories, interspersing of residential and business areas, ecological criteria for small gardens and so on.

In the 1960s there was considerable debate about the city's relationship to commercial development and trades, about land, development and all sorts of privileges which industry, commerce and small businesses could wrangle from the cities — they were, after all, the main taxpayers. If corporate taxes were to be replaced with environmental taxes, the city's relationship to its trades would change completely, and not necessarily for the worse. A high tax on land coverage would create an incentive for restoring old — and possibly chemically-contaminated — areas rather than building afresh on greenfield sites which have been assigned very high land development taxes. A national or European tax of this sort would have the added advantage of preventing competing localities from underbidding one another: to build anywhere on greenfield sites should become the most expensive option.

Changing the Framework

We have looked at energy, waste, water and land use, and found that the need for action at local level is great, but to date, progress has been relatively modest. If, however, meaningful changes were made at national or European level, there would suddenly be much more room for manoeuvre.

Changing the fundamental economic parameters, e.g. by ecological tax reform, would be a much more elegant and much more effective way of changing the overall framework than increasing the legislative and bureaucratic restrictions on private sector activities. Imagine much of the municipal waste problem disappearing once there is the firm expectation that secondary raw materials will gradually obtain a sizeable commercial value through taxation on primary materials: large amounts of paper, plastic, metal and glass would no longer be thrown away. An incentive system for composting could take care of the rest, leaving essentially toxic wastes to be removed and treated. Energy, transport, and water problems would be easier to solve. Municipal authorities would find themselves carried along in a direction taken at present only by those few cities like Curitiba, Brazil which can muster the political will and strength to embark on 'ecological replanning'.

There is a need, too, to strive for the technological innovations essential to the environmentally friendly city, and these are only likely to be attracted to economically profitable activities. If abuse of the land and pollution become very expensive, and human labour and clean trade become cheaper, then we shall have established the ideal conditions for a technical revolution in town planning or replanning, in infrastructure and in municipal services.

The altered framework could be similarly beneficial for the urban-rural relationship. Again, if transport, fossil and nuclear energy, water, abuse of land, high chemical inputs and air pollution become considerably more expensive, the production or procurement of energy, water and food will return with renewed vigour to the countryside immediately surrounding a given city. Contamination of the countryside with hazardous substances from the cities should decline and the producers' expected return from food prices could increase in relative terms.

One should not imagine that such developments will be automatic, speedy or idyllic. The foregoing is hardly more than a cautious forecast based on current trends and applying simple market logic to the city.

Chapter 14

Earth Politics After the Earth Summit

A New Challenge for Foreign Policy

Natural resources and the environment have always been a cause of conflict between peoples. They have sent nations to war and their diplomats to the negotiating table whenever granaries, hunting or fishing rights have been at issue. Wars, of course, have often left them a scorched earth, one of the most wanton forms of environmental destruction.

By contrast, modern environmental foreign policy assumes a different face. Nowadays the emphasis is on cross-frontier environmental pollution, the protection of international waters, the harmonisation of regulations and, more recently, climate protection and biodiversity. It is more and more widely recognised that national sovereignty in its traditional form, already limited through military alliances and economic inter-relations, is also being eroded by the international dimension of the environmental problems we face. For a fuller, and 'Triade' discussion of the new situation see MacNeill et al., 1991; also Sand, 1990; Hurrell and Kingsbury, 1992; Porter and Brown, 1992.

Since 1973 the EC's member states have step by step surrendered pieces of their sovereignty in environmental matters to the Community. In the first period, until 1987, this took place primarily in the areas relevant for competition, so that environmental directives were typically based on EEC Treaty Article 100. Since the Single European Act came into force in July 1987, the Community (now European Union) has been able to take the initiative on environmental matters in their own right (Article 130 S). With majority voting it is now even possible for a country to be outvoted and yet be bound by the provisions that have been agreed. Derogation from the European standards is permitted only where these standards are exceeded: they are a minimum legal requirement.

Since the end of the 1970s attempts have been made to reduce pollution beyond the Community, first by getting long-range cross-frontier air-pollution covered by treaty. The forum for this was the ECE, the UN Economic Commission for Europe. At first the Germans found it difficult to accept that an international treaty should prescribe the date and quantity by which much sulphur-dioxide emissions should be reduced. Only after the *Waldsterben* debate from 1982 on did the Germans play a positive, even active, role. The Geneva Agreement on long-range cross-frontier air pollution of 1979 was given substance by the Helsinki Protocol on a 30 per cent reduction in SO_2 emissions by 1993 (the '30 per cent club'). This was followed in 1988 by the Sofia Protocol which envisages that emissions of nitrogen oxide will be frozen at 1987 levels by 1994; seventeen of the signatory nations declared themselves prepared to reduce these by a further 30 per cent. In 1992 a Protocol on volatile organic compounds (VOCs) was finally added.

More than 100 international environmental agreements had been signed before the Earth Summit (see Hohmann, 1992). Some, such as the Convention on International Trade of Endangered Species (CITES), agreed in Washington in 1982 and the Ramsar Convention on the protection of wetlands, have a truly global scope. Most, however, have a limited geographical focus such as the Antarctica Agreement of 1991, the Law of the Sea Convention (which, however, does not predominantly cover environmental questions), various oil spill agreements, the Barcelona Convention on the Protection of the Mediterranean, the Rhine protection agreement, and the treaties for the protection of the North Sea, the Baltic Sea, the Alps and so on.

Accession to a convention remains, of course, a voluntary act. After accession and ratification signatory states have to observe well-defined obligations of restraint. The main weakness of international environmental treaties is sanctions as environmentalists, lawyers or even other nation states can do little to stop signatory states violating a treaty. Often violation is even beyond the realistic control of signatory states, as in the case of the CITES Convention where illegal trade in endangered wild animals continues to circumvent customs control by using false declarations, finding its way to irresponsible end-customers.

If public anger is aroused, it may become feasible to organise a boycott against products of a violating country. A recent example involving government rather than consumer action is the attempted US ban on imports of Mexican tuna because of porpoise and dolphins killed in Mexican tuna nets. This is also, of course, an example of the ecological dimension in North-South tensions.

Ecological North-South Conflicts

Ecology has brought a new factor into the already difficult North-South relations. Mutual blame dominates the relations, as we saw at the beginning of Chapter 1.

Industrialised countries consume much more than their fair share of global resources, as is indicated in Figure 1 on p. 4. Historically the industrial countries have been largely responsible for the build-up in the atmosphere of human-induced greenhouse gases (some 90 per cent of CO_2) and CFCs (around 98 per cent of emissions), which have been added into the atmosphere over the last 150 years. Even today they produce more than 70 per cent of CO_2 emissions and more than 90 per cent of the CFCs. The developing countries, which we now call upon to save the last of the rain forests, know all about this and see no reason why they should forego anything which could help them in their generally difficult or desperate economic situation. China, already responsible for as much as 13 per cent of total world emissions of CO_2, is planning to build many more coal-fired power stations. Somehow we shall have to 'buy' the co-operation of the developing countries, but so far have no useful experience as to how that could be brought about.

Many people in developing countries as well as in the former Communist countries of the East understand very well that environmental ruin is to their personal detriment, but governments see the need for action almost exclusively in the economic and technological domains. Pollution control is costly and can be afforded only after reaching decent levels of economic development.

A 'development first, environment second' attitude dominated political thinking in Third World capitals until the late 1980s. Even after the publication in 1987 of the Brundtland Report, priorities did not really change. 'Sustainable development' was mostly read as 'development, as sustainable as possible'. We in the North help to confirm this view by claiming that we need more economic growth to finance both our own environmental protection and additional ecological aid programmes as foreseen in Agenda 21 (see Chapter 8).

The developing countries notice the excitement and alarm in the North caused by the destruction of the tropical forests. Some politicians in the South see this as hardly appropriate coming from those nations which are primarily to blame for the poverty and consequent environmental damage. Other politicians who think ahead see it as a golden opportunity to bring change to the calamitous state of North-South economic relations and to get the North to hand-over large sums of money. As the environmental crisis is presented as a consequence of the poverty or debt crisis, ecology becomes a means of putting pressure on the North. In this way ideas developed in the 1970s for a new international economic order could be revived. The stabilisation of raw material prices, for example, is often proposed, as are obligatory payments from North to South using per capita consumption rates as a yardstick for contributions.

Nothing of this kind has materialised, of course. Funds flowing from North to South and debt relief should be offered, according to the North, only under strict 'green conditionality', i.e. against reliable promises by the South that so and so much nature will be conserved. The North has never been susceptible to any scheme involving automatic payments of any magnitude. Some voluntary 'debt for nature swaps' financed by Northern environmental groups have relieved a few countries, including Bolivia, Costa Rica, Ecuador and the Philippines, of marginal portions of their external debts and helped conserve some wildlife areas. Germany and other countries have completely written off the public debts of a few (mainly African) least developed countries and obtained somewhat vague commitments of sustainable development, while the World Bank created the Global Environment Facility (GEF) allowing soft loans for developing countries' environmental protection projects.

To people in the North both diagnosis and therapy look different from those of the South, as is indicated in Figure 35.

	DIAGNOSIS	THERAPY
The View from the South	The environmental crisis results from poverty in the South, wastefulness in the North, external debts and destructive trade relations.	Sustainable growth in the South; debt relief; fair trade relations; modest consumption in the North.
The View from the North	The environmental crisis results from over-population, poor management and lack of technology.	Birth control in the South; environmental impact assessment in development projects; transfer of technology & management skills; debt relief with green conditionality.

Figure 35: North and South differ sharply both in diagnosis and in therapy for the socio-ecological crisis. (See, e.g., Banuri, 1993).

This sharp divide over the socio-ecological crisis characterised the diplomatic situation at the time of the UN General Assembly's resolution 44/228 to convene the United Nations Conference on Environment and Development (UNCED). And Brazil invited the family of nations to hold the conference at Rio de Janeiro.

The UNCED Process

UN Resolution 44/228 practically coincided with the end of the Cold War. Was this sheer coincidence? Quite probably, but it is none the less undeniable that Mikhail Gorbachev declared that the global ecological crisis was a central reason for ending East-West confrontation. The end of the Cold War also presented a new situation for the South. All of a sudden it became pointless to play on the rivalry between East and West. Hopes blossomed that enormous peace dividends could now be harvested and directed towards Third World development, but it soon became clear that the East was changing from being a donor to a recipient of international aid and attracting the attention of the West more than the South ever had. The end of the Cold War therefore in effect weakened the position of the South to a considerable extent just at the beginning of the UNCED process. On the South's situation after the Cold War see Hartman and Vilanova (1992).

UNCED had many names. Some called it ECO 2, making the Stockholm UNCHE ECO 1. Some just called it Rio or the Rio Conference, but in the end the most popular and most adequate name for UNCED was the Earth Summit.

Maurice Strong, former Secretary General of ECO 1 was appointed Secretary General of UNCED as well, a unique procedure at the UN. Tommy Koh of Singapore, an old hand in UN affairs, chaired the series of meetings of the Preparatory Committee, and a hand-picked Secretariat in Geneva serviced the whole UNCED preparatory process with skill and devotion. It soon became clear that UNCED would become the largest diplomatic event since the end of the Second World War. More than 100 heads of state or of government announced their attendance as the substance of the Earth Summit appeared increasingly relevant and attractive.

It was planned that the Climate Convention, an apparent necessity since at least the first meeting in 1988 of the Intergovernmental Panel on Climate Change, would be signed at Rio. Likewise, the signing of the Biodiversity Convention (Chapter 9) was also planned. An Earth Charter was prepared for adoption at Rio, a solemn declaration of principle on environment and development; it was later relabelled the 'Rio Declaration'.

Centre stage, however, was taken by the Agenda 21, a comprehensive Programme of Action on Environment and Development (see Chapter 8). To make it operational, financial mechanisms and technology transfer supporting Agenda 21 were discussed in the UNCED preparatory process. Institutional arrangements at UN level to steer the implementation of Agenda 21 were also to be negotiated.

All in all governments, the secretariat and hundreds or thousands of advisers were taking on an enormous workload. The UNCED process became a huge undertaking. It involved literally several million people, some working on specific substantive issues, some on the organisation of the event, and some, directly or indirectly, on the creation of a broader public awareness. Much of the preparatory momentum came from non-governmental organisations (NGOs), many of them highly critical of what governments were doing (Ekins, 1992). Without that momentum and public pressure it would have been easy for some governments to leave everything to diplomatic routine and thereby let the conference fail, an outcome nearly assured by the deep divide between North and South over the central issues (see Figure 35).

As a matter of fact, during and after the last Preparatory Committee meeting in New York in March-April 1992 it looked very much as if total failure was programmed. By that time none of the central issues had been resolved, neither finances, institutional arrangements, climate, biodiversity or forests. The draft of Agenda 21 remained full of 'brackets', passages in the text which were contested by single countries or, more often, by the entire North or South respectively. The OPEC countries in particular demonstrated very little interest in UNCED's success and began to show great nervousness at the mere mention of climate, atmospheric pollution or even energy efficiency.

Although negotiations were concluded during April and May 1992, by special negotiating committees for the climate and biodiversity conventions, many observers, including nearly all German NGOs and journalists, were certain until its opening that the Earth Summit would not achieve anything of importance. They believed it would be a gigantic festival of vanity and nonsense requiring some 30,000 international air tickets, hundreds of tons of paper and brutal security measures affecting the local population. Many cancelled their year-old reservations in order not to be part of what they began to call the 'Summit of Hypocrisy'.

The Earth Summit

Reality turned out to be better and the Earth Summit was a success. The need for statesmen and their delegations to succeed appears to have been strong. Not least, the Europeans had learned something about the South. After the Group of 77 (developing countries) preparatory conference in Kuala Lumpur, April 1992, many parts of the European media acknowledged that the North was the main polluter and pressure was put on governments to accept some of the Southern views. Similarly, some of the Southern media, familiarised their public with the views of the North. The *Journal do Brasil*, the leading Brazilian newspaper, had a regular environmental supplement during the year before UNCED and sought to make its readers proud of their country's unique ecological treasures.

José Lutzenberger, Environment Secretary of the host country until March 1992, was an eloquent advocate for the endangered Brazilian environment and an ecological representative of Brazil at countless international gatherings where he nevertheless faithfully voiced Southern concerns (see Figure 35). He was dismissed shortly before the Earth Summit but was present in Rio at many of the Global Forum events and as a favourite interviewee for the Northern media.

The host country succeeded beyond all expectation in mastering the daunting logistics, and this helped to make delegates, observers and the participants in the Global Forum feel comfortable, which certainly contributed to the success of the conference.

Of course, Maurice Strong, Nitin Desai and their UNCED secretariat team worked tirelessly in the service of fair compromise between conflicting countries. Tommy Koh as Chairman of the Preparatory Committee symbolised governments' determination to make the conference a success. Pakistan in its role of speaker of the Group of 77 was able to re-establish the Group's unity and even to keep the OPEC dissenters on board. The EC managed to hold a progressive line despite the absence of its Environment Commissioner until June 1992, Carlo Ripa di Meana, who in the end did not come to Rio in protest against the weak compromise on carbon taxes (Chapter 11), and despite a relatively weak (Portuguese) presidency. The German and Dutch ministers Klaus Töpfer and Hans Alders were very vocal activists for the Community's environmental policy and helped make the Community repeat at Rio its commitment to stabilize CO_2 emissions at 1990 levels until 2000, a message in stark disagreement with the USA.

The USA found itself isolated in an unprecedented way, just three years after the collapse of Communism and a little more than a year after the Gulf War. During the negotiations about the Climate Convention the USA had refused to accept binding dates for CO_2 reduction. It declared itself unable to sign the Biodiversity Convention, a decision clearly coming from the White House, not from the EPA and its highly competent and devoted head, Bill Reilly. President Bush's speech at Rio was a masterpiece of environmental pretentiousness; he did not really address any of the global environmental problems caused in large part by his country, but instead boasted about domestic pollution control which had little to do with UNCED's agenda. Seemingly, the speech did not even impress the electorate at home to which it was, of course, mainly addressed.

In the view of the South and of most Northern NGOs it is the American way of life in its present wasteful form that is in fundamental conflict with sustainable development, and US isolation at Rio was above all caused by this simple fact. Ironically, Bush's negative attitude to UNCED's themes contributed to the success of the conference and facilitated political unity at the Earth Summit.

The substantive agreements reached or signed at the Earth Summit were just as important as the political atmosphere at Rio, although they fall far short of what the Earth really needed. The Climate Framework Convention, which was in fact signed by the USA, can be seen as a turning point despite the lack of binding dates. Article 2 clearly states that 'greenhouse gas concentrations (should be stabilised) at a level that would *prevent* dangerous anthropogenic interference with the climate system.' This level is to be reached in a timespan 'to allow ecosystems to adapt *naturally* to climate change' (emphasis added).

These statements can be compared with the best estimate by climatologists (e.g. IPCC, 1990) that we are running into an average global warming of $0.3\,°C$ per decade and considerably more locally unless a drastic reduction (not just a freeze) of greenhouse gas emissions is achieved. This $0.3\,°C$ per decade represent a formidable threat to ecosystems since the rate of temperature change would be too fast to allow them to adapt naturally. With perhaps a little more scientific evidence supporting the above estimates about global warming, Article 2 of the Convention should lead to rapid and decisive steps towards a reduction of greenhouse gas emissions, especially because Article 3 says that 'lack of full scientific certainties should not be used as a reason for postponing such measures'.

Article 4 consists of concrete commitments including extensive reporting on greenhouse gas sources and sinks, national or regional programmes to mitigate the greenhouse effect, promotion of climate-friendly technologies and processes, inclusion of climate protection into economic, social and environmental policy, climate oriented programmes of education and awareness building, and regular reports on actions taken.

Articles 7 to 10 establish the Conference of Contracting Parties, its Secretariat, a Scientific Committee and a Control Committee. The Conference of Contracting Parties is expected to agree Protocols to concretise the Convention. Chancellor Kohl in his speech at Rio not only reconfirmed Germany's commitment to reduce greenhouse gas emissions by 25 to 30 per cent (against 1990 levels) by 2005 but also invited the Conference of Contracting Parties to hold its first meeting in Germany.

Remarkable progress was also achieved on Agenda 21. It was adopted, which in itself was a considerable achievement. All brackets were removed and a somewhat vague financial commitment by Northern countries was obtained. The Global Environment Facility of the World Bank will receive more money and Third World representatives will have more influence on its lending policies. At the United Nations, a new Commission for Sustainable Development was established to supervise the implementation of Agenda 21. One should not, of course, over-estimate the impact this commission or the adoption of Agenda 21 will have. Three Development

Decades and a broad consensus on the needs for development at all UN Agencies during the 1960s and 1970s have not even narrowed the gap between North and South, so it is difficult to imagine that matters will be radically different this time. The Rio Declaration, a positively anthropocentric document on development and environment, was unanimously adopted but has hardly any binding power. Finally, the Earth Summit adopted Principles for the Protection of Forests, strongly pushed by European countries, and agreed to prepare a Convention against desertification.

The biggest diplomatic gathering of the Economic Century has certainly made the path towards the Century of the Environment considerably clearer, but in all its concrete decisions it was still very much an event of the Economic Century.

The Agenda After Rio

Every single document adopted at the Earth Summit shows the signs of political compromise, and to see the formal results of Rio as solutions would be a major misunderstanding. Public opinion needs to develop much further; sustainability and South-North equity and justice are still far away.

One of the inherent weaknesses of UNCED lies in the fact that it was a meeting of sovereign states. Sovereignty allowed countries like the USA, Saudi Arabia and Malaysia to block progress on issues where, to the degree that it existed, world public opinion clearly wanted more. National sovereignty, the symbol of the Century of the Nation State, is no longer tolerable as the dominant principle of international law (French, 1992).

The Northern media have a tendency to speak only of limiting the sovereignty of Malaysia and Brazil — namely in the context of preserving forests and biodiversity as the 'common heritage' of mankind. But there is an important credibility gap involved here, aside from the North's high consumption levels which we have already mentioned. In the early 1980s the South spoke of the common heritage of mankind in the context of the Law of the Seas, and at that time it was specifically Germany, the USA and the UK which abstained from the UN consensus, arguing that enterprises owning and developing advanced sea-bed mining technologies should not be discouraged by international restrictions.

Another weakness of the Earth Summit relates to its failure to address the debt crisis (see Chapters 4 and 8). Latin American environmentalists, among them José Lutzenberger, speak of the ecological debt the North keeps incurring towards the South and towards posterity.

It can be argued (see S. George, 1990, H. Sabet, 1992) that the financial debts have long been repaid via a combination of interest payments and lowered commodity prices (cf. Figure 22) and that, therefore, debt forgiveness would be the most rational policy. But classical foreign policy has no way of inducing creditors, who are mostly private banks, to do what is necessary. A complex mix of actors including the Paris Club, debtor countries, Northern governments, environmentalists and multinational agencies including the IMF and the World Bank, should get together and work on something broader and more ecological than the Brady Plan of 1992. Unfortunately the international financial community in the early 1990s is more concerned with the former Soviet Union's gigantic debts (advising, of course, more efficient exploitation of Russia's natural resources) and with Japanese financial adjustments after 30 years of boom than with the 'ecological debts'.

Earth Politics after the Earth Summit will by necessity involve new forms of international solidarity. Perhaps the 20,000 or more participants at more than 100 events in Rio de Janeiro's Global Forum may become the key agents of that change. They were living an international culture beyond the nation state and even beyond the dictatorship of economic reason. They were, in many different ways, longing for sustainable and new models of wealth.

PART FOUR:

SEARCHING FOR NEW MODELS OF WEALTH

We now leave the domain of Realpolitik and turn our attention to *vision*. Realpolitik alone tends to become dull and meaningless without a vision of what could be different and how one would *wish* things to be. Without vision, politicians like Bismarck, de Gaulle or Kennedy would have been mediocre figures. The new century, the Century of the Environment, will also need a compelling, global vision.

Searching for and building up this vision will be the work of generations of people. A single book can not do more than name the themes that need to be addressed during the Century of the Environment.

The fourth part of this book is devoted to that task. It starts quite close to our present real world with technologies for the environment. Going far beyond pollution control technologies, Chapter 15 ends by offering seven criteria for technologies that may dominate the Century of the Environment.

Technology is rooted in the sciences. The sciences constitute one of the central driving powers for any changes in our world, and they can therefore also be held responsible for some of the destructive changes occurring on Earth. Scientists cannot escape the question of their own responsibilities. This insight will lead us in Chapter 16 into signs of crisis in the self-justification of the sciences. Is there a new scientific revolution around the corner?

Work and labour are central to the Economic Century. How are they going to change their meaning in the forthcoming Century of the Environment? No doubt the monopolistic view of work as paid labour will be replaced by a more liberal view that incorporates the merits of neighbourhood work, child care, ecological engagement and other non-paid or underpaid work. Again, a new vision is required; Chapter 17 leads into this debate.

Finally we are speaking about perceptions of wealth. We need new models of wealth or of prosperity, which won't simply be wealth with less energy consumption but will also be a new way of looking at things. Having decent air to breathe may one day be perceived as a more important index of wealth than so many dollars in a bank account. We may be heading for fairly fundamental changes in our culture. Chapter 18 ventures a preliminary glance at this cultural change.

Chapter 15

Technology's Green Revolution

Environmental Technology: A Growth Sector

Technology has long been considered the environmental movement's 'enemy number one'. Nuclear power, road and air traffic, the chemical industry, the mechanisation of agriculture and genetic engineering are all symbols of what environmentalists are battling against. Engineers, for their part, have tended to think of conservationists as enemies of technology and progress. This confrontation seemed justified as long as technology was predominantly a means to further the exploitation of the natural world or to serve human convenience at the expense of environmental quality, but there has been some change. Environmental legislation has had its effects on the direction of technology. New firms and some old ones have discovered that they can make money out of environmental technology. Other firms have discovered that 'pollution prevention pays' (see pp. 145–46). The conflict between environmentalists and technologists has taken on a new perspective since this 'greening of technology' (Speth, 1990). Engineers no longer see conservation as a threat from crazed Luddites but as a public responsibility which they have come to accept, and for a growing number of environmentalists, some of whom are technically well trained, technology has become a means to the end of environmental protection.

Twenty years of environmental policy have made environmental technology a growth sector. Sewerage technology has come so far that treated industrial and municipal sewage need no longer pose any threat to fresh water and seas. The Rhine leaves Germany's most heavily industrialised state of North Rhine-Westphalia in a healthier condition than at its entry into the state. The Thames and the Ohio have benefited from similar cures, but there are many more rivers waiting for it, which means that there are almost unlimited markets for firms selling water purification equipment.

The chemical giant Bayer-Leverkusen runs its waste water through a treatment works based on tower biology after which the water can sustain delicate fish in aquaria, a highly effective living advertisement for the efficiency of the treatment.

Desulphurisation and denitrification ('de-nox') technologies are established air pollution control technologies, although they are not cheap. The Large Combustion Plants Order in Germany, adopted a few years before the respective EC Directive, implied investments of some DM 30 billion for West Germany alone. Ten times more may be required to clean up Eastern Europe's furnaces. Germany was foolish in the late 1960s to leave advanced de-nox know-how to the Japanese who now dominate the world markets with their patented technologies.

Advanced waste disposal technologies are also on the rise as a result of growing economic pressure. Incineration technology has made substantial progress, and, indeed, the use of modern techniques has made it relatively harmless. Incineration, however, should not be seen as more than a temporary solution for the disposal of refuse. Environmental groups rightly oppose it wherever it tends to be abused as a convenient excuse for maintaining wasteful life styles.

Technical progress has also led to improvements in areas which we identified in Part Two as scarcely affected by environmental policies. Between 1973 and 1985, for instance, Japan achieved a reduction in energy use, not least because of high energy prices, of 31 per cent, from 18.9 to 13.1 megajoules per constant dollar of GNP, while in Canada, with low energy prices, the best that could be managed was a reduction from 38.3 to 36 (Brown et al., 1988, p. 42). Canada therefore required about three times as much energy as Japan to produce the same amount of GNP. It is widely known that the artificial increase in energy prices in Japan and the resulting reduction in energy consumption has encouraged rather than inhibited the development of technology. An unprecedented growth occurred in 'brain power' industries, with a decline in heavy industry and while Canada's railways crumbled Japan's were extended.

Let us not fool ourselves. There are disadvantages to the otherwise welcome development of environmental technology to date.

Firstly, expenditure on environmental protection is defensive in that it does not produce consumer goods but merely mitigates the ill effects involved in manufacturing them (Leipert, 1989). Ultimately, of the successes described above, it is only the increase in energy productivity which, in a classical sense, is productive.

Secondly, the type of environmental protection we have been developing over the last twenty years remains unaffordable for most countries including those in East Europe which need it most.

Thirdly, industry in the developed world has long been able conveniently to transfer many of its environmentally unsound products and processes to developing countries (see the next section).

Fourthly, it is so far mostly a curative, 'end-of-the-pipe' rather than preventive approach to environmental protection. Some of these end-of-the-pipe technologies of the early years have, objectively viewed, even worsened environmental conditions. Tall smoke stacks, which eased the local situation, have caused serious damage to formerly unaffected natural habitats. Many technologies have brought in their wake new, and to some extent, still unsolved, problems. Sewage treatment produces huge amounts of sludge, the metal and toxin content of which limits its potential for agricultural use. The residue of waste incineration is normally special waste, as are the used filters from air purification equipment.

The continued growth of the environmental technology sector in its present shape is clearly not satisfactory. We ought to look for more radical improvements, and ones which can be applied in poor and rich countries alike. As we noted in Chapters 10, 11 and 12, this will not happen unless and until the right signals reach the market place.

Substitution, Relocation, Innovation

Japan's success in increasing energy productivity and clean production has to a considerable extent been bought at the expense of transferring polluting and energy-intensive industries to developing countries. The natural resources of Brazil, the Philippines, Indonesia and Malaysia are paying a substantial amount of Japan's ecological bill (cf. Chapter 8). Europe, too, exports a large and ever-growing proportion of its ecological problems.

Must it be thus? Do we have to have polluting and energy-intensive methods of production, which can be sent abroad in the effort to spare our own land? The answer is both positive and negative. It is negative in that we can do without certain goods and services, we can substitute polluting technologies or we can make them ecologically compatible. It is positive, in that these three strategies have limited reach and in that relocation can often be justified environmentally.

To illustrate these options, let us look at one example, the production of aluminium from bauxite, a process which will, of necessity, remain energy-intensive. No measure of technical innovation can change that. An ecologically responsible approach would include four potential solutions, the first of which is the most radical — doing without aluminium. The second would be to substitute the use of aluminium in certain circumstances with paper, glass or plastic, even with wood (which can now be bonded to achieve great strength). Of course, care must be taken to ensure that the substitutes do not themselves overly damage the environment.

The third approach would be to make the aluminium manufacturer and its local energy supplier as clean and efficient as reasonably possible and recycle aluminium as far as possible because aluminium from scrap requires some fifteen times less energy than smelting it from bauxite.

Finally, however, consideration should be given to relocating the production of aluminium in places where energy can be generated with minimal costs to the environment. Possible locations include sites close to sources of hydroelectric power in Norway, Canada, Greenland or Russia and other places blessed with waterfalls, a goodly quantity of rain and a reasonably robust environment. The relatively flat and ecologically sensitive Amazonian forests, by contrast, do not satisfy these criteria.

Aluminium is but one example. The four basic answers above apply to hundreds of other products and production methods: do without, substitute, improve the process or relocate environmentally. The problem with relocation, of course, is that it is usually done for quite different motives, and long before home-based strategies for substitution and environmentally sound production have been exhausted.

This is a central problem for Earth Politics. The object of the exercise appears to be a situation in which relocation follows ecological reasoning not opportunistic convenience. As long as this situation is not achieved and as long as cynical economists at the World Bank keep talking about 'under-polluted countries' which ought to cordially invite in polluting activities, there will be insufficient pressure to work on the first three solutions and the corresponding technological innovation.

The North must go ahead, even unilaterally, the first three of these with solutions. Put yourself in the position of the environment minister of a developing country, who has at last decided to confront the polluters. If the polluters can then argue that even in Europe the above solutions are not explored seriously, how is he or she to persuade the economy and technology ministers at the Cabinet tables?

During the UNCED process more and more developing countries began to erect barriers to the import of polluting technologies in much the same way as the Basel Agreement of 1989 which defined barriers against the international shipment of toxic waste.

This is an encouraging sign and one of the important effects of the Earth Summit that developing countries themselves have begun to take a fresh look at the *direction* of technological progress. In as much as the OECD countries have turned their backs on bulky and polluting industries, the South is understanding that innovation today means dematerialisation (as the Japanese call it), energy efficiency and knowledge intensity.

Policies to induce and foster this new direction should be chosen pragmatically. It is not advisable to copy Northern command-and-control legislation which does not even work satisfactorily in Mediterranean EC countries and so far fails to address the energy, water, resources and land use problems outlined in Part Two.

Redefining the Meaning of Productivity

Let us assume that pressure for a new and sustainable model of prosperity will increase and soon become the prevailing condition for technological progress. One possible shape which this economic pressure might adopt was indicated in Chapter 11 — a continuously increased price load on environmentally-problematic production factors. Then we should expect a slow but fundamental redirection of technological progress, a true 'Green Revolution' of technology which might be characterised by seven criteria.

1. *Cleanliness.* Only technologies which produce little or no emissions would be used. Avoidance of emissions would be achieved by process innovations, by the abolition of high emission technologies, or, in exceptional cases, through the capture of emissions at 'the end-of-the-pipe'.

2. *Energy Productivity and Solarisation.* Machines, space heating, lighting, transport and distribution systems would all be tailored to meet the highest standards of energy efficiency and energy productivity (see Chapter 5). The very concept of productivity would change. Today it is essentially reduced to labour productivity — which was increased through the industrialisation process by a factor of approximately twenty since 1850. Now it is time for energy productivity to grow, by a factor two easily, by a factor four with considerable effort, by a factor eight with enormous effort and over a period of at least 50 years, and by a factor sixteen or so over 100 to 150 years. Energy productivity increases of a factor eight would allow a simultaneously doubling of prosperity and cutting of energy consumption by a factor four; remaining energy needs could largely be satisfied with renewables (solarisation).

3. *Minerals and Water Productivity.* What was said about energy productivity also holds for minerals and water productivity. Both minerals and water have the advantage over energy that, at least in theory, they can be completely recycled. The durability of products, remanufacturing (rather than shredding and recasting) of automobiles, refrigerators and other durable goods and the systematic re-use of materials would become essential design principles. Drinking water cycles will be largely separated from water for industrial, agricultural and cleansing purposes.

4. *Ecological Land Use.* Agriculture, housing, industry and transport routes would be reorganised to have only minimal effects in terms of land deterioration, soil erosion and water pollution, and large parts of the land will be dedicated primarily to ecologically valuable uses including biodiversity reserves.

5. *Information Intensity.* Products and services, production and consumption processes are all becoming more information-intensive. There are great opportunities for increasing comfort and the quality of life with the help of science and technology, data systems and customer

information, miniaturisation (see e.g. Drexler and Peterson, 1991), culture and communication, all of which are information-intensive activities with minimal effects on the environment (cf. Chapter 18). The limits to information intensity generally lie at the receiver's end. Information technology will of necessity become increasingly concerned with responsible data-handling and protection, the receiver's capacity and willingness to digest and use available information, and with 'information pollution'.

6. *'Error Friendliness'*. As economics, technology and culture become ever more global in scope, the danger of the spread of errors threatens (Perrow, 1986). Even if the creeping destruction of the environment can be halted through legal and economic means, there remains the danger of major catastrophes and chain reactions, either civil or military. Policies, law and technology will work on counterforces which include democratic control, legal restrictions (mostly to protect the commons), modular design (to keep the effects of failures small). Total avoidance of error is both impractical and inhuman. Thus technology must aim to evolve 'error friendliness' (Ch. and E. v. Weizsäcker, 1986) as a design principle. Error friendliness goes beyond classical error tolerance (which is not much more than robustness). Like mutations and curiosity in biological systems, error friendliness also includes an element of innovation which is not the case with robustness. It is a fundamentally 'biological' or 'evolutionary' design principle.

7. *Suitability for the Informal Economy*. Technologies will increasingly be developed with the informal sector rather than industrial use in mind. While the demand recedes for short-lived, resource-intensive goods transported over long distances, in other words for typical industrial mass production, there should be a corresponding increase in demand for satisfying, meaningful and productive activities outside the formal economy. Backyard food, social care, home manufacture and repair, help among neighbours are some of the key activities for the informal sector, which is definitively not to be restricted to developing countries. Modern technologies for the informal sector are as yet at a very early stage because the informal economy has until now been seen only as a sign of chronic backwardness. But there is no reason whatsoever why this neglect should continue. (Readers who find this paragraph particularly revolting are invited to read Chapter 17.)

From Vision to Action

How can these criteria which are conjectured from ecological and social exigencies become reality?

Technology will always follow the market (within the limits set by scientific progress). Technology markets have, for many years, been led to a large degree by defence contracts. This state of affairs is now changing. However civilian technology markets, too, are often highly state-dependent through the award of contracts for postal services, transport and construction and through setting the legislative framework, not least in the field of environmental protection. Only a modest part of the technology market is defined by private consumption, and even this is subject to substantial state influence through such means as fiscal, education and social policy. To describe the state as far and away the most important agent in the technology market is not to overestimate the importance of the public sector but an accurate description of reality. Finding the answers in an existing and changing technology market, on the other hand, is primarily a matter for private business.

Implementation of the first four criteria can be advanced largely through state commitment (preferably EU-wide) to an ecological tax reform or else, in the highly developed countries, through a system of tradeable permits. The legislative basis would have to be brought into line with the criteria. The biggest question is how quickly the necessary framework can be introduced in different parts of the world.

I believe that given a decisive move away from over-use of resources, the fifth criterion, information intensity, will come into being of itself. In a democratic society it is only to be expected that interest within the information revolution will focus on the control and responsible handling of information.

The sixth criterion will have to find its way to fruition through our culture. The literary success of books by Charles Perrow (1986), Hans Jonas (1986), Joseph Weizenbaum (1985) and others indicates a cultural readiness to take error friendliness seriously. As a policy measure, the best instrument for the implementation of this criterion is a tightening of liability law and the introduction of compulsory liability insurance for an expanding range of major impact technologies, acknowledging, of course, the 'limits to certainty' (Giarini, 1988).

A further possibility, which seems utopian at present, would be the introduction of international rules comparable to anti-trust laws restricting the size of companies or of some of their operations, and limiting uniformity. A practical entry point for anti-uniformity rules could be found in the sphere of nature conservation and species protection; agricultural uniformity could be limited by the creation of a network of ecological refuges, either through limiting field sizes or by legislating for temporal or spatial diversity. This could be a multiform tool for conservation in Europe as well as in the American Midwest and Australia, especially if fair compensation were payable to farmers.

The development of technology for the informal sector will also depend on demand. At present, the informal sector (in developing countries) is almost always characterised by being short of cash. This, I believe, is a transitory situation. The future will rather look like the booming OECD countries' hobby market, but supportive measures in both South and North, such as permitting and encouraging people to do outside the official economy what they can do for themselves, would greatly strengthen and reinforce this trend.

All in all, it is safe to assume that in an era which sees all seven criteria satisfied there will be more and not less technology. High resource-use is in my view a sign of crude and inept use of engineering skills. As the future will not have at its disposal the wealth of resources currently available, it is inevitable that today's clumsy technologies will appear to be 'dinosaur technologies' whose extinction could have been forecast. Once this knowledge penetrates the consciousness of a significant number of captains of industry and politicians, the race will be on to overcome the dinosaur technologies and to gain the lead in creating the efficiency revolution in the use of scarce resources.

A Few Examples

The efficiency revolution does not belong to the world of science fiction but has for the most part been long available or long conceived. There are already a number of technological means available for the raising of energy productivity which cannot at present be introduced into the market because energy prices are too low. Included amongst these are the low wattage light bulb, which supplies the same amount of light with 15 watts as a normal 75 watt bulb; combined heat and power plants, which conserve the 30 per cent of heat energy otherwise lost by a power station; transparent heat insulation, which uses most of the energy provided by even diffuse daylight and traps heat extremely efficiently so that buildings can be constructed with virtually no commercial energy requirements; cars consuming two thirds less energy than today's average cars — a goal agreed for 2003 between Detroit and the Clinton administration. And finally, foodstuffs, the production of which calls for very small amounts of energy input, such as modest amounts of high quality meat from free-range animals in place of double quantities of insipid meat from intensively reared animals. Intensive rearing would, in any case, lose its profitability within an ecological framework.

More than just fuel efficiency can be expected of new 'piggy-back' systems, such as buses and suburban trains offering space for bicycles. For long-distance travel, double-decker railway coaches are conceivable in which small 'citycars' can be parked cross-wise on the lower deck and are able, given specially adapted platforms, to get on and off almost as quickly as the passengers who sit upstairs and enjoy much greater comfort than when squeezed into today's cars. A similar rapid-transfer system could be developed for freight containers.

These 'piggy-back' systems combine the energy and convenience advantages of rail travel over longer stretches with individual mobility over short distances. Commercial business too, can only gain, as goods are transported over long distances by rail with virtually no personnel costs for the company. As a prerequisite, management of rail networks must become Europe-wide and the network's weak points — such as Italy, where strikes by underpaid workers frequently disrupt services on an outdated network — must be taken care of.

Ecological land use demands new town-planning mechanisms and a re-integration of urban and rural space (cf. Chapter 13) and requires new mechanical, chemical and logistical technologies which involve definitively more and not less know-how than today's technologies. This nevertheless means the departure from a definition of technology which always demands 'as much machinery and as few people as possible'.

Technologies based on error friendliness and suitability for the informal sector are mutually related. Technology for the informal economy is hardly likely to involve large-scale disasters. Decentralised food and energy production, composting, repair, local recycling of materials and networks of (mutual) social care all have their informal economy components and are much error-friendlier than their centralised counterparts (see also Chapter 17).

Chapter 16

The Impact of Science

Dissecting, Torturing, Fading Out

Anatomy is a useful science in the service of medicine and the preservation of life, but the knowledge gained from that science is knowledge gained from dissecting corpses. The likelihood of death for living creatures increases in proportion to the depth of investigation. This is the everyday experience of 'life scientists'. The telescope allows us to observe the heron whilst letting it live; the scalpel will kill it but keep its cells alive. Preparation for the electron microscope kills the cells but leaves organic microstructures intact. Those, however, don't survive further biochemical or biophysical investigation.

Life scientists' everyday experience was a scientific strategy for Francis Bacon (1561–1626), public prosecutor, politician and latterly a physicist. Nature had to be mastered; to become man's slave. Nature had to be chased with hounds and tortured to give away her secrets. Such were the brutal prescriptions of a man who was amongst the first to predict that real progress would follow from the exploitation of the natural sciences. Bacon's spirit lived on in the advice of René Descartes (1596–1650) to his fellow men to make use of scientific knowledge in order to become masters and owners of nature.

Where science is made absolute, it can adopt truly brutal and destructive features. An instance of this is Stanley Milgram's (1965) well-known behavioural experiment in which he persuaded students to inflict pain on others. He claimed that, in the interests of science, he needed the help of his students in applying electric shocks to induce people to learn. On the other side of a glass screen, the subjects could be seen supposedly at work on a number of exercises. Every mistake was to be punished by a shock, explained Milgram, with the student controlling the level of electric charge. With each shock, the subjects cried out or reacted physically but carried on with their work. Some of the students applied such high levels of charge that they could have expected the subjects to suffer severe pain, if not physical injury, but of course the real subjects of Milgram's experiment were the students themselves. He wanted to find out the level of cruelty of which people were capable in the service of science. The subjects behind the glass screens were actors who simulated pain, reading the levels of the charges supposedly, but not actually, being applied.

Killing animals in the interest of scientific progress is one aspect of science, life sciences in particular. In the world's experimental physiological and pharmaceutical institutes, such killing is the rule rather than the exception. It is true that there is legislation for animal protection, for example, prescribing the use of anaesthetics where possible. But, should the nature of the experiment demand a conscious animal, it is not difficult to obtain permission. Ethical considerations therefore arise not only from the sometimes explosive results of science but also from the methods used in research.

The problems of scientific methodology are not solely problems of ethics. The search for truth has its own problems. Through its measuring techniques, even through the very act of posing certain questions, scientific research delves into the sphere of reality. Reality is dissected, manipulated, faded out and devalued, even often substantially changed. Every opinion poll changes reality, even when conducted faultlessly. Every experimental design skilfully fades out and excludes parts of reality, and 'no theory ever corresponds precisely with all the facts in its field' (Feyerabend, 1975).

Scientific work is meant to be published. For publication the cast-iron criterion is reproducible results. Other laboratories must be able to check and confirm them. This quality criterion constitutes a high ethical value to many scientists: it elevates the scientific community above many other professions whose truthfulness is never checked and controlled. However, reproducibility implies methodological sacrifice. The singular, the irreversible, the ephemeral and the tenuously interwoven are expelled from the peer-reviewed scientific world. Not completely, however, because science can also lay down its observations of the ephemeral by committing them to film or tape, but in such preservation, the essence of the ephemeral of any given situation is lost. 'Imagination, breadth of vision, joy in discovering relationships and meaning, all of which are necessary in scientific endeavour, die away in the artificial world of methods which puts certainty on top', writes Hartmut von Hentig (1988).

There is no denying the power of scientific rigour. The bluff of charlatanry and complaisance can be exposed such as the claims by Trofim D. Lysenko of having conducted experiments on the inheritance of acquired characters, experiments which could not be reproduced in the West. Lysenko's 'results' appealed strongly to Stalin and his ideologues as they seemed to confirm the socialist credo of the malleability of the human nature.

The understanding that good science is ideally placed to reveal and root out charlatans plays a powerful role in the solidarity of the scientific community, but the self-admiration and pleasure taken in revealing and rooting out scientific frauds can go a long way to closing scientist's eyes to other dangers and narrowness of thinking, which go hand in hand with methodological coercion according to Feyerabend.

Destructive Impacts

As we have seen, science encompasses some cruelty and some partial exclusion of reality. Moreover, as most people are well aware, science has an extraordinary power to change the world. The industrial revolution, modern weapons systems, the population explosion (being the result of improved hygiene, medicine and the ability to feed a great many more people than was possible in the days of the hunter-gatherers), modern comfort and present day mass communication are all products of systematic use of scientific discoveries.

'Knowledge is power,' wrote Francis Bacon in his *Novum Organum*. It is not surprising that many critics see the roots of the present environmental crisis in Bacon, Galileo and Descartes, and in the triumph of scientific thinking. 'Modern (Galilean) physics is murderous from its very roots, and ultimately, suicidal,' writes Klaus Müller (1977, p. 59), himself a physics professor. 'Exaggerated reliance on scientific methods and on rational analytical thinking has led to attitudes and behaviours which are deeply anti-ecological,' writes Fritjof Capra — also a physicist — in *The Turning Point* (1982). And Carolyn Merchant (1981) lends a feminist perspective to the critique. She says that 'we must re-examine the formation of a world view and a science which, by reconceptualizing reality as a machine rather than a living organism, sanctioned the domination of both nature and woman.' Countless other observations spring to mind. They all express something important, something about the dangerous, even explosive side of the sciences of which most of us are more or less aware. Scientists, technologists, economists, politicians and laypeople all are well advised to take the dangers very seriously.

And yet it seems to me that the critics are painting too gloomy a picture. People's capacity for learning is being undervalued. Physics could only risk becoming suicidal if it were perpetually propagated by the zeal for primitive 'progress': the progress of the ever more, ever faster, ever more precise. Certainly it was possible for centuries to fall victim to the illusion that only this was progress. The 'conquest' of the oceans, of the sky, of outer space and of the world of atoms and molecules in the days of the respective pioneers was undoubtedly seen as progress and not as destructive. It is within the ability of mankind to redefine progress and to call destruction by its real name. Where a new sense of sustainable progress emerges, scientific endeavour will eagerly help pursue the new goals.

One point should be made, however; such a redefinition of progress is not going to be achieved through moral appeals alone. We need to recognise (and change) the dynamic processes which are so forcefully and inescapably harnessing the sciences for that cult of the ever-more, ever-faster, even where 'more' and 'faster' means destruction.

He Who Pays the Piper ....

There are two main driving forces behind science's further development, the 'internal' and the 'external'. The internal is the curiosity of the scientist, the 'inordinate satisfaction' of the researcher, as the physicist and mathematician Carl Friedrich Gauss once called it, and the exchange of ideas among scientists. Scientists are inclined to see only this inner impetus, to elevate it, and to regard themselves as independent and free. But in so doing scientists hopelessly underestimate the tremendous power of external forces.

What 'free' scholar would remain free to conduct his or her research, if there were no payment for that work? And who is it that ensures the comfortable salaries of millions of scientists? True, it is mostly public budgets from which research and academic teaching is paid, allowing for a degree of academic freedom. But why should the public sector do so? Is it for the sake of scientists' inordinate satisfaction? Certainly not. The state's expectation is that multiple interests will be served by science and academic education. The state and the private sector require education, training, research and development. The expectation of economically quantifiable results from science forms the economic basis of the science industry. It is only in this context that we can understand the explosive growth of scientific activity.

The political left has for many years seen the sciences as a productive force. Conservatives have found it more convenient for a long time not to emphasise the relationship between science and economic productivity and rather to depict the scientist's work as a free, non-profit activity. This did not prevent conservative market economies from utilising scientific results much more efficiently than the socialist ones.

Today the commercialisation of science is no longer ignored by anybody. The scientific community is either slightly embarrassed by the fact but discreetly recognises it, or, in its search for research contracts openly advertises it. What many representatives of the scientific community find disturbing is the exploitation of research results by the military. Since the atomic bombs on Hiroshima and Nagasaki, responsible scientists the world over have been plagued by the fear that the fruits of their work would one day be taken over by the military or by terrorists. Even those who had knowingly worked for the military — from fear that

Nazi Germany would steal the march on them — were after the war aghast at what had happened. 'We have done the Devil's work,' said J. Robert Oppenheimer, the 'father of the atom bomb', to a visitor. 'We must now return to reasonable work, and dedicate ourselves exclusively to basic research.' (quoted by J.J. Salomon, 1974, pp. 81–93). This was an understandable and honourable reaction, but no answer to the real problem. Albert Einstein and Otto Hahn were as fundamental in their research as it was possible to be, and yet their work led eventually to the atomic bomb.

Scientists who want to avoid the problem cannot simply retreat into pure research. In the words of Hubert Markl, then President of the German Research Association, 'We should educate our scientists not only in good methodology, but equally in their shared responsibility for the applications of their work.' I should like to add that scientists need to become quite clear about the external influences dominating their workplace, so that the convenient notion of purely internal driving forces is seen for what it is — a myth.

What Scientists Themselves Can Do

What should scientists do, in concrete terms, if they are to accept responsibility for the applications to which science is put? Firstly, they should devote a significant amount of time to researching the consequences of their discipline. These consequences are, after all, an integral part of reality. The reality of penicillin lies in its medical impacts. Should it cease to be effective, say, because of bacterial resistance, it would soon be moved from the pharmaceutical shelves into dust-accumulating collections of curios.

Negative impacts are likewise a part of reality. Environmental damage, risks, and impairment of social harmony are all too familiar manifestations of the reality of technology. If there were no ill effects, technology would be seen in a quite different light. For the sake of completeness in our comprehension of reality, science needs to concern itself with the many ramifications of its impacts, the so-called 'impact trees'. These impact trees themselves delve into new scientific territory.

Research into this new territory is not helpful, however, and can be absolutely counter-productive to academic careers. There are hardly any university positions for interdisciplinary impact researchers, there are only a few peer review journals and research contracts are scarce. Most research money is given for and channelled through the peers of disciplinary research. Technology assessment, e.g. by the US Congress's Office for Technology Assessment (OTA) is an exception. The OTA's small budget is probably larger than the combined technology assessment budgets of all EC member countries taken together (including the European

Parliament's STOA, Science and Technology Options Assessment). The funding and career situation for impact scientists is better at the large research installations, many of which have moved a long way from nuclear research (their typical origin) to complex non-military programmes.

The reason for the scarcity of funds and careers in impact research is certainly not the lack of fascinating scientific questions. The physics involved in splitting the atom is far less exciting today than research into the complex questions of energy demand (real or imagined) or risk assessment. Molecular agricultural plant research tends to be scientifically less challenging than research into eutrophication or biodiversity in agricultural areas or the scientifically-based development of attractive diets for feeding the hungry. In fact, 'basic research' seems to offer less in the way of new scientific frontiers than work on complex, applied problems. Historically we should be aware that the glory of basic research (alluded to in Oppenheimer's remark cited on p. 188) stems from the post-war period when politically innocent basic research was contrasted with the work of applied scientists in the service of Hitler or Stalin, or, indeed, of the needs of American war production to which Oppenheimer referred. Today few countries provide a reason for politically-motivated retreat into basic research.

Scientists' responsibility today includes, as I have said, the general readiness to work on the problems of the modern world, and indeed the problems which science itself has engendered. Science should not close its mind to the destruction of the Earth's biological diversity, to population growth, climatic risks or any of the thousands of local environmental problems, and it should also fight for better funding of the related research. The fact that these problems tend to have their immediate roots in political and economic affairs and are not of a purely scientific nature implies that many more scientists need to adopt a conscious commitment to work in the political field where appropriate.

There are all sorts of ways of doing this. These include the popular presentation of problems within the scientist's discipline; active membership of scientific associations which have espoused the principles of responsibility, such as Pugwash, the International Physicians for the Prevention of Nuclear War, and the Society for Social Responsibility in the Sciences; making and maintaining overseas contacts, especially with Eastern European and developing countries; interdisciplinary co-operation in academic teaching and recognition of students' achievements beyond the narrow confines of disciplinary curricula; engagement in research into impacts; commitment within academic, research and funding bodies for more research into impacts, as outlined above; and active political involvement via issue groups, professional associations or political parties.

It goes without saying that such committed engagement should not jeopardise the scientific virtues of independent thinking, intellectual integrity and openness to scrutiny.

Commitment can also consist in the scientists informing themselves of the practical applications of their work and establishing contact with those responsible. If we are ever to succeed in breaking the vicious circle of 'ever-more, ever-faster' we need to do so at the point of origin. If we can identify the forces of false exploitation, we should be in a better position to redirect them into an environmentally benign direction, as outlined in Part Three of this book. Scientists should not try to dissociate themselves from this huge political task.

The development of new fields of science and technology can itself be an aim of responsible commitment, fields which will prove themselves useful in a century in which saving the environment enjoys the highest priority. In order to imbue this new territory with the seriousness of good science, the individual researcher is going to need pluck, a pioneering spirit and a co-operative nature and will have to put up with the scorn of peer-group members who are not plagued with methodological doubts and to whom the application of results from their daily routine guarantees a comfortable salary and perhaps some sizeable royalties. Scientists who have a good academic position are, objectively, rarely pioneers, even if, subjectively, they consider themselves to be so.

Another Scientific Revolution Ahead?

Science has always been proud of its pioneering work. Above all, the 'scientific revolutions' (Thomas Kuhn, 1962) set themselves, without exception, against the spirit of the scientific and social establishment. It is quite possible that we are today on the threshold of a new revolution which may encompass all spheres of knowledge. There are indications that this is the case. The distinction drawn by Descartes between mind and matter, on which Newtonian physics rested, has already been overtaken by quantum theory, and, more drastically, by neurobiology and information theory. The Newtonian world view in which things move in constant space and through time was shaken up by Henri Bergson and Alfred North Whitehead, and has lost further validity since Einstein's theory of relativity and the works of for example, Ilya Prigogine (1979), Carl Friedrich von Weizsäcker (1992), François Jacob (1970) and Humberto Maturana and Francisco Varela (1984). There are growing signs of new thinking, by, for instance, Gregory Bateson (1979), Fritjof Capra (1982) and David Bohm (1980). A number of fundamental problems, important for the study of complex systems, are in a scientifically unsatisfactory state, although not insoluble, for example philosophical questions of information, chaos, entropy and the structure of time.

The rejection of a mechanistic view of the world and of modern functional rationalism unites those in the vanguard of new thinking. They are inclined to sweep away the old. There are, however, good reasons why this would be wrong.

Firstly, scientific revolutions in Thomas Kuhn's sense integrate the old and make it understandable in the context of the new. Therein lies a difference between political and scientific revolutions.

Secondly, we are utterly dependent on the technology born of modern rationality; to sacrifice it to any new age fashion would be catastrophic.

Finally, the new way of thinking should be characterised by seeking symbiosis and communality rather than weeding out dissidents.

Some cultures have the expectation that narrow, mechanistic scientific thinking will fade away and yield to a new, more integrative thinking. I believe that the century of the environment will allow us no other choice, and yet I cannot escape the feeling that much needs to be done before we can hope to see this transformation taking shape. Representatives of the new thinking tend to spend too little time dealing with the strength and positive side of the technocratic philosophy and too much time in gaining mutual encouragement from the (usually correct) diagnosis of its weaknesses.

A Revival for the Humanities

One kind of development towards new scientific thinking which is in no way revolutionary can already be observed today. This is a renaissance of the humanities.

The natural, technical and economic sciences have prospered in our century. They have served expansion, the taming of nature and an increase in wealth. They represent knowledge which is of practical use, rather than knowledge which helps our orientation in the world. They will still be in demand in the Century of the Environment when questions of adjustment to ecological realities arise. But once our societies begin to broadly realise that 'the slowest ship in convoy' is not technology *per se* but its integration with culture, justice and the social fabric, then there will arise an almost irresistible re-evaluation of the humanities.

Already we can observe a reawakening of interest in history, philosophy, languages, cultures and religions, but the humanities in their present pure state could not justify a re-examination. They have very little relationship to today's and tomorrow's scientific and technical realities.

For Pascal and Goethe, philosophy and contemporary science constituted a unity. Today there reigns the mutual lack of comprehension and communication, so well depicted in C. P. Snow's *Two Cultures* (1960). In the last 50 years it has been well nigh impossible for non-scientists including scholars in the humanities to engage in conversation with scientists. And what philosopher could compel the natural sciences into dialogue? The only group to have achieved anything more than informal dialogue with scientists has been the legal profession, which has used the state's authority to set limits and rules to the application of science and technology.

Of late, the natural and technical sciences have had to struggle for acceptability (and industry has donated millions for 'acceptance research', in the naïve assumption that acceptability can be bought by psychological tricks). Many scientists are increasingly willing to recognise and moderate the hazardous results of their success. This is something new and opens up new avenues for dialogue with the humanities. Both sides still need to understand that we are in the Economic Century and that economic quasi-rationality remains the main force behind science and technology. There is no place in the dialogue for philosophers who ignore this, and scientists who ignore the fact are not being honest with themselves.

A renaissance of the humanities requires more than a veneer of understanding of history and a contrite willingness to converse on the part of scientists. It demands interdisciplinary, not just multidisciplinary, co-operation. It demands the development of new integrative research fields rather than new disciplines. It demands that the careers of those involved in the humanities, science, technology and social sciences are moulded to new inter-related themes rather than to single subjects. It demands from business, from the state and from our culture that we acknowledge and honour these changes as necessary.

For the humanities, a revival represents an enormous challenge. The humanities cannot escape the demand that they play a major part in the shaping of the culture of the new century, the Century of the Environment. They must open their doors to Earth Politics.

Chapter 17

Freedom of Work

What Is Work?

'Work' is one of the essential issues both in politics and in anthropology. It would be quite inappropriate to try to deal comprehensively with such an important and contentious topic in a book on environmental politics. What may be feasible is to attempt to illustrate some areas in which work and the environment are inter-related. Even this more modest approach, however, cannot avoid calling into question today's common understanding of work since this form of work is almost inextricably bound up with the kind of unsustainable growth and destruction of nature described in this book.

Work enables human beings to make use of and upgrade the values of nature. In many traditional agriculturally based cultures it was largely possible to do this without damaging nature (see Chapter 7), but productivity was low, just sufficient to sustain a relatively small population and a modest standard of living.

It is understandable that economics since Adam Smith has regarded raising the level of productivity as one of its prime tasks. The division of labour was found to be a prerequisite for this rise in productivity. The introduction of modern technologies demanded factories to which the workforce needed to walk or travel, and specialists whom the farm or the village could neither train nor retain. Thus the creation of work in the modern economy came at the same time to mean the uncoupling of work from its direct relationship with subsistence (see also Chapter 8).

Industrial production, once divided from the sustainable subsistence economy, required raw materials in large quantity. Both in the early and high stages of industrial development, work consisted primarily in gaining access to raw materials, mining and processing them.

The division of labour, industrial work and a general speeding up of work processes brought to the people wealth, power and a new feeling of self-esteem. The cry 'God is dead', the glorification of machines, the political self-awareness of the workforce, the colonisation of the world, the unrestrained search for the treasures of the earth and the creeping devaluation of subsistence work are all facets of the sense of progress, which is the hallmark of the great age of industrialisation. Of course it must be said that different sectors of society profited to highly differing degrees, capital owners more than the workers, the city more than the land, men more than women.

At any rate, especially since the workers' movement began to help shape events, the concept of work took on a positive connotation. Thereafter little else was meant by work than gainful employment (Arendt, 1956). Work in its earlier forms — on the farm, in the home and even crafts — began to be devalued and lose respect. Farmers and craftsmen still retained an unassuming middle-class role. Housework on the other hand was demoted to the role of 'reproduction' notably by 'progressive' or socialistic social sciences. Reproduction, meaning sleeping, eating, loving and child-rearing became a subordinate supply service for 'real' production. Nature fared the same.

While subsistence work had to maintain a caring relation towards the environment, industrial work had no visible reason to do so. Even on the farm, keeping a sustainable management became a lesser concern than short-term business administration. Skilled artisans no longer had time to lavish time on the pieces they were working on. House-keeping became progressively independent of the seasons and scarce supplies. In this stream of progress it was impossible for human work to maintain its traditional sustainability orientation. Thus there are sound ecological reasons to investigate critically the nature of work in its present form.

There are at the same time social reasons for criticising what is nowadays understood by work. Firstly to *have* work has effectively come to be a privilege. More than half the world's people who are capable of work and willing to seek employment do not have a regular job. Faced with this dreadful fact, one cannot simply get on with the agenda and put the unemployed off with talk about the next boom: whether or not one is employed is far too important a question of daily life and of self-respect.

Secondly, jobs as such now account for only a small part of human activity. With the 38.5 hour week, six weeks holiday a year, an average of two weeks' sickness leave, special leave and official bank holidays, and 40 years' work in a lifetime, the average employee in Germany works for only about one-seventh of his or her waking hours or one-tenth of his or her life. Six-sevenths of the waking hours are devoted to other activities. Even if travelling time to and from work and the time spent on vocational training are counted as work, the scales are still tilted heavily in favour of other forms of activity.

Thirdly, whereas in earlier times, roughly when people were first given family names, a job (miller, smith, tailor) both identified and fulfilled a person; nowadays, employment, especially that of women, often consists of short-term jobs and says little about the person. Just imagine if we acquired our names today, would we want to take our present jobs and call our families, for example, Programmer, Audiotypist, Cashier?

Finally, and above all, even now the formal economy based on employment would be totally helpless if the 'informal sector' did not still exist. Sleeping, eating, loving and bringing up children are not subordinate activities we could do without but the indispensable foundation of all human existence. Economic theory has a shocking tendency to repress this simple fact.

For all these reasons, even in the context of Realpolitik, it must be permitted to break the taboo which surrounds and protects work in its present economic form and think in terms of a future in which wealth depends far less on having a job and on consuming what is produced by the formal economy.

What Is Wealth?

Chapter 10 referred to Christian Leipert who in drawing up his account of 'defensive expenses' describes many manifestations of illusory prosperity. Take a well-known example: two cars pass each other quietly on a country road. Nothing happens and they contribute little to the gross national product. But then one of the drivers, not paying attention, wanders over to the other side of the road and causes a serious accident involving a third approaching car. 'Terrific!' says the gross national product: air ambulances, doctors, nurses, breakdown services, car repairs or a new car, legal battles, visits from relations to the injured, compensation for loss of earnings, insurance agents, newspaper reports, tidying up the roadside trees — all these are regarded as formal, professional activities which have to be paid for. Even if no party involved gains any improvement in his or her standard of living and some actually suffer considerable loss, our 'wealth', namely our gross national product, still increases.

As a scientific justification for this fallacy, the argument is often made that unpleasant events like accidents are an inevitable part of our lives and cannot be eliminated through economic planning. The argument goes that we have no choice other than to quantify the contributions to restoring our wealth by ambulances, doctors, car repairs etc. But that is only part of the truth. In the first place there are ways of living and means of transport which increase or decrease the likelihood of accidents. Second, in planning for the future, decisions are often made which increase the gross national product without necessarily doing anything for the general well-being. This brings us to the second example.

Figure 36:   We spend only one tenth of our total hours--or one seventh of our waking hours--in employment.

A mother is considering whether or not to breast-feed her new-born child. She has a job as a supermarket cashier, which is not at all fulfilling, but tolerably well paid. In order not to lose the job, she stops breast-feeding a few days after delivery and the baby gets used to the bottle. Now she has to buy milk, boil bottles and sterilise them. Let us assume that, in an ideal world, the baby's father is able and prepared to do all this. The real costs are yet to come: for example, no longer benefiting from the mother's milk which helps to develop its immune system, the baby is more susceptible to illness, often has tummy-ache and stops its parents from sleeping. There are frequent consultations with doctors, perhaps some serious treatment. And there are child-minders or day-nurseries to be paid for. The gross national product, which takes no account of the tummy-ache or the sleepless nights, has benefited royally from the mother's decision in favour of her work.

In the main, gross national product simply measures all products and services which are sold on the market. The examples given show that health, happiness and personal fulfilment are not of necessity closely linked to a growth in GNP or employment. Under certain conditions they can even increase simultaneously with a decline in gross national product or employment. Small children and the environment seem to do best if they do not figure in the gross national product at all (or hardly at all).

If it were possible with less employment systematically to improve the environment, reduce illness and cause less destruction, then clearly greater health and happiness, or indeed greater prosperity, could be achieved with a smaller gross national product. There are two ways in which this goal could be achieved.

Firstly, all negative or simply 'defensive' services should be omitted from the definition of prosperity so that a new kind of wealth can be calculated (see, e.g. Hueting et al., 1991).

Secondly, human activities relevant to this new wealth should be put on an equal social and (where possible) financial footing, irrespective of their relationship to the formal economy.

The question of definition cannot be explored in depth in this book, but a few words about the incentives needed to raise the level of welfare are perhaps in order. Until now our political and cultural incentives have almost always been designed to increase the gross national product. Pensions are calculated according to years of employment. Social prestige, a very strong incentive, is clearly tied to employment, not to breast-feeding, gardening or working illegally. Vocational training and continuing education are almost totally geared to securing and keeping employment.

Society's narrow-mindedness in this area is unfair to the unemployed (who are not in the habit of being inactive), unfair to mothers, housewives and house-husbands and an obstacle to an environmentally sustainable form of prosperity. This third point goes right to the heart of this chapter and will be further explored in the following section.

It is encouraging in Germany that a law was introduced in 1989 by which one year of maternity leave can be added for each child to the years of employment in the calculation of pension benefits. A Supreme Court ruling of 8 July 1992 on women's informal labour during the early post-war period indicated that German social policy will be forced to continue on this road. So it may not be too far-fetched to anticipate a time when state decisions on pensions and education will emphasise and reward the creation of net wealth regardless of the formal employment structure. At the same time, and in the long term more importantly, our culture has to evolve or rediscover an awareness of this concept of net wealth, in which social worth and a sense of personal happiness is not solely determined by a job's contribution to the gross national product but by its ecological, social and 'net economic' benefits (Daly and Cobb, 1989, pp. 401–455). Formal and informal economy ought once again to be on a par with each other.

Environmental Protection in Your Own Hands

Conventional environmental protection is assumed to mean large-scale investment and 'end-of-the-pipe' installations, a view which is encouraged by both state and industry. We can be proud of the vast sums which have flowed into environmental protection and continue to do so. Hundreds of thousands of jobs have been created, many of them producing exports (see the section 'Jobs and the Environment' at the end of this chapter). In the context of our present economic system, increased turnover through environmental protection is considered good. On the other hand, the reverse strategy of preventing damage in the first place and therefore spending less on environmental restoration means less work, lower turnover, lower earnings and a lower GNP and is therefore regarded as bad.

In reality such a healthy contraction, in so far as it is technically possible, could be advantageous for genuine well-being in our high-technology society. We have too little experience to judge the success of a strategy based on economic contraction, but this novel experience is essential for Earth Politics to succeed. There follow a few examples of ecologically and socially advantageous ways in which we can become leaner and fitter and how human activity would evolve within such a strategy.

Energy: A lot can be done in terms of DIY (see the next section). It is possible, for example, to build in insulation against heat loss. Energy requirements are reduced and the gross national product would decline, but well-being would increase (provided, of course, that sufficient ventilation and energy efficient heat-exchange prevents bad air indoors and excessive exposure to Radon). Some 30 per cent of the work in installing solar panels on roofs, hot water systems derived from passive solar energy, heat pumps and biogas equipment can be done on a do-it-yourself basis, which is plainly not possible in obtaining energy from the electricity socket or the oil tank. Once these facilities are installed, the self-reliance achieved will reduce dependence on external sources. If the capital costs of purchase and installation are not more than 30 per cent of the cost of saved energy, the gross national product will decrease in parallel with the benefits for the environment, health and happiness. On farms which have guaranteed quantities of raw material for bio-gas installations, it is profitable to generate their own energy even compared to the unrealistically low prices of today's markets.

Health: A healthy way of life, knowledge of herbs and lay medicine were for thousands of years the primary way of protecting health. Medicine was on hand for war, serious accidents and certain specific illnesses. But life expectancy was low; thanks to improved hygiene, medicine and good nutrition it has greatly increased. But one thing is fairly certain: nowadays there is too much doctoring going on — even if it takes place with the consent of most patients. It would not be unreasonable if, let us say, 30 per cent of present-day professional medical care were to be replaced by various forms of self-help. Such a set-back for the gross national product would not affect health and happiness of the majority (the medical profession representing the minority). Indirectly, it would even be of benefit for the environment, as much more attention would be paid to healthy living, while the impact of the health industry on energy consumption, hazardous wastes, traffic congestions and so on would be reduced at the same time.

Long-term care: Putting the elderly and the sick into nursing homes or 'retirement residences' is often unnecessary and degrading. If families had more time, consignment of the sick and the elderly to the isolation of life in a home could easily be postponed for some years. The advantage for the environment is much the same as with health.

Repairs: We have to bid farewell to the throw-away society. This means returning to the old habit of repairing things; such repairs should not be performed exclusively by skilled workers and technicians but also by ordinary people working for themselves. This, in turn, leads to a reduction in the gross national product and a better environment.

'Freedom of Activity'

Working for oneself clearly relates to what in development economics is called subsistence work, but it deserves a fresh look and a modern connotation. For this it may benefit from a new terminology. In German, Christine von Weizsäcker (1978) coined the term 'Eigenarbeit' signifying work that belongs to you that you shape mostly yourself and that may also shape you ('eigen' means one's own). 'Eigenarbeit' or 'Eigenwork' is done for your family or for yourself, for your neighbours and for future generations. It is often unpaid but may under fortunate circumstances also be paid, in cash or in kind; remuneration in kind relates it to subsistence work, e.g. gardening, repair and family work. *Eigenwork* is awfully vulnerable to exploitation by others (notably by husbands and boy-friends) because there is a natural tendency to do it anyway, but then, people would probably feel much poorer still if they had nothing in their lives which can be exploited.

Subsistence and *Eigenwork* need to be protected against the grip the formal economy is taking on land, time, family life, independence and human identity. As was argued in Chapter 8, such protection may be a matter of life or death in developing countries. In affluent countries it is a question of promoting and protecting the kind of work which accords with the wishes and abilities of the people. Most people today do have a desire to be professionally employed, but this does not by necessity imply a preference for full employment 40 hours a week on one unchanging job for a lifetime. And it implies even less any willingness to let the sphere of *Eigenwork* be destroyed. To fulfil the desire of millions for a decent living and for satisfactory work is simply a different task from 'creating full-employment'.

An important element of freedom is endangered when *Eigenwork* is destroyed, repressed or marginalised. Perhaps the traditional freedom of chosing one's education and profession ought to be transformed into a broader 'freedom of activity'. 'Activity' embraces gainful employment, *Eigenwork*, moonlighting, 'shadow work' (Ivan Illich's term for undesired and unpaid work in the service of the official economy, e.g. commuting; see Illich, 1980), sport, education and training, and any kind of leisure activity. 'Activity' can be paid or unpaid, satisfying or unsatisfying, legal or illegal, productive or unproductive. The freedom of activity (or perhaps liberty of activity) should also extend to the liberty *not* to work, where this is not morally unacceptable (such as failure to give first aid). This very broad concept of activity deliberately allows it to retain a neutral overtone, unlike work and employment which usually sound very positive, or moonlighting or shadow work which usually sound negative.

Freedom of activity can mean the free choice of education and training; the free choice of one's job; the freedom to choose periodic, part-time and *ad-hoc* work; the freedom to undertake informal, unregistered yet paid neighbourhood and community work (with some specifications so as not to encourage excessive tax evasion); and the freedom to self-reliance. None of these freedoms imply anything like an entitlement to a job, higher education or money.

Some consumer and client protection clauses need to be rewritten, but it need not always be the same schematic approach which applies to consumer protection relating to industrial production at present. There is a world of difference between marketing, on the one hand, two million tins of baked beans or tuna and, on the other, a neighbour's selling someone some green beans or eggs. One case of botulism from one mass-produced tin warrants an outcry of indignation by the public and the press. It is worth calling back the whole shipment. The laws are very strict in this area, and supervision tight. One case of food poisoning from eggs or trout purchased directly from a neighbouring farmer, on the other hand, is only a local event, of little interest to the general public. Here too, rules need to be applied, but existing civil and criminal law and, of course, legal standards for farm hygiene and for the use of agrochemicals, should suffice.

The freedom to choose individual periodic or part-time work could lead to individual work 'menus', provided that they correspond to what is on offer in the job market. Trade unions and professional associations don't like this kind of individuality, but it should by all means be possible to maintain their *legitimate* interests (quality standards for work, protection of the individual worker, political strength *vis-à-vis* the employers), while illegitimate interests (such as the elimination of unwelcome competitors) are suppressed.

The freedom to enjoy self-reliance is equally in conflict with the monopolistic claims of the state or the trade and professional associations. But there are powerful precedents: while nearly everybody can obtain a driving licence, we don't accept a professional drivers' monopoly. In health, nutrition, education, the social services, skilled manual work, energy provision, environmental protection and resource handling, the level of self-reliance can be quite high. In Eastern Europe and many developing countries this is a sad and unwanted reality, but where it is freely chosen it will be seen as an improvement in the quality of life. Only in a few areas (such as policing, the law, defence, and certain basic education or public works services) does a state monopoly make sense. Certain standards which are regarded essential, as in the case of the driving licences, can just as easily be accommodated.

By following the daring path towards 'freedom of activity' we would solve a number of problems, but new ones would be created. In particular, the overall size of the employment 'pie' would shrink as people would make more use of their options for DIY. This is because they would spend less money obtaining their sufficiency of goods and services. Yet the contraction of the formal economy and the shrinking employment pie do not imply any loss of well-being. After all, people's well-being does not ultimately come from *selling* goods and services but from *obtaining* them.

It all ends up, as is so often the case, as a question of distribution. An average reduction of working hours could even go hand in hand with lower unemployment figures if the individualised labour market leads to a better match than today between supply and demand. If social security were partially decoupled from participation in the formal economy, and if the self-esteem of people was increasingly linked to meaningful DIY (no longer to gainful employment alone), the fears of people with smaller job engagements to slide down the social scale would no longer be justified.

It is not possible in half a chapter to do justice to the highly controversial debate on work flexibilisation, moonlighting and real wealth in conditions of a slow growth or even a decline of the formal economy, but it would have been dishonest to avoid the debate altogether.

Jobs and the Environment

Let us conclude this chapter by offering some more conventional facts and thoughts on work and the environment (see Renner, 1991). Environmental technology was described in Chapter 15 as a growth sector.

In the traditional sense of work as employment, environmental work is on the rise throughout the world. In Germany it may account for approximately 700,000 jobs that relate directly to environmental protection, and the number is growing.

There are ways and means of encouraging this development, for example through special state programmes for employment and the environment. The basic idea is for the state to create jobs in the environmental sector, raising the necessary funds to do so either through higher taxation on polluters or the Keynesian approach of deficit spending which it is hoped will be paid off later through a higher national income. A third, more conventional, strategy would be further to tighten environmental laws to such an extent that private industry is forced to employ more people in the area of environmental protection.

According to current economic theory, all the three strategies — if carried out by a single nation in isolation — lead to economic losses due to the competitive situation in international trade. The problem can be looked at in a different way, however. If there are other strategies available such as ecological tax reform, which appear to achieve the same degree of environmental protection but without jeopardising international competitivity at the same time, one should not resort to artificial job creation at the expense of the economy. What might be justifiable, at least for a transitional period, would be conversion from military programmes (which are, of course, state-run) towards environmental protection by the state.

In the long term, there is not much prospect in either the public or the private sector for jobs in remedial 'end-of-the-pipe' environmental protection. If the strategies discussed in this book become a reality, the number of jobs even in environmental protection will actually decrease because the technological and cultural transformation envisaged is meant to lead to the prevention of environmental damage through process and attitudinal changes rather than through generating additional activity. Thus a sustainable economy may indeed be an economy with a shrinking formal economy (Hueting et al., 1991), but not one with less well-being.

Chapter 18

New Models of Wealth

What Was the Question Again?

Imagine someone going to Hyde Park Corner and speaking about the need for new models of wealth, models based on far lower consumption of natural resources. He or she would be greeted with derision. 'But we have wealth already,' you hear them mutter, 'except in times of recession. And we have environmental legislation, rather too much of it perhaps. What else do we need? Don't preach to us about self-denial.' Thus speak the realists. The fact is, however, that despite all the existing environmental protection, the actual decisions made by business, government and consumers all entail increased consumption at home and exploitation of the environment and natural resources at home or abroad. Despite our outward show of belief in environmental protection, we remain firmly in the thrall to (short-term) economics, the driving force of this century. The necessity for new models of wealth, sustainable and copyable ways of life is diametrically opposed to present reality, and yet it is inescapable.

Let us remind ourselves that we are losing some 3,000 square metres of forest and 1,000 tonnes of top soil *every second*. The extinction of species is rampant. We are threatened both by the greenhouse effect and depletion of the ozone layer. The industrialised countries consume roughly ten times as much energy, water, land and raw materials per capita than the developing countries. If consumption of these items were to be quintupled world-wide, the earth could not survive. It is absolutely vital that we in the North adjust to using less. Our present model of wealth, which we take for granted and assume is the starting point for even better times, is not sustainable. If we continue to ignore this peril we will ignite a political and ecological disaster which will make the Second World War look like a brief skirmish.

Seeking new, sustainable models of wealth is not an idealistic daydream but an absolute imperative if we are to avoid disaster. We cannot begin to recognise the seriousness of the situation if we do not look beyond our national boundaries, and the Earth Summit has fortunately facilitated our transcending traditional national myopia.

But if matters are so dire, why do I persist in using the words 'models of *wealth*'? Why not simply talk of reversal and austerity? The answer is very straightforward: because it is possible to reduce our energy, mineral and water consumption by half or even three-quarters, to halt further land degradation and to achieve a transition to clean technologies without foregoing well-being, and also because political consensus on austerity is simply impossible to imagine. But it needs to be made crystal clear to the defenders of wealth and convenience that if we do not, all of us, quickly turn towards sustainable models of wealth, the devastating and costly collapse of the old system of wealth and freedom will just be a matter of time.

What of the Role of the Economy?

In the introductory chapter I referred to the Economic Century as a transitional stage and called for a change of direction as the Century of the Environment dawns. And yet the concrete proposals throughout this book are directed towards economic pragmatism, economic sustainability and people's preference for the good life. How does this fit? Let me offer two answers.

The first relates to the sketchy philosophy of history offered in the first chapter. The transition from one stage of cultural evolution to another is never clear-cut. It was the concept of '*national* economy' (in English known as political economy) which paved the way from the dominance of the nation state to the dominance of economic thinking. For the demise of the princely courts, a century earlier, it was vital that the people should become the 'sovereign' — a term which nowadays has an antiquated ring. The religious wars in central Europe were not stopped by any abrupt end of religious beliefs but by the strange sounding formula *cuius regio, eius religio* (the land adopts the religion of its ruler) which paved the way for the dominance of those rulers' princely courts.

That is to say, plans for the future which are not firmly anchored in the present are politically unsound and in this century environmental policies which are incompatible with economic thinking are simply fantasies doomed to failure.

The second answer goes somewhat deeper. Economic reason, after all, has a more enduring logic than princely courts or denominational wars (a small comfort, perhaps, to the people of Northern Ireland and Bosnia). Even if saving the environment becomes the dominant principle, economic reason will not disappear. The forces of economic incentives, of material gratification, of egotism, envy and the profit motive and of the desire for power are not going to disappear overnight, but will of necessity fit into a sustainable framework. Moreover, economics can learn from mistakes.

Once prices and other economic parameters come close to 'telling the ecological truth', economic reasoning will cease to be destructive to the environment. Resource efficiency and the protection of the environment will in the long term turn out to be economically sound. Small wonder, then, that the new models of wealth can be considered models to contribute to long-term prosperity.

But What Are the New Models of Wealth?

What do they actually look like, these new models of wealth? The first answer might come as something of a surprise: the 'models' do not exist as anything like stable prescriptions. Rather, they are going to represent the historical process of economic and cultural change away from today's spendthrift way of life.

The second answer is purely formal but offers a negative definition. The new models of wealth will allow far less pollution and consumption of natural resources per capita, but people will be more open than today at recognising that less can be more. Less wasted energy and less rubbish means benefits today. Less smoke and less noise mean a higher quality of life. But there may be a day also when less hurry, less moving around, less material turnover will be appreciated as a higher standard of living.

There is more. Environmental protection is transformed from being an economic cost to an economic benefit, as Chapters 11 and 12 seem to suggest. This leads to the hope for a much more pervasive identification with the ecological goals on the part of the population at large. The 'negative' answer of *less* resource consumption subscribed to by the moral minority would easily be turned into positive feelings among the majority about a 'new elegance' in dealing with scarce resources.

The appreciation of a new elegance may lead us a little further in clarifying what I have just called a purely formal answer. The new models of wealth — this is the third answer — are likely to consist of millions of individual ways of making use of and appreciating the new ecological boundaries. Individual readers may enjoy imagining how their lives might change when heating oil, car and air travel, meat, plastics, metals and other things become more expensive, and information, services (even sophisticated ones), recreational and cultural activities become noticeably cheaper; when manufacturers advertise their goods for their durability, recyclability and ease of repair; when public transport — both long-distance and local — functions considerably better than at present; when self-reliance and *DIY* (see Chapter 17) are encouraged rather than repressed; when working patterns become more flexible; when cities become greener and more hospitable and the countryside becomes more diverse and entertaining; when a transformed educational system rises to the challenge of new work patterns and lifestyles.

A new culture will emerge from the millions of different answers to such questions. The very nature of the questions means that we are not talking here about a sad decline into material poverty but about genuinely new forms of prosperity.

To reinforce this message, I would even go so far as to talk quite openly of luxury in the Century of the Environment. The desire for extravagance and luxury will not die away as a result of the environmental crisis, just as it did not disappear as a result of the French, Russian and Chinese revolutions. Luxury will still exist, but in a different guise. Refined tastes in gourmet food, furniture, social life, culture and the arts all appear to be ecologically acceptable. Even such luxuries as horse-riding, sailing, good hotels and large estates (with high levels of biodiversity) are not particularly detrimental to the environment and could give as much pleasure to the fortunate few as motor-racing with Maseratis, swimming in oil-heated pools or quick trips to Bermuda.

It will always be a legitimate aim of social policy to combat extravagance and to help the needy, but social policy can hardly make use of the ecological argument when the luxury in question is adjusting to ecological necessities.

Private luxury may be the most glaring symbol of luxury. The everyday convenience that surrounds the businessman, from short-haul flights and unlimited car use to spacious, aggressively air-conditioned suites of rooms or conferences in first-class hotels are no less of a threat to the environment. Here too an ecological change is due. In expensive hotels hot showers might be metered and charged for, while a couple of phone calls or drinks from the mini-bar might be free. Ecological architecture for office design could evolve and travel by car and plane might be limited by the use of tele-conferences and an improved railway system.

In the longer term it is quite conceivable that the concepts of wealth and luxury will become progressively decoupled from the consumption of natural resources. Our present notion of obtaining wealth and luxury through ever greater consumption is not only ecologically unsustainable but also a highly questionable means of fulfilling our needs. Indeed William Leiss (1979) has pointed to the 'limits to satisfaction' and Ivan Illich (1970, 1972, 1980) never tires of demonstrating new 'counter productivities' in the carousels of the consumer society and its services. Related works by Hazel Henderson (1981), James Robertson (1989), Klaus Meyer-Abich (1979), Mary Clark (1989), Jean-Pierre Dupuy (1977), Lester Milbrath (1989) and others show in an impressive variety that much of the satisfaction taken from resource consumption is fallacious. It is not terribly surprising, therefore, that other forms of satisfaction are on the rise again, such as the company of friends, fulfilment through spiritual, religious and artistic experiences, and an aesthetic pleasure at the healthy regeneration of nature. A steady advance of such experiences can be expected if prices of natural resources are moving towards 'telling the ecological truth' and, therefore, the supply of material goods does not collapse.

Some readers will feel a growing unease when reading these lines. Who is going to decide what people should do (or not do) to satisfy their needs? Are we heading for ecotyranny?

Ecotyranny in the Century of the Environment?

Discussing new models of wealth implies highly contentious political issues. My views in this respect are quite unambiguous: I strongly reject any form of ecotyranny.

Economic stringency, whether in time of war or peace, has always been the ideal breeding ground for dictatorships. Democracies, on the other hand, were far more likely to thrive and expand when there was enough to go round. It is all too obvious that the ecological constraints which, whether we like it or not, will force us into a Century of the Environment, would be an ideal pretext for states, groups of states or even multinational corporations to establish some kind of ecotyranny.

Dictatorships have always had (or obtained through manipulation) a popular or moral excuse to legitimise their ascent to power. The centuries described in the first chapter as characterised by religious wars, principalities and nation states offer plenty of evidence for this. The present century is the first for a long time in which the rejection of totalitarianism has been elevated to a moral principle, but this has been the case only because ever more material wealth was available for distribution. In enjoying this pleasant new situation, our economic culture became oblivious to the limits of this strategy and kept promising ever higher levels of consumption. It will be a considerable feat indeed to preserve and maintain the pleasant and anti-totalitarian principles of individual freedom, democracy and justice at a time when there will be less material wealth to go around.

Inevitably, the state will be tempted to set quota on limited resources, to control every detail of the economy and to regulate what, 'for the sake of the environment', its citizens may or may not do. Experts on 'the quality of life' could define exactly which needs are allowed to be satisfied. Environmental administration could well develop into a mega-machine (according to Lewis Mumford). An ecological Brave New World may be in sight. And as the environmental crisis is worldwide, it could, in theory, very easily lead to a state of worldwide agreement on totalitarian ecological principles. The escape route of emigration would be blocked.

How can ecotyranny be prevented? Three policies will have to be pursued.

Firstly, ecological transformation should start in good time, while there is still plenty of room for manoeuvre and before the urgency of the situation subordinates all other considerations. Secondly, we should promote those environmental policy instruments which besides being effective leave much room for individual response, and we should refuse those which are repressive. Finally, we should start to concern ourselves now with liberties which will have to be protected once the exigencies of the Century of the Environment become everyday realities.

The first of these two policies were the subject of this book. The third explores new territory. Which kind of liberties and rights will need to be developed and protected? I can only offer a few preliminary suggestions.

Human rights must not be eroded; on the contrary, they should be further developed to include the rights of future generations (Brown-Weiss, 1989) and the explicit right to a healthy environment.

Ecological restrictions should be expressed in general terms (e.g. in prices of generic commodities) rather than in detailed rules and regulations. The subsidiarity principle, which states that higher authority should only act when called on to do so by a subordinate level, should be respected as a cornerstone of government policy. Self-reliance should be promoted. Indeed, whole villages, districts and regions should be protected from excessive state intervention or economic dependence; this will even imply limitations on trade. Patterns of work and time-budgets should increasingly reflect individual choice. The legal system should further develop to protect citizens and small economic units against repression by political and economic superpowers. Anti-uniformity laws ought to be developed for products, processes, landscapes, education and so on.

At first glance all this may appear very idealistic. People today are used to the harsh reality of constantly competing for market shares, export markets and technological advantage. Fine words about subsidiarity principles and the right of future generations will not stop firms being taken over by Japanese banks or surrendering to the aggressive marketing of Asian export companies. If such lofty principles are to be adopted, then they should preferably be adopted worldwide, but someone has to make a start. It may turn out that there is a similarity with the position of human rights in the past: at first glance those states look stronger which ignore and repress them, but over time they lose out because they lack social coherence and innovation. The 'Four Tigers' and China are already aware of the ecological crisis building up in their confines and are becoming more open to adopting stringent environmental policy measures.

Education and Culture

Culture and education change over the centuries and also leave their stamp on the centuries. We take many of our values from the traditions of thought within our culture. As we now approach the century of the environment and want to develop new models of prosperity, we will have to push our culture a stage further and direct the education system towards the new tasks ahead.

That is easier said than done. The education system today is not at all prepared for the new task, either in terms of structure or of content. It is based on school subjects and disciplines, and directed principally towards the acquisition of qualifications. Testability and objective measurement of achievement rank high. Education for responsibility is certainly an avowed aim, but the everyday reality and pressure of high school life (on the European continent) allow little time in which to put this into practice. Ecology, if it forms part of the curriculum, comes under the headings of biology and geography, but learning about wetland ecology and mineralogy is not sufficient to meet the challenges presented by the environmental crisis. Whole subjects need to be redefined, co-operation between teachers of different subjects needs to be made easier, and teacher-training (including on-the-job training) completely revised.

Moreover, career structures of every kind need to be completely overhauled, as does the level of academic understanding and the *modus operandi* of educational establishments. The ecological restructuring of businesses, households and local authorities could mean an exciting new role for adult education. There is an inherent creative tension between the international nature of the environmental crisis and its visible effects locally. In schools, no subject will remain unaffected, except perhaps sport, music and the classics.

Irritating and unsettling as another set of reforms might be, it would nevertheless have one big advantage over earlier educational reforms: this time the pupils themselves would be involved, rather than standing on the sidelines. It is their future, after all, which is at stake.

We would also need a new view of civilisation and culture in the Century of the Environment. The natural world, plants and animals must come to be valued in their own right — as they already are in many religions. They must cease to be seen simply as commodities.

As a sign of a new culture, which could become vital to our survival in the new century, there might arise a credo of diversity, of ecological sustainability, of long-term thinking, of a slower pace of life, of error-friendliness (cf. Chapter 15), of a consciousness of boundaries (yet with a sense of world-wide citizenship), of things beyond financial worth, of self-reliance, of communal solidarity and a sense of the value of the commons. Both our values and the monetary value of goods and services would undergo a fundamental change, and many items and activities would be removed completely from the sphere of financial transaction.

All this, however, is in no way a vision of a return to the Middle Ages or the Stone Age. The experience of advanced technology, prosperity, global and cosmic horizons will not be lost.

As this book draws to a close, it offers up a new cultural direction for humanity, a debt that Europe surely owes to the world. The Earth deserves to be recognised as our common home. As every culture knows, to destroy one's own home is folly indeed.

Bibliography

Agarwal, Anil and Surita Narain. 1991. 'Global Warming in an Unequal World', *International Journal of Sustainable Development*, Vol. 1, pp. 98–104.

Alcamo, Joseph (Ed). 1992. *Fair Wind, Foul Wind: Coping With Crisis in Eastern Europe's Environment*. Laxenburg (Austria): IIASA.

Anderson, Kym and Richard Blackhurst. 1992. *The Greening of World Trade Issues*. New York: Harvester Wheatsheaf.

Anon. 1990. 'Green taxes: Where there's the muck there's the brass. Many European countries are looking into the idea of using taxes to encourage greener behaviour.' *The Economist*, 17 March 1990. pp. 28-31.

Arendt, Hannah. 1956. Vita Activa. Stuttgart: Kohlhammer.

Arizpe, Lourdes. 1988. 'Culture in International Development.' *Journal of the Society for International Development*, Vol. 3, pp. 17–19.

Ayres, Rubert U. 1991. *Eco-Restructuring*. Laxenburg (Austria): IIASA.

Bacon, Francis. 1952. Novum Organum. Advancement of learning. Chicago: *Encyclopedia Britannica*.

Baldock, David et al. 1986. *Agriculture and Environment: Management Agreements in Four Countries of the European Communities*. Luxembourg: EC Publications.

Baldock, David et al. 1989. *Reform of the Structural Fund — An Environmental Briefing*. London: World Wildlife Fund UK.

Ballard, Charles L. and Steven G. Medema. 1992. 'The Marginal Efficiency Effects of Taxes and Subsidies' in *The Presence of Externalites: A Computational General Equilibrium Approach*. Department of Economics, Michigan State University. East Lansing MI:

Bandyopadhyay, Jayanta and Vandana Shiva. 1987. 'Chipko: Rekindling India's Forest Culture.' *Ecologist*, Vol. 17, pp. 26-34.

Banuri, Tariq. 1993. 'The Landscape of Diplomatic Conflicts' in Wolfgang Sachs (ed.), *Global Ecology*. London. Zed Books Ltd.

Barde, Jean Philippe and David Pearce. 1991. *Valuing the Environment*. London: Earthscan.

Barney, Jim et al. 1980. *The Global 2000 Report to President Carter*. Harmondworth: Penguin.

Bateson, Gregory. 1979. *Mind and Nature. A Necessary Unity*. New York: E.P. Dutton.

Baumol, William J. and Wallace E. Oates. 1979, 1988. *The Theory of Environmental Policy*. Cambridge: Cambridge University Press.

BDI. 1990. [German Industry Federation]. *Die Zukunft unserer Umwelt*. Brochure. Köln: BDI.

Bello, Walden. 1989. *Brave New Third World? Strategies for Survival in the Global Economy*. San Francisco: Institute for Food and Development.

Benedick, Richard Eliot. 1991. *Ozone Diplomacy. New Directions in Safeguarding the Planet*. Cambridge (USA): Harvard University Press.

Bergmann, Eckehard and Dieter Ewringmann. 1989. *Ökosteuern, Entwicklung, Ansatzpunkte und Bewertung*, in Hans Nutzinger and Angelika Zahrnt. *Umweltsteuern — Abgaben in der Diskussion*. Karlsruhe: C.F. Müller.

Berner, Robert A. and A. C. Lasaga. 1989. 'Modelling the geochemical carbon cycle.' *Scientific American*, March 1989, pp. 54-61.

Binswanger, Hans Christoph et al. 1983. *Arbeit ohne Umweltzerstörung*. Frankfurt: Fischer.

Bleischwitz, Raimund and Helmut Schütz. 1992. *Unser trügerischer Wohlstand. Ein Beitrag zu einer deutschen Ökobilanz*. Wuppertal: Wuppertal-Institute for Climate, Environment and Energy.

Bohm, David. 1980. *Wholeness and the Implicate Order*. London: Routledge & Kegan Paul.

Bonus, Holger. 1984. *Marktwirtschaftliche Konzepte im Umweltschutz*. Stuttgart: Ulmer.

Boorstin, Daniel J. 1983. *The Discoverers*. New York: Random House.

Brown, Lester et al. 1989-92. *State of the World 1988, 1989*, etc., respectively. New York: W.W. Norton.

Brown-Weiss, Edith. 1989. *In Fairness to Future Generations: International Law, Common Patrimony and Intergenerational Equity*. Tokyo: UNU; Dobbs Ferry NY: Transnational Publishers.

Button, Kenneth J. and David W. Pearce. 1989. *Improving the Urban Environment: How to Adjust National and Local Government Policy for Sustainable Urban Growth*. Oxford: Oxford University Press.

Byrne, John, and Daniel Rich (Eds). 1992. *Energy and Environment: The Policy Challenge*. New Brunswick NJ: Transaction Publications.

Cairncross, Frances. 1991. *Costing the Earth: What Governments Must Do; What Consumers Need to Know; How Business Can Profit*. London: The Economist Publications.

Capra, Fritjof. 1982. *The Turning Point: Science, Society, and the Rising Culture*. New York: Simon and Schuster.

Carson, Rachel. 1962. *Silent Spring*. Boston: Houghton & Mifflin.

Carson, Walter H. (Ed). 1990. *The Global Economy Handbook*. Boston: Beacon Press.

Cecchini, Paolo et al. 1988. *The European Challenge: 1992. The Benefits of a Single Market*. Aldershot: Gower.

Clark, Mary E. 1989. *Ariadne's Thread: The Search for New Modes of Thinking*. New York: St. Martin's Press.

Cline, William R. 1992. *Global Warming: The Benefits of Emission Abatement*. Paris: OECD.

Club of Rome. 1991. *The First Global Revolution*, edited by Alexander King. New York: Pantheon.

Commission of the European Communities. 1985. *Perspectives for the Common Agriculture Policy*. COM(85) 333 final, 15 July 1985. Brussels: EC Commission.

Commission of the European Communities. 1985. *White Paper on the completion of the Internal Market*. Communication from the Commission to the European Council. COM(85) 310.

Commission of the European Communities. 1991. *Proposal for a Council Directive introducing a tax on carbon dioxide emissions and energy*; COM(92) 226 final, of 2 June 1992. Brussels: EC Commission.

Commission of the European Communities, [DG VII]. 1992. *A Community Strategy for Sustainable Mobility. Green Paper on the Impacts of Transport on the Environment*. COM (92) 46 final, 6 April 1992. Brussels: EC Commission.

Commission of the European Communities. 1992. *Towards Sustainability. A European Community Programme of Policy and Action in Relation to the Environment and Sustainable Development*. Brussels: EC Commission.

Commoner, Barry. 1990. *Making Peace with the Planet*. New York: Pantheon Books.

Cropper, Maureen L. and Wallace E. Oates. 1992. 'Environmental Economics: A Survey.' *Journal of Economic Literature*, Vol. 30, pp. 675–740.

Daly, Herman. 1991. *Steady-State Economics*. 2nd. ed. Washington: Island Press.

Daly, Herman and John B. Cobb. 1989. *For the Common Good: Redirecting the Economy Toward Community, the Environment and a Sustainable Future*. Boston: Beacon Press.

De Fries, Ruth and Thomas Malone (Eds). 1989. *Global Change and Our Common Future*. Papers from a forum. Washington: National Academy Press.

De la Court, Thijs. 1990. *Beyond Brundtland: Green Development*. London and Atlantic Highlands NJ: Zed Books.

Dower, Roger C. and Mary Beth Zimmerman. 1992. *The Right Climate for Carbon Taxes: Creating Economic Incentives to Protect the Atmosphere*. Washington: World Resources Institute.

Drèze, Jean and Amartya Sen. 1989. *Hunger and Public Action*. Oxford: Clarendon.

Drexler, K. Eric and Chris Peterson. 1991. *Unbounding the Future: The Nanotechnology Revolution*. New York: William Morrow.

Dunlap, Riley E. and Angela Mertig (Eds). 1992. *American Environmentalism*. Philadelphia: Taylor & Francis.

Dupuy, Jean-Pierre and Jean Robert. 1977. *La trahison de l'opulence*. Paris: PUF.

Durning, Alan B. 1989. *Poverty and the Environment: Reversing the Downward Spiral*. Washington: Worldwatch Institute.

Durning, Alan Thein. 1992. *How Much Is Enough? The Consumer Society and the Future of the Earth*. New York: W.W. Norton.

Durrell, Lee. 1986. *State of the Ark: An Atlas of Conservation in Action*. New York: Doubleday.

Ehrlich, Paul R. and Anne Ehrlich. 1990. *The Population Explosion*. New York: Simon and Schuster.

Ekins, Paul (Ed). 1986. *The Living Economy: A New Economics in the Making*. London: Routledge & Kegan Paul.

Ekins, Paul. 1992. *A New World Order: Grassroots movements for global change*. London and New York: Routledge.

Elkington, John. 1990. *Green Consumer: A Guide for the Environmentally Aware*. New York: Viking Penguin.

Elkington, John and Tom Burke. 1988. *The Green Capitalists: Industry's Search for Environmental Excellence*. London: Gollancz.

Feyerabend, Paul. 1975. *Against Method. Outline of an anarchistic theory of knowledge.* London: NLB.

Fowler, Cary and Pat Mooney. 1990. *Shattering: Food, Politics, and the loss of Genetic Diversity.* Tucson AZ: University of Arizona Press.

Fox, Michael W. 1992. *Superpigs and Wondercorn: The Brave New World of Biotechnology and Where It All May Lead.* New York: Lyons & Burford.

French, Hilary. 1992. *After the Earth Summit: The Future of Environmental Governance.* Washington: Worldwatch Institute.

Friedman, Milton. 1962. *Capitalism and Freedom.* Chicago: University of Chicago Press.

Fröbel, Folker et al. 1977. *The New International Division of Labour: 1981.* Cambridge: Cambridge University Press.

Fukuyama, Francis. 1991. *The End of History and the Last Man.* New York: Free Press.

Gallopin, Gilberto et al. 1974. *The Limits to Poverty: The Bariloche Report.*

George, Susan. 1992. *The Debt Boomerang.* Boulder CO: Westview.

German Bundestag. 1991. *Protecting the Earth. A status report with recommendations for a new energy policy.* Study Commission of the 11th German Bundestag. Bonn: German Bundestag.

German, Bundestag. 1992. *Climate Change — a threat to global development.* Bonn: Economica Verlag.

Giarini, Orio and Walter R. Stahel. 1989. *The Limits to Certainty: Facing Risks in the New Service Economy.* Dordrecht and Boston: Kluwer Academic.

Glaeser, Bernhard (Ed). 1984. *Ecodevelopment: Concepts, Projects, Strategies.* Oxford and New York: Pergamon Press.

Global 2000 Report: see Barney et al. 1980.

Global Tomorrow Coalition (Walter H. Corson, Ed). 1990. *The Global Ecology Handbook: What You Can Do About the Environmental Crisis.* Boston: Beacon Press.

Goldemberg, José, et al. 1987. *Energy for a Sustainable World.* Washington: World Resources Institute.

Goldsmith, Edward et al. 1992. *The Future of Progress: Reflections on Environment and Development.* London: The International Society for Ecology and Culture.

Goldsmith, Edward and Nicholas Hildyard. 1985-1989. *The Social and Environmental Effects of Large Dams.* 3 Vols. Camelford, Cornwall: Ecosystems.

Goodland, Robert and Herman Daly. 1992. *Ten Reasons Why Northern Income Growth Is Not the Solution to Southern Poverty.* Washington: Environment Department, World Bank.

Goodland, Robert, et al. 1991. *Environmentally Sustainable Economic Development: Building on Brundtland.* Paper No. 46. Washington: Environment Department, World Bank.

Gore, Al. 1992. *Earth in the Balance: Ecology and the Human Spirit.* Boston: Houghton Mifflin.

Gould, Jay M. and Benjamin Goldman. 1990. *Deadly Deceit: Low-Level Radiation, High Level Cover-Up.* New York: Four Walls Eight Windows.

Gribbin, John. 1990. *Hothouse Earth: The Greenhouse Effect and Gaia*. London: Bantam Press; New York: Grove Weidenfeld.

Grupp, Hariolf. 1986. 'Die sozialen Kosten des Verkehrs'. *Verkehr und Technik* Vol. 9/10.

Häfele, Wolf et al. 1981. *Energy in a Finite World*. Cambridge, (USA): Ballinger.

Hahn, Robert and Gordon Hester. 'Where did all the markets go? An analysis of EPA's emission trading program'. *Yale Journal of Regulation* Vol. 6, pp. 109-153.

Haigh, Nigel. 1989. *EEC Environmental Policy and Britain*. Harlow Mdx: Longman.

————. 1991. *Manual of Environmental Policy: the EC and Britain* (continuously updated). Harlow, Essex: Longman.

————. 1992. *The EC and Integrated Environmental Policy*. London: IEEP.

Hansmeyer, Karl Heinrich, and Hans Karl Schneider. 1989. *Zur Fortentwicklung der Umweltpolitik unter marktsteuernden Aspekten*.* Cologne: Finanzwissenschaftliches Institut.

Hardin, Garrett and J. Baden. 1980. *Managing the Commons*. San Francisco: Freeman.

Hartman, Chester and Pedro Vilanova (eds.). 1992. *Paradigms Lost: The Post Cold War Era*. London and Concorde, MA: Pluto Press.

Helm, John L. (Ed). 1990. *Energy Production, Consumption, and Consequences*. Washington: National Academy Press.

Henderson, Hazel. 1981. *The Politics of the Solar Age*. New York: Doubleday.

Hennicke, Peter et al. 1985. *Die Energiewende ist möglich*. Frankfurt: Fischer.

Herrera, Amilcar O. (Ed). 1976. *Catastrophe or New Society? A Latin American World Model*. Ottawa: IDRC.

Hohmann, Harald (Ed.). 1992. *Basic Documents of International Environmental Law*. 3 Vols. London: Graham & Trotman.

Hotelling, Harold. 1931. 'The Economics of Exhaustible Resources'. *Journal of Political Economy*, Vol. 39, pp. 137–175.

Huber, Joseph. 1991. *Unternehmen Umwelt. Weichenstellungen für eine ökologische Marktwirtschaft*. Frankfurt: Fischer.

Hueting, Roefie et al. 1991. *Methodology of Sustainable National Income*. Report of the Netherlands Central Bureau of Statistics. Voorburg: Netherlands. Also available (1992) from WWF International. Gland: Switzerland.

Huppes, Gjalt, et al. 1992. *New Market Oriented Instruments for European Environmental Policies*. London: Graham & Trotman.

Hurrell, Andrew and Benedict Kingsbury (Eds). 1992. *The International Politics of the Environment*. Oxford: Clarendon.

Hynes, Patricia. 1989. *The Recurring Silent Spring*. Elmsford NY: Pergamon.

Illich, Ivan. 1972. *Tools for Conviviality*. New York: Harper & Row.

————. 1981. *Shadow Work*. London: Marion Boyars.

Intergovernmental Panel on Climate Change. 1991. *Climate Change: The IPCC Response Strategies*. Washington: Island CA.

————. 1992. Supplement Report. Geneva: IPCC Secretariat.

Intergovernmental Panel on Climate Change (J.T. Houghton, et al., Eds.). 1990. *Climate Change: The IPCC Scientific Assessment*. Washington: Island CA.

International Chamber of Commerce. 1989. *Environmental Auditing.* Paris: ICC.
————. 1991. *Business Charter for Sustainable Development.* Paris: ICC.
International Chamber of Commerce, Commission on Taxation. 1992. *The Use of Economic and Fiscal Instruments in Environmental Policy.* Position paper, adopted in May 1992. Paris: ICC.
IUCN, UNEP, WWF. 1991. *Caring For the Earth: A Strategy For Sustainable Living.* Gland (Switzerland) and Nairobi: WWF.

Jacob, François. 1970. *La logique du vivant: Une histoire de l'hérédité.* Paris: Gallimard.
Jäger, Jill. 1988. *Developing Policies for Responding to Climate Change.* Summary of Villach and Bellagio discussions and recommendations. Stockholm: Beijer Institute (Stockholm Environment Institute).
Jänicke, Martin et al. 1989. 'Structural Change and Environmental Impact. Empirical Evidence on 31 Countries in East and West.' *Intereconomics* Vol. 24, pp. 24–34.
Janzen, Daniel. 1989. 'The Death of Birth.' Lead Article of *Time Magazine* No. 1, 1 January 1989.
Jesinghaus, Jochen. 1988. 'Instrumente der Umweltpolitik. Vergleich Japan/ Bundesrepublik.' *Spektrum der Wissenschaft,* February 1988, pp. 44-45.
Jochem, Eberhard. 1992. 'Potentials to Reduce Greenhouse-Gas Emissions by Rational Energy Use and Structural Changes' in G.I. Pearman (Ed). *Limiting the Greenhouse Effect: Controlling Carbon Dioxide Emissions.* Chichester NY: Wiley.
Johnson, Stanley and Guy Corcelle. 1989. *The Environmental Policy of the European Communities.* London: Graham & Trotman.
Johannson, Thomas, B. Bodland, R. H. Williams (eds.). 1989. *Electricity—Efficient End Use and New Generation Technologies and their Planning Implications.* Lund: Lund University Press.
Jonas, Hans. 1985. *The Imperative of Responsibility: In search of an Ethics for the Technological Age.* Chicago: University of Chicago Press.
Jouzel, J. et al. 1987. 'Vostok ice core: A continuous isotope temperature record over the last climatic cycle (160 000 years).' *Nature,* 329; pp. 403-408.

Kapp, K. William. 1950. *The Social Costs of Private Enterprise.* Cambridge, (USA): Harvard University Press.
Kharbanda, O.P and E.A. Stallworthy. 1990. *Waste Management: Towards a Sustainable Society.* Westport CT: Auburn House /Greenwood Press.
Khor, Martin. 1992. 'Development, Trade and the Environment: A Third World Perspective' in Edward Goldsmith et al. (Eds). *The Future of Progress.* Clifton, Bristol: The International Society for Ecology and Culture.
Krämer, Ludwig. 1991. *Umweltrecht der EWG.* Baden-Baden: Nomos.
Krause, Florentin et al. 1980. *Energie-Wende.* Frankfurt: Fischer.
Kuhn, Thomas. 1962. *The Structure of Scientific Revolutions.* Chicago: Chicago University Press.
Lappé, Frances Moore and Joseph Collins. 1977. *Food First: Beyond the Myth of Scarcity.* Boston: Houghton Mifflin.

Leipert, Christian. 1989. Short version in English: 'Social costs of the economic process: the example of defensive expenditures.' *J Interdisc. Economics* Vol. 3, pp. 27–46.

Leiss, William. 1979. *The Limits to Satisfaction*. Toronto: University of Toronto Press.

Lenssen, Nicholas. 1991. *Nuclear Waste: The Problem That Won't Go Away*. Worldwatch Paper 106. Washington: Worldwatch Institute.

Leventhal, Paul L. and Milton M. Hoenig. 1986. *Nuclear Installations and Potential Risks. Hidden Danger: Risks of Nuclear Terrorism*. Paper presented to a Council of Europe Hearing, Paris, 6 January 1987, Document No. AS/AUD/RAD (38) 12, dated 30 December 1986.

Lewis, Martin W. 1992. *Green Delusions: An Environmentalist Critique of Radical Environmentalism*. Durham NC: Duke University Press.

Liedke, Gerhard. 1972. 'Von der Ausbeutung zur Kooperation. Theologisch-philosophische Überlegungen zum Problem des Umweltschutzes' in E.U. von Weizsäcker (Ed). *Humanökologie und Umweltschutz*. Stuttgart: Klett.

Lorius, Claude et al. 1985. 'A 150 000 year climatic record from Antarctic ice.' *Nature*, 316, pp. 591–596.

Lovejoy, Thomas. 1989. 'A Projection of Species Extinction.' in Jim Barney et al. (Eds). *The Global 2000 Report to the President*. Harmondsworth: Penguin.

Lovelock, James. 1979. *Gaia: A New Look at Life on Earth*. Oxford: Oxford University Press.

Lovins, Amory. 1977. *Soft Energy Paths*. Harmondsworth: Penguin.

Lovins, Amory and L. Hunter Lovins. 1990. *Least-Cost Climatic Stabilization*. Old Snowmass CO: Rocky Mountain Institute. Rpt. in *Annual Review of Energy*, Vol. 16.

Lux, Kenneth. 1990. *Adam Smith's Mistake: How a Moral Philosopher Invented Economics and Ended Morality*. Boston: Shambala.

MacKenzie, James J. et al. 1992. *The Going Rate: What it Really Costs to Drive*. Washington: World Resources Institute.

MacNeill, Jim, et al. 1991. *Beyond Interdependence. The Meshing of the World's Economy and the Earth's Ecology*. Oxford and New York: Oxford University Press.

Maddox, John. 1972. *The Doomsday Syndrome*. New York: McGraw-Hill.

Maier-Rigaud, Gerhard. 1988. *Umweltpolitik in der Offenen Gesellschaft*. Opladen: Westdeutscher Verlag.

Markl, Hubert. 1989. 'Natur als Kulturaufgabe.' in Lutz Franke (Ed). *Wir haben nur eine Erde*. Darmstadt: Wiss. Buchgesellschaft.

———. 1989. *Wissenschaft zur Rede gestellt*. Munich: Piper.

Martinez-Alier, Juan with Klaus Schlüpmann. 1987. (Paperback: 1990) *Ecological Economics, Energy, Environment and Society*. Oxford: Basil Blackwell.

Maturana, Humberto R. and Francisco J. Varela. 1992. *The Tree of Knowledge: The Biological Roots of Human Understanding*. Rev. ed. Boston: Shambala.

McNeely, Jeffrey. 1988. *Economics and Biological Diversity: Developing and Using Economic Incentives to Conserve Biological Resources*. Gland (Switzerland): IUCN.

Meadows, Donella et al. 1972. *The Limits To Growth*. Report to the Club of Rome. New York: Universe Books.

——. 1992. *Beyond the Limits: Confronting Global Collapse, Envisioning a Sustainable Future*. Post Mills VT: Chelsea Green.

Merchant, Carolyn. 1980. *The Death of Nature: Women, Ecology and the Scientific Revolution*. San Francisco: Harper & Row.

Mesarovic, Mihailo D. and Eduard Pestel. 1975. *Mankind at the Turning Point*. The Second Report to the Club of Rome. London: Hutchinson.

Meyer-Abich, Klaus Michael. 1986. *Wege zum Frieden mit der Natur*. Munich: Hanser.

Meyer-Abich, Klaus Michael and Dieter Birnbacher. 1979. *Was braucht der Mensch, um glücklich zu sein?* Munich: Beck.

Mikesell, Raymond F. and Lawrence F. Williams. 1992. *International Banks and the Environment. From Growth to Sustainability: An Unfinished Agenda*. San Francisco: Sierra Club Books.

Milbrath, Lester. 1989. *Envisioning A Sustainable Society: Learning Our Way Out*. Albany: State University of New York Press.

Milgram, Stanley. 1974. *Obedience to Authority: An Experimental View*. London: Tavistock.

Mintzer, Irving M. (Ed). 1992. *Confronting Climate Change: Risks, Implications and Responses*. Cambridge: Cambridge University Press.

Mitter, Swasti. 1986. 'Toys for the Boys.' in *Journal of the Society for International Development*, Vol. 3, pp. 66-68.

Moll, Peter. 1991. *From Scarcity to Sustainability. Futures Studies and the Environment: the Role of the Club of Rome*. Frankfurt and New York: Peter Lang.

Mukerjee, Radhakamal. 1967. *The Economic History of India: 1600–1800*. Allahabad: Kitab Mahal.

Müller, A.M. Klaus. 1977. 'Geschöpflichkeitsdefizite in Naturwissenschaft und Theologie,' in Johannes Anderegg (Ed). *Wissenschaft und Wirklichkeit*. Göttingen: Vandenhoeck & Ruprecht.

Müller, Edda. 1986. *Innenwelt der Umweltpolitik*. Opladen: Westdeutscher Verlag.

Mumford, Lewis. 1970. *The Culture of Cities*. New York: Harcourt.

Myers, Norman. 1984. *The Primary Source: Tropical Forests and Our Future*. New York: W.W. Norton.

National Academy of Science. 1991. *Policy Implications of Greenhouse Warming*. Washington: National Academy Press.

Nisbet, Evan G. 1991. *Leaving Eden — To Protect and Manage the Earth*. Cambridge: Cambridge University Press.

Norberg-Hodge, Helena and Peter Goering (Principal Eds). 1992. *The Future of Progress*. See Goldsmith, Edward et al. 1992.

Nordhaus, William D. 1991. 'To Slow or Not to Slow: The Economics of the Greenhouse Effect.' *The Economic Journal*, Vol. 101, pp. 920-937.

Oates, Wallace E. 1988. 'Should Pollution Be Taxed?' *Economic Impact,* 4/88, pp. 27-31.

OECD. 1991. *State of the Environment.* Paris: OECD Publications.

Ogata, Shijuro et al. 1989. *International Financial Integration: The Policy Challenges.* New York: The Trilateral Commission.

Ohnesorge, F.K. 1989. 'Die Sicht der Toxikologie' Ernst U. von Weizsäcker (Ed). *Gutes Trinkwasser — wie schützen?* Karlsruhe: C.F. Müller.

Oppenheimer, Michael and Robert H. Boyle. 1990. *Dead Heat: The Race Against the Greenhouse Effect.* New York: Basic Books.

Opschoor, Johannes B. and Hans Vos. 1989. *The Application of Economic Instruments for Environmental Protection in OECD Member Countries.* Paris: OECD Publications.

Pearce, David. 1991. 'The Role of Carbon Taxes in Adjusting to Global Warming.' *The Economic Journal* Vol. 101, pp. 938-948

Paehlke, Robert C. 1989. *Environmentalism and the Future of Progressive Politics.* New Haven CT: Yale University Press.

Pearce, David and R. Kerry Turner. 1990. *Economics of Natural Resources and the Environment.* Hemel Hempstead: Harvester Wheatsheaf.

Pearce, David, et al. 1989. *Blueprint for a Green Economy.* London: Earthscan.

Perrow, Charles. 1984. *Normal Accidents: Living With High-Risk Technologies.* New York: Basic Books.

Peters, Rob and Thomas Lovejoy (Eds). 1992. *Global Warming and Biodiversity.* New Haven: Yale University Press.

Picht, Georg. 1989. 'Die Wertordnung der humanen Welt' in Lutz Franke (Ed). *Wir haben nur eine Erde.* Darmstadt: Wiss. Buchgesellschaft.

Pigou, Arthur Cecil. 1920. *The Economics of Welfare.* London: Macmillan.

Polanyi, Karl. 1957. *The Great Transformation: The Political and Economic Origins of Our Time.* Boston: Beacon Press.

Pollock, Cynthia. 1986. *Decommissioning: Nuclear Power's Missing Link.* Washington: Worldwatch Institute.

Porter, Gareth and Janet Welsh Brown. 1992. *Global Environmental Politics.* Boulder CO: Westview Press.

Priebe, Hermann. 1988. *Die subventionierte Unvernunft.* 3rd ed. Berlin: Siedler.

Prigogine, Ilya. 1979. *From Being To Becoming: Time and Complexity in the Physical Sciences.* New York: Freeman.

Prognos. 1987. (P. Bullinger, et al., Authors). *Umweltwirkungen des Eisenbahnverkehrs unter besonderer Berücksichtigung des Hochgeschwindigkeitsverkehrs.* Basel: Prognos AG.

Rechsteiner, Rudolf. 1992. 'Sind hohe Energiepreise volkswirtschaftlich ungesund?' Manuscript for the Wuppertal Institute for Climate, Environment and Energy.

Renner, Michael. 1991. *Jobs in a Sustainable Economy.* Washington: Worldwatch Institute.

Repetto, Robert, et al. 1992. *Green Fees: How a Tax Shift Can Work for the Environment and the Economy.* Washington: World Resources Institute.

Repetto, Robert, et al. 1987. *Natural Resource Accounting for Indonesia.* Washington: World Resources Institute.

Rifkin, Jeremy. 1990. *Entropy: Into the Greenhouse World*. New York: Bantam Books.

Robertson, James. 1990. *Future Wealth*. London: Cassell; New York: Bootstrap.

Roszak, Theodore. 1992. *The Voice of the Earth*. New York: Simon & Schuster.

Rothkrug, Paul and Robert L. Olson. 1992. *Mending the Earth: A World for Our Grandchildren*. Berkeley: North Atlantic Books.

Ruttan, Vernon W. 1992. *Sustainable Agriculture and the Environment: Perspectives on Growth and Constraints*. Boulder CO: Westview.

Ryan, John C. 1992. *Life Support: Conserving Biological Diversity*. Washington: Worldwatch Institute.

Sabet, Hafez. 1992. *Die Schuld des Nordens: Der 50-Billionen-Coup*. Frankfurt: Horizonte Verlag.

Sachs, Wolfgang (Ed). 1992. *The Development Dictionary: A Guide to Knowledge as Power*. London: Zed Books.

Sachs, Wolfgang (Ed). 1993. *Global Ecology: A New Arena of Political Conflict*. London: Zed Books.

Sagan, Carl and Richard Turco. 1990. *A Path Where No Man Thought: Nuclear Winter and the End of the Arms Race*. New York: Random House.

Sahlins, Marshall. 1972. *Stone Age Economics*. Hawthorne NY: Aldine de Gruyter.

Sale, Kirkpatrick. 1991. *The Conquest of Paradise: Christopher Columbus and the Columbian Legacy*. London: Hodder & Stoughton.

Salomon, Jean Jacques. 1974. 'Forschung und die Verantwortung des Wissenschaftlers in unserer Gesellschaft' in Friedrich Cramer (Ed). *Forscher zwischen Wissen und Gewissen*. Berlin: J. Springer.

Sasson, A. (Ed). 1991. Biotechnology in Developing Countries, Present and Future. Paris: UNESCO.

Sand, Peter H. 1990. *Lessons Learned in Global Environmental Governance*. Washington: World Resources Institute.

Schipper, Lee and Stephen Meyers et al. 1992. *World Energy: Building a Sustainable Future*. Stockholm: Stockholm Environment Institute.

Schipper, Lee and Stephen Meyers et al. (Eds). 1992. *Energy Efficiency and Human Activity: Past Trends, Future Prospects*. Cambridge: Cambridge University Press.

Schmidheiny, Stephan with the Business Council for Sustainable Development. 1992. *Changing Course: A Global Business Perspective on Development and the Environment*. Cambridge (USA): MIT Press.

Schmidt-Bleek, Friedrich. 1994. *Wieviel Erde braucht der Mensch?* Basel: Birkhäuser.

Schmidt-Bleek, Friedrich and Heinrich Wohlmeyer (Eds). 1991. *Trade and the Environment*. Laxenburg (Austria): IIASA.

Schneider, Stephen H. 1989. *Global Warming: Are We Entering the Greenhouse Century?* San Francisco: Sierra Club Books.

Seifert, Eberhard K. and Juan Martinez-Alier (Eds). 1992. *Entropy and Bioeconomics*. Proceedings of the 1st International EABS Conference. Milan: Nagard.

Shiva, Vandana. 1989. *Staying Alive: Women, Ecology and Development*. London. Zed Books.

Simon, Julian L. 1989. *Population Matters: People, Resources, Environment, and Immigration*. New Brunswick NJ: Transaction Publications.

Slesser, Malcolm. 1972. *Politics of the Environment*. London: George Allen & Unwin.

Smart, Bruce (Ed). 1992. *Beyond Compliance: A New Industry View of the Environment*. Washington: World Resources Institute.

Smith, Adam. 1776. *An Inquiry into the Nature and Causes of the Wealth of Nations*. New edition Edwin Cannan (Ed). New York: Modern Library.

Snow, C.P. 1969. *The Two Cultures and a Second Look: An expanded version of the Two Cultures and the Scientific Revolution*. Cambridge: Cambridge University Press.

Soto, Alvaro (Executive Ed) et al. 1992. *For Earth's Sake*: A Report from the Commission on Developing Countries and Global Change. Ottawa: IDRC.

Speth, James Gustave. 1990. *The Greening of Technology*. Washington: World Resources Institute.

SRU. 1985. *Umweltprobleme der Landwirtschaft*. Stuttgart: Kohlhammer.

Starke, Linda. 1990. *Signs of Hope: Working Towards Our Common Future*. Oxford and New York: Oxford University Press.

Stern, Paul C. et al. (Eds). 1992. *Global Environmental Change: Understanding the Human Dimensions*. Washington: National Academy Press.

Stigliani, William. 1988. *Changes in valued capacities of soils and sediments as indicators of non-linear and time-delayed environmental effects*. Laxenburg (Austria): IIASA.

Stren, Richard, et al. 1992. *Sustainable Cities: Urbanization and the Environment in International Perspective*. Boulder CO: Westview Press.

Sukopp, Herbert, and Ulrich Hampicke. 1985. 'Ökologische und ökonomische Betrachtungen zu den Folgen des Ausfalls einzelner Pflanzenarten und gesellschaften.' *Schriften des Deutschen Rats für Landespflege* Vol. 46, pp. 595-608.

Swanson, Timothy M. and Edward B. Barbier (Eds). 1992. *Economics for the Wilds*. London: Earthscan.

Svedin, Uno. 1991. 'The Contextual Features of the Economy- Ecology Dialogue' in Carl Folke and Tomas Kåberger (Eds). *Linking the Natural Environment and the Economy*. Essays from the Eco-Eco Group. Dordrecht: Kluwer Academic.

Taylor, Ann. 1992. *Choosing Our Future: A Practical Politics of the Environment*. London: Routledge.

Teufel, Dieter et al. 1986. Externkosten des Autoverkehrs. UPI-Bericht Nr. 15. Heidelberg: Umwelt-und Prognoseinstitut.

Tiedje, James M. et al. 1989. 'The planned introduction into the environment of genetically engineered organisms. Ecological considerations and recommendations.' *Ecology* 70, pp. 298-315.

Timberlake, Lloyd. 1984. *Natural Disasters — Acts of God or Acts of Man?* London: Earthscan.

Tisdell, Clement A. 1991. *Economics of Environmental Conservation: Economics for Environmental and Ecological Management*. Amsterdam: Elsevier.

Tolba, Mostafa K. 1992. *Saving Our Planet: Challenges and Hopes*. London and New York: Chapman & Hall.

Trzyna, Thaddeus C. and Roberta Childers. 1992. *World Directory of Environmental Organizations*. Sacramento: Institute of Public Affairs.

Tsuru, Shigeto and Helmut Weidner. 1985. *Ein Modell für uns? Japanische Umweltpolitik*. Köln: Kiepenheuer & Witsch.

Twidell, John and Tony Weir. 1990. *Renewable Energy Resources*. London: Chapman & Hall.

Umweltbericht 1990. (Environment report by the Federal Environment Minister), 7 volumes. Bonn: Bundesminister für Umwelt, Naturschutz und Reaktorsicherheit.

Umweltbundesamt, 1989. Daten zur Umwelt 1988/1989. Berlin: Fed. Envir. Office.

UN. 1992. *United Nations Framework Convention on Climate Change*. Annex I to the Report of the Intergovernmental Negotiating Committee. A/AC.237/18 (Part II)/Add.1. New York: UN.

UNCED. 1992. *The Global Partnership for Environment and Development: A Guide to Agenda 21*. New York: UN Publications.

UNCED. 1992. *Report of the UN Conference on Environment and Development*. A/CONF/151/26. 5 Vols. New York: UN.

UNEP. 1985. *Environmental Refugees*. Nairobi: UNEP.

UNEP. 1992. *Convention on Biological Diversity*. 5 June 1992. Na. 92–7807. Nairobi: UNEP.

UNFPA. 1992. *World Population Report 1992*. New York: UN.

VCS. 1989. *Der Ökobonus. Vorschläge zur Realisierung des Modells*. Herzogenbuchsee (Switzerland).

Verbruggen, H. 1991. 'Contours of a sustainable trade system.' *International Spectator*, Vol. 45, No. 11, November 1991.

Verhoeve, Barbara et al. 1992. Maastricht and the Environment: the implications for the EC's environmental policy of the Treaty on European Union signed at Maastricht on 7 February 1992. London: Institute for European Environmental Policy.

Vester, Frederic. 1990. *Ausfahrt Zukunft*. Munich: Heyne.

Weinschenck, Günther and Rolf Werner. 1989. *Einkommenswirkungen ökologischer Forderungen an die Landwirtschaft*. Frankfurt: Landw. Rentenbank.

Weizsäcker, Carl Friedrich von. 1977. *Der Garten des Menschlichen*. Munich: Hanser.

———. 1992. *Zeit und Wissen*. Munich: Hanser.

Weizsäcker, Christine von. 1992. 'Diverse Notions of Biodiversity,' in Wolfgang Sachs (Ed). *Global Ecology: A New Arena of Political Conflict*. London : Zed Books.

Weizsäcker, Christine von and Ernst U. von Weizsäcker. 1979. 'Recht auf Eigenarbeit statt Pflicht zum Wachstum.' *Scheidewege* Vol. 9, pp. 221–234.

————. 1986. 'Fehlerfreundlichkeit als Evolutionsprinzip.' *Universitas* Vol. 41, pp. 791–799. English version: Ernst and Christine von Weizsäcker. 1987. 'How to Live With Errors? On The Evolutionary Power of Errors.' *World Futures: The Journal of General Evolution* Vol. 23, pp. 225-235.

Weizsäcker, Ernst U. von. 1987. *Not a Miracle Solution, but Steps Towards an Ecological Reform of the Common Agricultural Policy.* Bonn: Institute for European Environmental Policy.

Weizsäcker, Ernst U. von and Jochen Jesinghaus. 1992. *Ecological Tax Reform: A Policy Proposal for Sustainable Development.* A Study prepared for Stephan Schmidheiny. London and Atlantic Highlands NJ: Zed Books.

Weizsäcker, Ernst U. von (Ed). 1986. *Waschen und Gewässerschutz.* Karlsruhe: C.F. Müller.

————.1988. *Gutes Trinkwasser — wie schützen?* Karlsruhe: C.F. Müller.

————.1988. *Weniger Abfall — Gute Entsorgung.* 1991. Karlsruhe: C.F. Müller.

Weizsäcker, Ernst U. von, et al. (Eds). 1983. *New Frontiers in Technology Application: Integration of Emerging and Traditional Technologies.* Dublin: Oxford: Tycooly.

Westin, Richard A. 1992. 'Understanding Environmental Taxes.' Manuscript, Law Center, University of Houston Texas.

Westing, Arthur H. (Ed). 1986. *Global Resources and International Conflict: Environmental Factors in Strategic Policy and Action.* Oxford and New York: Oxford University Press.

Wicke, Lutz. 1986. *Die ökologischen Milliarden. Das kostet die zerstörte Umwelt — so könnenwir sie retten.* Munich: Kösel.

Wicke, Lutz. 1991. *Umweltökonomie.* 3rd. ed. Munich: Vahlen.

Wilson, Edward. 1992. The Diversity of Life. Cambridge (USA): Harvard University Press. — Belknap Press.

Winter, Georg. 1989. *Business and the Environment.* New York: McGraw-Hill.

World Bank. 1992. *World Development Report 1992. Development and the Environment.* Oxford and New York: Oxford University Press.

World Commission for Environment and Development. 1987. *Our Common Future.* The Brundtland Report. Oxford and New York: Oxford University Press.

World Energy Council. 1993. Energy for Tomorrow's World. The realities, the real options and the agenda for achievement. London. Kogan Page.

World Resources Institute (Allen L. Hammond, Editor-in-Chief). 1990. *World Resources 1990-91: A Guide to the Global Environment.* Oxford and New York: Oxford University Press.

World Uranium Hearing. 1993. Poison Fire, Sacred Earth. Proceedings of the WUH, Salzburg, 13-17 Sept. 1992. Munich (Schwanthaler Str. 88): World Uranium Hearing.

WWF (Chris Rose and Phil Hurst). 1992. *Can Nature Survive Global Warming?* London: Media Natura Ltd.

Yergin, Daniel. 1991. *The Prize: The Epic Quest for Oil, Money and Power.* London: Simon and Schuster.

Young, John E. 1992. *Mining the Earth.* Worldwatch Paper No. 109. Washington: Worldwatch Institute.

Index